D0394000

YOUR CAT
THE OWNER'S MANUAL

CONTENTS

Foreword by Dr. Jane Brunt   ix

Introduction   1

PART ONE
FRESH STARTS AND NEW BEGINNINGS   5

Chapter 1	WHERE TO BEGIN: REALISTIC EXPECTATIONS	9
Chapter 2	WHAT KIND OF CAT DO YOU NEED/WANT?	19
Chapter 3	LOOKING FOR LOVE IN ALL THE RIGHT PLACES	37
Chapter 4	BASIC GEAR AND COOL CAT STUFF	49
Chapter 5	KITTEN- AND CAT-PROOFING YOUR HOME	69

PART TWO
HOME CARE TO KEEP PETS HEALTHY AND SAFE   81

Chapter 6	WHAT IS GREAT TO EAT AND WHERE TO FIND IT	85
Chapter 7	HEALTHY CATS ARE BUSY CATS	101
Chapter 8	ESSENTIAL HOMEWORK FOR GOOD HEALTH	111
Chapter 9	AVOIDING PREVENTABLE *CATA*STROPHES	127
Chapter 10	TIME, MONEY, AND CAT CARE	139

PART THREE
THE SOCIAL ANIMAL: TEACHING GOOD BEHAVIOR 149

Chapter 11   SHAPING AND TRAINING GOOD BEHAVIOR   153
Chapter 12   HOUSE RULES FOR GOOD CATS   163
Chapter 13   SOLVING LITTER BOX PROBLEMS   181
Chapter 14   CORRECTING BAD BEHAVIOR   193
Chapter 15   TRAINING FOR FUN AND SAFETY   203

PART FOUR
IN SICKNESS AND IN HEALTH 211

Chapter 16   FINDING A GOOD VETERINARIAN   215
Chapter 17   FOCUS ON PREVENTIVE CARE   229
Chapter 18   HOW TO HANDLE AN EMERGENCY   245
Chapter 19   GETTING THE BEST MEDICAL CARE   261
Chapter 20   SPECIAL CARE FOR AGING AND
              SPECIAL-NEEDS CATS   275

Acknowledgments   289

Resources   291

Index   297

About the Authors   305

FOREWORD

If you love cats as I do, then you need this book. In it, you'll find everything you need to know about caring for your cat, and even if you think you know everything, I'm here to tell you that you probably don't. And neither do I!

But Dr. Marty Becker knows *a whole lot*! And he wants to help you . . . and your cat.

I've long known of and admired Dr. Becker for his advocacy on behalf of pets and the people who love them. In this book, Dr. Becker offers just what this doctor ordered, with surprises and solutions on every page to address the many joys and occasional challenges of keeping a cat with less time and less space than our forebears could ever have imagined. Backed by more than thirty years of hands-on experience, along with an unquenchable desire to know the best veterinary medicine has to offer, Dr. Becker puts it all down on paper in his own lively and entertaining style.

The result is truly as advertised: An "owner's manual" that covers it all, from nose to tail and inside and out. A modern guide to the modern cat lover's life, using an educated, science-based, and cooperative approach to keeping everything going smoothly with your cat.

Do you really need the help? As a veterinarian, I can tell that what I see every day suggests that you probably do. Cats are just not getting what they need. Studies show that pet lovers spend more time with their dogs, and dogs see the veterinarian far more often than cats do.

When it comes to preventive care—the kind of visits that save money and prevent misery—cats really lose out. And that's just wrong: if I could see cats when they're healthy, I can often help keep them from getting sick.

That's why I'm so happy to see Dr. Becker turn his talents to our feline companions. Knowing what makes a cat tick and how to recognize when things just aren't right is the key to having a long and happy relationship with your cat, and you'll find that stressed time and time again in this wonderful book.

So sit down, snuggle in with your cat, and read on. You'll both be better off for it!

Dr. Jane Brunt
CATalyst Council Executive Director
American Association of Feline Practitioners Past President

Dr. Brunt is one of the country's leading experts on feline care and is executive director of the CATalyst Council, an educational organization advocating for better, more knowledgeable care for cats. Dr. Brunt founded the Cat Hospital At Towson (CHAT) in Baltimore, Maryland, the first feline-exclusive veterinary hospital in the state. She is frequently featured in the media as a cat-care expert and regularly serves as a spokesperson for initiatives regarding cat health and welfare.

YOUR CAT
THE OWNER'S MANUAL

INTRODUCTION

I'm going to start off with a confession: growing up, I never used to think that much about cats.

Before you put this book down and wonder why I'm writing about cats now, let me tell you two things: first, it has been decades since I felt that way; and second, you have to know that I grew up on a dairy farm.

The animals on our farm were all well-treated, they all had jobs (so did us farm kids), and they all worked as hard as we did to survive. And while we worked pretty closely with many of our animals, the cats were...well, independent contractors. They were barn cats, and they hung out because a farm is a good place to live if you like to eat rodents, which is what barn cats did—and still do, in many places. This relationship has endured for thousands of years, ever since people started farming. Our farming attracted vermin, and our vermin attracted cats.

As humans, we have domesticated many animals, but you can argue that the cat domesticated himself; hanging with us was a choice cats made, not the other way around. Even though they chose us, cats drew the line at how far domesticated they would be, which is why so many cats still live wild today. No other animal works both sides of the wild-tame line as well as a cat.

Growing up as a farm kid, I appreciated cats mostly for the job they did. But in the decades since I left farming and became a veterinarian,

I learned to appreciate them as companions, and to love them as well. As a veterinarian, I became a strong advocate for cats, in terms of their health and their safety, and I have dedicated much of my time to making their lives better, so the people who love them can enjoy their companionship more.

I've written a lot about cats over the years, and shared many tips with my TV, radio, Internet, and print audiences. But with this book, I'm doing what I've wanted to do for years: put everything cat lovers need to know all in one place.

So what *do* you need to know? You'd think after so many thousands of years together, people would have cats all figured out by now: how to choose and feed one, how to train one, how to choose supplies, how to manage basic home care, how to recognize a veterinary emergency, and how to get a veterinarian's help. And, as is so important in these get-thrifty times, how to spend well and wisely.

Yeah, we ought to know all of that by now. Really, we should. But we don't.

I can tell you this from my side of the exam-room table as a practicing veterinarian: many cat lovers really don't know everything they need to about their cats, except for the one thing we all know—we love our cats, and our cats love us.

I've spent more than thirty years as a veterinarian, and half of that as an expert on *Good Morning America* and, more recently, on *The Dr. Oz Show*. All of this experience, and I still get many of the same questions I did my first day of the practice. I'm still answering those questions every day, not only from people who see me at the veterinary hospitals (yes, I still practice, because I love it), but also from people who recognize me in an airport (I travel about half my life) and even from friends and neighbors.

Part of the problem is that while cats haven't changed that much, our relationship with them has changed a great deal in a short amount of time. As I mentioned, I grew up on a dairy farm in Idaho, one of those storybook places where we had a little bit of everything growing and needing care. Even as a young boy, I was involved in caring for animals—and my dad meant it when he said to treat them right. One of my first farm jobs was collecting eggs from our chickens, and I figured out I could get all those hens out of the nest if I just walked into the coop and yelled, "Boo!" They'd run, and collecting those eggs would be easy, or so I thought...until my dad caught me at this and let me know what I was doing would not fly.

That was an early lesson. Next up: my youthful amazement at watching a veterinarian come out to our farm and bring back a cow from what seemed near death with a simple procedure. A miracle!

Is it any wonder I do what I do and love it? Animals, the people who love them, and the profession that cares for them both—these are the reasons I was put on this earth, I know.

But back to cats. While the cats of my youth were hardworking mousers, the cats most of us have today are "born retired." And many of them live completely indoors. While that's generally considered an advantage—indoor cats generally live longer than free-roaming cats— life indoors has challenges. Many cats are bored, and many cats are fat, and both of these situations can and often do lead to health problems.

What you need to help your cat is this manual.

Yes, I know a lot of people pride themselves on never reading the manual. But life is so complicated these days that if you don't read the manual you're missing out. With a new smartphone, you may be missing that tip that's going to save you lots of time. With a new cat, you may be missing out on a great way to spend that time you saved...

...with your cat.

You're going to have "America's Veterinarian" with you on every page, answering every question old and new with answers that have been prac-ticed and researched with the best veterinarians in the world.

You and your cat are worth it, and I'm happy to help.

Dr. Marty Becker,
"America's Veterinarian"

PART ONE
FRESH STARTS AND
NEW BEGINNINGS

Everyone has a unique idea of the "perfect" cat, and how a cat lover arrives at that vision doesn't seem to have a lot to do with logic—it has to do with love. And that's fine, really. Aside from being careful about the few cats or kittens with truly severe health or behavior problems, you really can just follow your heart when it comes to choosing a feline companion.

This is just one area where cats have a definite advantage over dogs. Getting a dog is like walking through a minefield with so many dangerous missteps that you cannot see: breeds that are a horrid match for many lifestyles, some breeders (large puppy mills as well as smaller operations that are either careless or clueless) you must avoid for your own good and for the good of the dogs, and even the occasional rescue or shelter dog who just has too much baggage to handle. That's why, when I was writing *Your Dog: The Owner's Manual*, I devoted huge sections to helping you choose a dog, paying very careful attention to both the big picture (breed-related health and temperament problems, and bad breeders versus good ones) and the small picture (problems with an individual puppy or dog).

But with cats, I'm going to tell you: If you want a female adult cat with tuxedo markings...go for her! If you dream of a big, long-haired orange male tabby kitten, no problem!

With just a few cautions—yes, there are kitten mills just as there are puppy mills, but they're easily avoided—you really can have the cat of your dreams. Check the shelters! Check with rescue groups! Adopt two—contrary to popular belief, most cats are very social. They not only enjoy but also need company.

Blinded by love? It's pretty much okay. Love will get you a long way—even love at first sight. And I know all about that. After all, I've been married for more than three decades to a woman I adored from the day I met her. And she and I have both been known to take home pets on impulse, although that last part is pretty typical among us veterinarians. We tend to collect hard-luck cases. (My very funny friend, Dr. Tony Johnson, an emergency and critical care specialist at the Purdue University College of Veterinary Medicine, has an entire family of pets all named for what they were suffering from when he met them in the ER. There's Arrow, the cat who'd been shot by one; and Crispy, the burn-victim cat; and I'm sure I don't have to explain about his dog, Tripod.)

That tugging of heartstrings is a fine impulse, and I want you to act on it, more than once, when it comes to cats (with marriages, stick to one, or at least one at a time). After you get your cat or kitten home, then the work (and the fun!) begins. And that's what this section is all about.

Now, let's get choosing.

Look at you: you need a cat. And, just as important, there's a cat out there who needs you. Preferably (or should that be purr-fur-ably?) two.

If the collar doesn't fit, you must admit: cats are not small dogs.
They need and deserve to be treated like cats, both behaviorally
and medically.

Chapter 1

WHERE TO BEGIN: REALISTIC EXPECTATIONS

Some people are born into cat-loving families, while others have cats thrust upon them through marriage to a cat lover, an inheritance from a family member, or sometimes a cat who just shows up at the door. And then there are those who independently make the decision to take up life with a cat. However you came to love cats, welcome. You are a member of an exceptional club. You are entering into a unique relationship that can be joyful, entertaining, sometimes frustrating, but in the end always rewarding. Life with a cat is special, if you know what to expect and how to play the feline rules. Dogs can bend to human will. Cats? They'll bend a little, but not much.

Cats are surrounded by myths and misconceptions. It's no wonder that they are often misunderstood. I want to help you separate fact from fiction when it comes to this interesting and intriguing animal.

Remember: cats are not small dogs.

When you are reading about different cat breeds or reading the personality descriptions of cats at a shelter, you may come across some that are described as "doglike." It's true that some cats, like dogs, will follow you around, play fetch, or go for walks on leash. But that is where the resemblance ends. Cats differ from dogs in many ways.

First of all, their nutritional needs are different. Cats are what biologists call "obligate carnivores," which means they must have meat in their diet to survive. Lots of meat. While dogs can exist on a diet that contains large amounts of grain, cats need meat protein to be at the top of their game. Meat contains a nutrient called taurine that is essential for heart and eye health and normal cell, muscle, and skeletal function. Cats can't synthesize taurine on their own, so they must get it from their diet. Cats also have other nutritional requirements that vary from those of dogs, such as the type of vitamin A they can use. That's why you should never feed your cat the same food you give your dog. Cats don't need carbs; when they go on a diet, it is high protein like the Atkins diet, which is often referred to as the Catkins diet.

A cat's physiology is different, too. Cats metabolize drugs differently than dogs or people. It's very dangerous to give a cat the same drug you or I or the small dog next door might take, even if it's for the same type of problem. Take pain, for instance. I've seen clients kill their cats by going to the medicine chest and giving their cats aspirin or Tylenol (acetaminophen). The same holds true for parasite treatments. Never apply a flea or tick treatment or a shampoo made for dogs to your cat. Always call your veterinarian first and ask if a particular medication is safe for your cat and at what dose.

Another difference between dogs and cats is the way cats express pain. Well, it's not really different. It's almost nonexistent. It's much easier to notice pain in a dog because we tend to interact with dogs directly. We take them on walks and we see whether they're limping, for instance, or moving more slowly. Or see them hesitate to jump up on the couch or the bed, or climb into the car or up the stairs. With cats, it's much more difficult to see the changes in mobility that signal injury or arthritis. Unless you happen to see your cat while he's doing his business in the litter box, you might not notice that he's having more difficulty squatting or no longer does that Rockettes-high kick to cover his scat. You also might not notice that he doesn't jump to the top of the bookcase or cat tree anymore, and you might like it that he no longer jumps on the kitchen counter. Notice that he hasn't been able to groom himself very well lately? Perhaps all you notice is that he's been sleeping more lately, and hey, that's what cats do, isn't it?

Because cats are both predator and prey, they make a point of hiding any kind of weakness. They know instinctively that displaying pain puts them at risk from other predators, so they do their best to mask it. There's a big neon sign in the wild that flashes "Sick Is Supper!" so cats have evolved to keep pain hidden. That stoicism works to their disadvantage when it comes to veterinary care. The signs that a cat is in pain are so subtle that most people miss them, unless they are keen observers of their cats.

I know this is only the first chapter of the book, but the following mantra is so important it deserves to be stressed: *Cats can't take care of themselves, and they need to see a veterinarian regularly.* It's a mystery to me why people are so much less likely to provide veterinary care for their cats than their dogs. Cats are the most popular pets in America, yet veterinarians are seeing a decline in veterinary visits for cats. That's a shame, because cats need and deserve great veterinary care to ensure that they live long, happy, healthy lives. They might be intelligent and independent creatures, but they can't doctor themselves— at least not yet. Providing your cat with regular veterinary care is a good investment, and it's one of the responsibilities you owe your cat when you bring him into your life. Cats have been called the "pet of convenience" for how easy it is to care for them, but they shouldn't be considered self-supporting, because they do rely on us for adequate food, water, shelter, preventive care, and treatments for accidents and illnesses. There are literally millions of cats living in homes suffering needlessly from arthritis, asthma, urinary problems, dental disease, metabolic conditions, parasites—I could go on and on—just because their owners didn't know what to look for or to take them to the veterinarian (who does know what to look for) for regular examinations, preventive health care, and treatment.

Making Veterinary Visits Fun

I think one of the reasons people avoid taking cats to the veterinarian is because the visit can be stressful to both cat and person. It doesn't have to be, though. Here are three easy steps you can take to help your kitten or cat feel comfortable on the way to the clinic and during the examination.

(Continued)

Buy a carrier that loads from the front and the top (with two doors, in other words) and that is easy to break into two parts (so the cat can be left in the bottom half during a veterinary exam). Accustom your kitten to a carrier. Leave the carrier sitting open in the house so your kitten can explore it, nap in it, even eat meals in it. We call it making the carrier "fun furniture." Line it with a blanket or towel to make it extra comfy, and put treats inside it as an occasional surprise. Get a product called Feliway, which is a synthetic version of the feline cheek pheromone (cats use this like the Good Housekeeping Seal of Approval, applying it themselves to everything of which they approve) and spritz the bedding inside of the carrier from time to time and especially before taking a trip to the vet. When your kitten does need to go for a ride in the carrier, the experience won't be scary. You can use the same techniques with an adult cat.

Schedule veterinary visits at a time when your kitten or cat hasn't just eaten. She'll be less likely to suffer motion sickness and more interested in getting tasty treats from veterinary staff. Bring something that is familiar and smells like home to the cat.

Make the first appointment with the veterinarian a fun one. No shots, just a weigh-in and some treats and petting from the staff. Think of it as a "getting to know you" visit. Trips like this are also a great opportunity to teach your cat that car rides can be pleasant.

OTHER CAT MYTHS AND THE TRUTH

If you've never had a cat, you may have some misconceptions about the feline species. Here are eight myths you may have heard about cats, along with the real scoop on what they're like.

1. Cats Are Standoffish

One of the most common beliefs about cats is that they are independent and aloof, preferring their own company to that of people. Nothing could be further from the truth. It's true that cats in general are less "needy" than dogs, but most cats love spending time with their people, whether they're playing with toys or just sitting in a lap motor-purring. Know that being a lap cat is genetically influenced. Feline behaviorists used to think you could turn any cat into a lap cat, but it's not so. When cat lovers understand that sitting within eighteen inches is being friendly enough for some cats, they'll feel better about not having a full-on lap cat and accept their pets as they are.

2. Cats Are Not Affectionate and Don't Need Attention

This is another common misconception about cats. Cats are great companions for people who are away from home during the day, and it's true that cats are more able than dogs to stay on their own if you must be away overnight, but don't assume that they can get by with little or no attention. On the whole, they like it better when you're around. It's not unusual for cats to follow their people around like little shadows and to hop into a lap just as soon as one is available. Cats can even develop separation anxiety if they are left alone too frequently or for long periods. But don't expect all cats to enjoy prolonged stroking and petting—sometimes it overstimulates them. Massaging often works better than endlessly stroking the fur.

3. Cats Require Access to the Outdoors to Be Happy

Cats love the outdoors, no doubt about it, but it's full of dangers for them: speeding cars, marauding dogs, crazy cat attacks, parasites, and poisons set out for pests, to name just a few. But with the right environmental enrichment and regular playtime and exercise, indoor cats can live happily and never miss the great outdoors.

4. Cats Can't Get Along with Dogs

We tend to think of them as dire enemies or cartoon warriors, but more often than not, cats and dogs can be fast friends. It's not unusual to see them curled up together for a nap, grooming one another, or playing a game of tag. Foster interspecies friendships by introducing cats and dogs at an early age, while they are still open to new experiences. Even older cats and dogs can become best buds, though, with proper introductions. Don't just throw them together like you would two stepchildren from polar opposite parts of the world. That can be stressful and dangerous for all involved. Planning and patience win the day.

If you have a dog and are planning to add a cat to your household, start by confining the cat to a small area such as a guest bath or bedroom. He'll feel safe there, but he will still be able to hear and smell your dog. Spend lots of time with him in his safe room so he doesn't feel isolated.

In a couple of days, your cat will be feeling more comfortable in his new home, and you can schedule a first meeting with the dog. Put the dog on leash and open the door to the cat's room. Put the dog in a sit-stay or down-stay position, and don't let him lunge at the cat. Let the cat decide whether or how closely to approach the dog. Don't feed them that day before this exercise and give tasty treats to both animals for good behavior.

For the next couple of weeks, keep the dog on leash when the cat is present, and make sure the cat always has an escape route if he doesn't want to be near the dog. Increase the amount of time they spend together, and keep giving plenty of rewards and praise for behaving nicely toward each other. When they're calm around each other, you can take off the leash and let them begin what may well become a life-long friendship.

5. Cats Can't Be Trained

Surprise! With the right motivation, which for most felines means rewards for correct behavior, cats are highly trainable. You can teach a cat just about anything you want to teach him, as long as it doesn't require opposable thumbs or barking for a treat. The benefit of training is that it is an interspecies communication system. Once you learn how to train your cat, there's almost no behavior problem you can't overcome.

6. Cats Spread Toxoplasmosis and Women Who Are Pregnant Should Get Rid of Their Cats to Protect the Fetus

Not true at all! Do you think that female veterinarians and veterinary technicians stop working with cats during the nine months of their pregnancy? No way. In fact, they have no higher levels of exposure to toxoplasma than the general population. With certain easy precautions, the risk of infection to the developing fetus is virtually nil.

There's more on this in Chapter 9, but the important takeaway is this: no matter what well-meaning relatives and friends (and even some doctors) tell you, you don't have to get rid of your cat when you're expecting.

Have someone else clean the litter box, and if that's not possible, wear gloves when you do so. Cook meat well, and wash your hands thoroughly after handling meat. The risk of getting toxoplasmosis from gardening is much greater, and you should always wash vegetables well, and wear gloves when gardening. These precautions will minimize risk, and your cat can stay to help raise your child. (Pets are good for children, you know.)

7. Cats Will Harm Babies by Sucking Their Breath or Lying on Them and Smothering Them

If you didn't follow the advice for dumping your cat during pregnancy, chances are someone will insist you need to do so when you have an infant in the house. This mistaken fairy tale of killer cats probably began because cats enjoyed curling up near babies and sharing their warm, soft bedding. When the babies died from other causes, the cats got the blame for the death. The truth is that women, babies, and cats have lived together safely for thousands of years. Of course, you should always supervise your baby and cat when they are together, and it's best that they don't share a bassinet, but you don't have to worry that your cat has it in for your baby.

8. Cats Eat Grass and Other Plants Because They're Sick

Nope, they're just connoisseurs of the green stuff. Cats love the taste and texture of grass, young shoots sprinkled with dew or rainwater. Grass also provides roughage that helps to work food through the system, so eating grass needn't be discouraged. In fact, if you have an indoor cat, you should plant grass for him or her.

ENJOYING A CAT FOR WHAT HE IS

Having a cat is like bringing a bit of wild nature right into your home. The little lion who lounges on your sofa is not really so far removed from his big cousin, the king of beasts. When you watch your house cat stalk a grasshopper and then see a lion on television stalking a zebra, the similarity is unmistakable.

No matter what their size, cats are lethally armed warriors cloaked in elegant camouflage. Their loosely connected spines allow them to coil up in a ball, then spring up or out, landing softly and silently. Their retractable claws whip out like switchblades when they're needed and stay sheathed when they're not. Large, close-set eyes, natural night vision, and a broad head and short jaw allow them to spot prey and deliver a perfectly placed killing bite. Cats are adapted to every environment, from forests and plains, to mountains and jungles, to deserts and snowy steppes.

I'm not trying to scare you, far from it. I want to open your eyes to the wonder that is the cat. When you live with one of these miniature predators, you have a front-row seat to nature at work, right there from your sofa. If you can accept that a cat will always carry a little bit of the wild inside him, a little bit of an unpredictable nature, you will come to appreciate him all the more.

Specially Designed for Forward Movement

Cat claws are designed to move a cat in a forward direction. And if that direction is up a tree, it's difficult to head back down. The gracefully powerful movement of a cat heading up a tree is counterbalanced by the crashing and (if he's lucky) controlled free fall he'll use to get down.

Most cats do find their way back down, of course, which is a good thing these days. With municipal budgets being what they are, few fire departments are allowed to respond to the "cat in tree" calls anymore.

We don't recommend that you get out that tall ladder, either. The chances of you getting seriously hurt while reaching for a scared cat—and scared cats aren't safe to handle, even if they're yours— are generally better than your cat getting injured when he decides it's time to head down for dinner. You may be able to whet his appetite by opening a can of tuna, salmon, or mackerel and letting the wonderful fishy smell drift upward.

Kitten or cat? Male or female? One cat, two,...or more? There are pros and cons both to starting young and to adopting an adult, and advantages as well to starting two cats at once.

Chapter 2

WHAT KIND OF CAT DO YOU NEED/WANT?

You want a cat. You're ready for a cat. You know what it takes to keep a cat, and to keep a cat happy. You look at those "pet of the week" pictures and think, "I ought to run to the shelter now!" Or you look at Petfinder.com and scan the ads like it's a dating site. This one? Nah, too much fur. This one? Hmmm, "no kids." That one? Sweet face, but what about the calico one here? Click. Click. Click.

Choice, choices, choices. They're endless and you can make a lot of good ones. But you can't know what will work for you, your family, and your lifestyle until you narrow the choices.

Now, as a veterinarian, I've treated all kinds of cats. Males, females, docile to downright ornery, kittens to feline AARP members, long-haired to no-haired (either hairless breeds like the Sphynx or ones suffering from medical conditions). While there have been a few individual cats I could have lived without knowing—and like every veterinarian, I have the scars to prove it—I can't say there's any type of cat I don't love.

But I do see a lot of mismatches, and I feel just awful when a relationship's not working out. Many times problems can be fixed, or at least managed with some—and sometimes a lot—of effort. Life is full of compromises, true, but if you start out with some commonsense foundations when you're looking for a cat, you'll have a better chance of making that perfect match.

KITTEN VS. CAT: PROS AND CONS

When most people think about getting a cat, a kitten is the first thing that springs to mind. Think again! Kittens are a kick, no doubt about it, but they're not always easy to live with. Few things are as adorable as a kitten at play, but even fewer things are as destructive as a kitten at play.

Kittens climb up the back of the sofa and launch themselves off it. They climb up the curtains to get a better view out the window. They leap up to the fireplace mantel and knock over one of the pair of antique vases you inherited from Grandma—or, worse yet, a family member's cremains and then use the contents as a makeshift litter box (I've actually known this to happen!). And kittenhood can last up to three years before the little bundle of cuteness even thinks about settling down into sedate cathood.

Anyone who decides to get a kitten should be aware that this tiny feline firecracker will need a lot of attention, exercise, and play to help him stay out of trouble. He needs consistent, appropriate outlets for his youthful exuberance. Whereas puppies have an oral fixation, kittens have a climbing/scratching one. Most of all, he needs an owner who can set limits in a kind and intelligent way so the kitten learns what is acceptable behavior and what is not.

What's good about kittenhood? Lots of things. Kittens are like modeling clay. If they get a good start with plenty of handling at a young age, you can shape them through training—yes, cats can be trained!—to become the cat of your dreams. Young kittens are especially receptive to touch between two and eight weeks of age. With early exposure to kind and gentle human hands, plus kittygarten classes (they do exist, and they're great for socialization!) before they are twelve weeks old, kittens are less likely to develop behavior problems as they grow up.

No Catnip for Kittens

Not all cats like catnip. The ability to appreciate the herb is genetic, with slightly more cats in the fan club than not. These hardwired preferences aren't immediately apparent, though, since kittens under the age of three months don't react to catnip at all.

Among those cats who do like catnip, you'll find two basic kinds of reactions: your cat may seem to become either a lazy drunk or a wired-up crazy. Credit a substance called nepetalactone, which is found in the leaves and stems and causes the mood-altering behavior.

You don't have to house-train a kitten. They come fully programmed to dig before elimination and will look for a scratchable (freshly turned, soil-smelling) substance from three weeks old. Up until then, Mother Cat is licking their rumps to stimulate elimination. All you need do is make the box available and block off any other choices until the lightbulb goes off.

Kittens are full of life. One of the things I love best about kittens is their crazy energy, the feline equivalent of a sugar high. Toss a small ball or dangle a peacock feather and they fly around the room like animated hockey pucks (or old video games of Pong), bouncing off walls and turning flips. Watching a kitten at play is more entertaining than any reality show.

Kittens are endearing. With their big eyes, they draw us in, then mark us as their own, rubbing their cheeks against us and leaving a secret scent of pheromones that tells other cats "Mine! All mine." And who can resist the softness of their pawpads, whiskers that seem internally lit, and that glorious fur coat?

What Big Eyes You Have, My Dear!

I don't know about you, but I just melt when a kitten stares up at me with those big, beautiful eyes. Those eyes, which are huge in proportion to a kitten's body size, may be one of the reasons we are attracted to kittens and feel protective toward them. Kittens are born with their eyes closed because the eyes are still developing, but even at birth they are already 75 to 80 percent of their eventual adult size. The eyes open when the kittens are about ten days old, and they continue to grow, although not to the same extent as organs like the heart or liver. Don't stare straight into a cat's eyes. It is very rude in cat language. Only humans stare into eyes. Dogs find it a challenge as well. A cat kiss is different from what humans might think—start unfocused, eyes half closed, then blink slowly and you've done the kitty kiss.

By the way, the reason why cats often head toward the only person in the room who doesn't like cats? Because that person is probably the only one who isn't looking at the cat!

Kittens bring out our protective side. There's a special bond people develop with a kitten. Don't get me wrong. We can develop special relationships with adult cats, too, but it's not unusual to feel a certain investment in a kitten. He's little and vulnerable and relies on us for his very survival. That can forge a bond like no other.

It's easy to see why people are attracted to kittens, but don't overlook the benefits of life with a more mature mouser. If the mere thought of kitten antics makes you tired, and you'd like a more restful companion, consider adopting an adult cat, one that is three years or older. No kitten, however cute, can beat an adult cat in providing calm, loving companionship. While kittens are undoubtedly entertaining, adult cats have an advantage in the behavior department. They are past the destructive stage and into the lap-sitting age. They know the litter box drill and are usually already spayed or neutered and vaccinated. And if you get your cat from a shelter, they might be able to tell you up front about the cat's personality and habits: likes other cats or hates them, loves dogs or hates them, great with men and women, not appropriate for families with young children.

Don't think you'll be getting a golden oldie. Cats can live to be fifteen years or older, so a three-year-old cat is just getting started in the game of life. Even a ten-year-old cat has plenty of good years left in him. Bringing home a preowned cat with high mileage has special benefits. People who have adopted late-in-life cats marvel at their kind, loving, and more relaxed nature and unconditional love.

Worried about big vet bills? The good news is that middle-aged cats and even those entering their geriatric years are generally very healthy. Indoor cats can live long lives with little veterinary intervention as long as they eat a high-quality diet, are kept clean and parasite free, get appropriate preventive health care, and receive regular veterinary exams.

If you like the idea of acquiring an adult cat but have an interest in a particular breed, consider adopting a retired show or breeding cat. Breeders like to find "retirement" homes where these cats can still get the attention they are used to, even though they are no longer in the show ring. Consider this type of adoption, too, if it's important to you to know a cat's medical and behavioral history. To find a retired show or breeding cat, talk to breeders at shows, join a cat-oriented e-mail list and explain what you're looking for, or contact breeders through one of the many cat registries.

When it comes to life span, life is full of uncertainties. Sometimes a kitten may not live as long as the healthy middle-aged cat you adopt. You just never know, so don't rule a cat out simply on the basis of age.

The best thing about acquiring an adult cat of any age is that what you see is what you get. His personality is already established: placid or playful, outgoing or reserved, equable or anxious, talkative or quiet. Choosing an adult cat means being able to choose the cat that best suits your own personality and lifestyle. When you make that perfect match, both you and the cat win.

ADOPTING PAIRS (ADULT OR KITTEN)

If one cat is good, does that mean two are great? You bet! We give cats the time we can spare and the love we can share from our busy schedules, but that's not always enough. Sometimes a furry friend of the feline persuasion helps to fill a cat's day when his people are away. They can both hear the flutter of a fly's wings or hear a mouse creeping in a crawl space…you can't. They can get crazy on catnip together, groom each other with those raspy tongues, or chase each other playfully in a game of zoom-around-the-room, or just lie on the cat tree together soaking up the sun.

One of the many myths about cats is that they prefer to live alone, but that's not necessarily true. A pair of cats will play together, groom each other, and share catnap time. Two kittens will wear each other out, then collapse in a heap.

Just know that introducing cats isn't going to be without difficulties. Shelter and colony studies show it takes one year for a new (adult) cat to be accepted into a group, so when people want to get another cat, they have to expect challenges for a while. (Burmese and Ragdolls and Birmans are different; they seem to see "one of their kind," and feline experts have seen them "fall in love" as soon as another one of their breed arrives.)

Want an even better reason for acquiring cats in pairs? Veterinary studies show that when cats have company, both are healthier. Animals with buddies are sick less often, require shorter stays when they are hospitalized, and live longer.

A pair of cats can be from the same litter or close to the same age. The friendship usually works best if they are of the opposite sex. Two males or two females may each seek to be top cat, even if they are spayed or neutered.

Another pairing that works well is an older cat and a younger cat. The presence of a kitten can enliven an adult cat who may have lost some of his spark or put on a little pudge. And an older cat can teach a kitten the ropes: the best places in the house to hide and climb, the best way to demand a meal, how to choose the best lap for sitting, or how to follow the sun. It's a win-win-win!

Odds Are Out

When it comes to cats, remember that three can be a crowd and that for a cat, being that odd one out is no fun. Cats seem to get along best in even-numbered groups. When there's an odd number of cats, one cat may get picked on or develop aggression toward the other cats in self-defense.

DO YOU WANT A PEDIGREED CAT?

Most cat lovers share their homes with "the cat next door": one of the millions of random-bred cats who come in every coat color and pattern imaginable: orange, tabby, calico, tuxedo, pointed like a Siamese or ticked like an Abyssinian, to name just a few. It almost seems as if there's no reason to purchase a pedigreed cat such as a Persian, Maine Coon, Siamese, Himalayan, or one of the many other exotic cat breeds. But looking beyond appearance, choosing a pedigreed cat offers some advantages.

A pedigreed cat is one whose ancestry can be traced for generations back to forebears with the same characteristics—a cat with a family tree, in other words. You might buy a pedigreed cat for any number of reasons. One is the variety of unusual coat types they sport. These cats range from the practically bald Sphynx, who has the comforting feel of a soft, fuzzy hot water bottle, to the velvety waves of the Cornish Rex. The Exotic looks like a Persian, but his short coat is easier to groom.

You may be attracted to cats who stand out for their beautiful markings. They include the Birman, with white mitts on her paws; the Siamese, whose color points range from dark seal point to palest lilac; and the spotted Egyptian Mau.

Other pedigreed cats are just a kick to live with. The Abyssinian is intelligent, inquisitive, and active. You are most likely to find him surveying his domain from the top of the refrigerator or taking you for a walk so he can meet his adoring public. The playful but bossy Turkish Angora lords it over other animals in the household, including dogs, and may even enjoy a good swim. Japanese Bobtails play fetch, "sing" and talk to their families, and make good travel companions.

Sure, you can find these behaviors and sometimes the look of a certain breed in random-bred cats, but the advantage of a pedigreed cat is consistency. If you want a cat with a specific look or personality, this is the way to go. And pedigreed cats from reputable breeders have been bred for good health and temperament. The truth is, it's hard to go wrong with any cat, but a pedigreed cat allows you to expand your options, and that's always a good thing.

ORIENTAL VS. HEAVY: BODY TYPES AS AN INDICATOR OF ENERGY LEVEL

Have you ever heard the saying "All cats look alike in the dark"? That might be true when the lights are off, but cats actually come in several different body types. Even more interesting, body type can clue you in to the cat's likely activity level, from layabout to lively. What? You thought cats slept eighteen hours a day? Well, that's pretty much true, but it's the six hours they're awake that you have to worry about. Some cats are satisfied to do nothing but adorn your sofa during their waking hours and lick themselves in hard-to-reach places as a self-grooming ritual, no doubt about it. But others you're more likely to find jumping across the stairwell to get a better view out the window, perched atop the shelf in your bedroom, or swinging from the chandelier. In general, here's what you can expect from cats slinky to solid.

You know those cats who look like supermodels? The ones with the angular heads, tubular bodies, long legs, and long tails? They are busy, curious, talkative, and, yes, energetic. If you didn't know any better, you might think they were fragile, but you would be mistaken. Hiding beneath that skinny-kid-at-the-beach look is a solidly muscular body, ready for action. These are the cats you'll find walking on a leash, loudly commenting on your activities, and just generally running the household. Cats who fit this description are described as Oriental and include the Siamese, her close relatives the Balinese, Oriental Shorthair, Oriental Longhair, and the Cornish Rex. Again, you can find random-bred cats with these characteristics, although perhaps not to the physical extremes of their pedigreed pals.

Other slender and athletic cats are the Abyssinian, the Somali, the Japanese Bobtail, and the Turkish Angora. They have a little more substance than the Oriental breeds and are often described as having a "foreign" body type. And like their Oriental cousins, they are highly active. The Aby, for one, is a pistol, and the Japanese Bobtail is said to start getting into trouble earlier than other cats. When cats like this aren't climbing to the top of a grandfather clock and reaching for the whirling blades of the ceiling fan, you can often find them riding on their person's shoulder or going for a walk on leash.

Feline Fact

While cats (pedigreed cats, especially) do range somewhat in body type from slinky to bulky, all cats share the same basic design that makes them top-notch track stars. The average domestic cat can reach speeds of about thirty miles per hour. Cats also excel at the high jump. From a sitting position, they can jump six times their own length (this would be like the average human jumping from the ground to the top of a three-story building). Their powerful thigh muscles coil and release incredible energy, allowing them to escape the bounds of the earth and fly—at least high enough to get them to the top of that counter or shelf.

Cats with what's known as a semiforeign body type start to look more sturdy than slim. Their activity level tends to be moderate, but cats are like the rest of us; they are individuals, and some like to dance to a faster beat than others. The Devon Rex and the Sphynx are likely to be energetic, for instance, while the Egyptian Mau and the Tonkinese are playful but not necessarily high octane.

The cats that most of us are probably familiar with have stocky bodies with heads that are rounded or slightly wedge-shaped. They're known for having calm, easygoing personalities, but that doesn't mean they don't like to play. Besides the domestic shorthair and domestic longhair—sometimes known as random-bred cats—this type includes American Shorthairs, British Shorthairs, Bombays, Chartreux, and Scottish Folds. Expect these cats to enjoy play in short bursts, especially if you introduce them to a kitty fishing-pole toy or the joys of chasing a peacock feather around the house. In between playtimes, they are satisfied to snooze on the sofa.

The most restful cats tend to be those with compact, rounded bodies. Breeds that fall into this body-type category include the Persian, the Exotic (a short-haired Persian), the Burmese, and the Manx. They are built for lap-sitting, not leaping. The Manx, who enjoys climbing to high places, is the exception to the rule.

Then there are the big cats. No, not lions and tigers, just domestic cats that have been, well, supersized. Hefty breeds such as the Maine Coon, Bengal, Norwegian Forest Cat, Ragdoll, and Siberian fall into this category. Some of these jumbo-size cats can weigh twelve to twenty pounds. They are easygoing but agile and athletic, and they can often be found peering down from the highest spot in the room.

How Many Bones?

No one really can say how many bones a cat has, and the Manx is one of the reasons why. A long-tailed Maine Coon cat will have more vertebrae than a Manx with no tail, or a Manx mix with just part of a tail. And a cat with extra toes—they're called polydactyl—will have extra bones as a result.

The range is usually put between 230 and 250, with the average cat counting about 244 bones, if cats could or cared to count.

Anyway you count it, the average cat has about thirty more bones than we do. But we have something cats don't: collarbones. Not that a cat would consider that a disadvantage. Without a collarbone, cats can fit their bodies through openings the size of their heads. Assuming they aren't overweight, of course.

Two cats with identical tails and paws will still have a different bone count if one of the pair is male and the other female. That's because males have a tiny bone called the os penis.

THE FUR FACTOR

One of the best things about living with a cat is stroking his soft, beautiful fur. Whether he has the kinky coat of a Cornish Rex, the long, straight coat of the Persian, or the short, thick coat of the typical domestic shorthair, a cat's fur is a pleasure to touch.

The luxurious coat of the cat is made up of hairs that are produced by cells beneath the skin called follicles. A follicle consists of a hair bulb—where the hair originates—and a follicular sheath. The hair passes through the sheath to emerge at the skin's surface. Cats have up to three types of hairs, and the type of coat they have depends on variations in the size and numbers of those hairs.

Guard hairs are the first line of defense against cold and wetness and help to protect the skin from injury. Coarse, thick, and straight, they taper to a fine tip. More insulation and protection is provided by wiry, midlength awn hairs. The undercoat is made up of downy-soft secondary hairs. Up close, they look crimped or rippled. The secondary hairs, which are the most numerous of the three types, help to regulate the cat's body temperature.

Saved by a Whisker

Whiskers, also known as vibrissae or tactile hairs, are thick, stiff hairs located on either side of the muzzle, above the eyes, and on the lower back side of the front legs. Whiskers are arranged in neat

(Continued)

rows, with the shorter ones at the front, the longer ones at the rear. These specialized hairs can detect slight air movements and help the cat feel his way through the environment, especially in the dark. One way they do this is by allowing him to measure the width of an opening he might like to squeeze through. If his head and whiskers can fit through, the rest of his body can, too. It's like having a built-in ruler that works on a dead run.

Some cats have genetic mutations that cause them to have coats that are curly (the Devon Rex and the Cornish Rex) or wiry (the American Wirehair). Cornish Rex cats lack guard hairs altogether, and in the Devon Rex the guard hairs are soft instead of coarse. Although the American Wirehair's springy coat can feel like steel wool, it is surprisingly fragile and needs special care.

Now for the bad news. The messy truth about cats is that they shed, and shedding is one of the top complaints of pet owners. Sometimes it seems that there is more fur on our clothing and furniture than—on them! It's true that some cats shed less than others, but even "naked" cats such as the Sphynx leave sparse, fine hairs in their wake. The related belief that some cats such as the Rex or Siberian won't trigger allergies isn't true. Some of these cats can cause a less potent allergic reaction that allows mild allergy sufferers to share their lives with them, but all cats produce saliva, urine, and dander (dead skin flakes), which are the real sources of allergens, not fur.

That doesn't mean that you can't live with a cat if you're the allergic type. And it doesn't mean that you can't live with a cat if you're the fussy housekeeper type. Most people can live with pet allergies, with the help of an allergist (the human kind), and most people can reduce the amount of fur they find on their floors, furniture, and clothing. These strategies and techniques can help to keep sneezes, sniffles, and flying fur under control:

❖ **Wipe the cat's coat daily with a damp towel or large disposable scent-free wipes.** This helps to keep the coat free of dander. If you're highly allergic, assign this task to someone in the family who isn't allergic to the cat.

❧ **Brush the cat weekly or even daily** to remove dead hairs that will otherwise float off the cat and onto your belongings. I particularly like a product called a FURminator, which can take so much hair off the cat that you'd swear your cat is going to be bald. You should only use the FURminator sparingly (about once a month) but use a brush much more often. The great thing about regular grooming is that you can get rid of excess cat hair at the time and place of your choosing. Much better to have piles of hair in the laundry room than thousands of cat hairs sprinkled all over the house like fallen snow.

❧ **Even better, wipe or groom the cat outdoors** or in a garage, reducing the amount of fur found indoors.

❧ **Get a sticky-tape roller** like what you see at the vet's office from any pet store, or try a product such as the Pledge Fabric Sweeper for Pet Hair. Get in the habit of using electrostatically charged products such as Swiffer on your floors to pick up fur. Better to use a Swiffer and toss dust, dander, pollen, and spores in the trash than to have those things hitchhike on your cat and end up causing skin problems for the cat—or allergy problems for you, when your pet curls up next to you like he's a four-legged dust bunny.

❧ **Consider bathing your cat.** I know; you've heard all your life that cats hate water, but if you acquire your kitten at an early enough age, you can teach him to become accustomed to and even enjoy bathtime. Honest! Ask your veterinarian to recommend shampoos, conditioners, wipes, and more.

❧ **Vacuum frequently.** Use a vacuum cleaner with a HEPA filter, which traps very small particles, such as cat dander. This is another job for a person without allergies. If you can't pawn off this chore on another family member or a housekeeper, wear a face mask while you vacuum, as well as when you groom the cat. And here's a tip for when you have company: well-meaning cat owners don't vacuum right before guests arrive. Regardless of the vacuum used, this will lift the cat allergens, which are very light and will remain in the air for hours. Your guests will actually suffer more than if you didn't vacuum at all.

❧**Purchase a HEPA air filter or air purifier.** Cat allergen is very light, small, and sticky, so it floats more than other allergens, making it more likely to be trapped by the filter.

❧**Keep over-the-counter antihistamines on hand.** Liquid formulas work fastest, followed by the chewable type. For severe allergies, ask your allergist about prescription antihistamines and decongestants. Medications that can help include nasal sprays, topical steroid sprays, and eyedrops. A cat-friendly allergist can help you find a combination that works best based on your symptoms and sensitivities.

❧**Reduce the surfaces that can trap allergens.** Leather or vinyl furniture is better than fabric, and wood or tile floors are better than carpet. Use washable throw rugs, and launder your bedding in hot water.

❧**Invest in kitty couture.** No, I'm not kidding. Dressing your cat in a T-shirt, sweater, or body suit helps to keep your home a fur-free zone. If you introduce your kitten to the fashionista lifestyle while she's young, she'll soon come to expect getting dressed as a regular part of the day. And since your cat is wearing clothing at home, no one will know unless you tell them. It will be our little secret.

❧**Make your bedroom a cat-free zone.** If you're not willing to do that, at least keep the cat off your bed. When that's not possible or desirable, use dust mite covers on mattresses and pillows. Cat allergen particles are tiny, and the covers can help prevent them from getting into bedding. Then accustom yourself to a stuffy nose and puffy eyes. For most people, the companionship is worth it.

The Shot That May Stop the Suffering

About 10 percent of people are allergic to cats. An allergic reaction occurs when the immune system interprets benign substances, such as cat dander, as invaders and launches a counterattack. Currently the only solutions are to stay far away from felines, get multiple injections of kitty allergens to help the body build up a tolerance, or just suffer through it.

If you try all the techniques above to keep your house clean, and still suffer dreadfully from allergies, consider allergy shots. This involves starting with an injection of a dilute dose of an allergen and slowly building up to a maintenance level that's continued, usually monthly, for three to five years. Allergy shots aren't a cure, but they redirect the immune system away from an allergic-type immune reaction to a more normal immune reaction.

The downside is getting injections and the investment in time required. Most physicians require patients to receive the injections in their office as a safety precaution in case an allergic reaction occurs.

Factors to consider are that allergy shots work better in young people and in people who have only a few sensitivities rather than being sensitive to everything across the board.

But there may be hope! Immunologists have developed a vaccine by isolating the protein shed by cats that causes the most allergic reactions and, more specifically, by determining which segments of the cat protein binds to and activates immune cells. The researchers have made synthetic versions of these segments, called peptides. A mix of seven peptides makes up the vaccine. The idea, the researchers write, is that the human immune system will encounter these peptide strands, which fit into the immune cells like a key to a lock, and recognize them as harmless. That action stops the human sniffling-and-sneezing inflammatory response in its tracks—no buildup with an endless series of shots needed—even when the peptides are attached to real cat proteins. An early clinical trial on eighty-eight patients resulted in no serious side effects. A single injection reduced the skin's inflammatory reaction to cat allergens by 40 percent. To get the equivalent response with current antipollen allergy treatments, patients would need to get twelve weeks of treatment with pollen extract. The vaccine is being developed by Adiga Life Sciences, a company established at McMaster University, with clinical trials continuing to determine the optimal dose for the vaccine.

Is There Such a Thing as a Hypoallergenic Cat?

You may have heard about specially bred cats with a mutant gene that prevents them from producing Fel d 1, the protein that causes people to be allergic to cats. Or that certain cat breeds such as the Rex varieties or the Siberian don't cause allergies. Are they fur real?

The short answer is no for most people. No matter what you read on the Internet, all cats—short-haired, long-haired, curly-coated, wire-coated, hairless, or mutant—produce saliva, urine, and dander that carry allergens.

People with mild allergies may be able to tolerate some cats and not others, for a combination of reasons. Some cats make less antigens than others, and some houses contain less pollen, mold, or dust mites than others, reducing the total effect of allergens in the environment. But what about that mutant gene that knocks out Fel d 1? Although that particular protein causes most of the difficulty, cats produce other proteins that can also cause trouble.

Before you decide to try your luck with a reputedly hypoallergenic cat, remember that allergies can change or build over time. Still, your best bet is to seek out a light-colored, short-haired, spayed female cat. Male cats produce more allergens than female cats, and there is some evidence that dark-colored cats produce more allergens than light-colored cats. In fact the worst bet for allergies is probably a dark, intact, male cat.

A healthy kitten or cat has clear eyes and a clear nose; a glowing, lush coat; and a loving, curious attitude.

Chapter 3

LOOKING FOR LOVE IN ALL THE RIGHT PLACES

There are lots of ways to acquire a cat. You can get one from a neighbor whose cat had kittens; adopt one from a shelter or rescue group; or purchase one from a responsible breeder whose goal is to produce healthy, happy pedigreed kittens. And sometimes a cat chooses you; just comes right up to your front door and invites himself to stay. Here's what to look for in a cat or kitten and how to decide where to get him.

WHAT A HEALTHY CAT OR KITTEN LOOKS LIKE

A kitten can be as cute as all get-out, but if he's not healthy, you're bound for heartbreak. Luckily, a healthy kitten is pretty easy to spot. First off, he's active and alert. Kittens have two speeds: full blast and fast asleep. If it's kitten nap time when you visit a breeder or shelter, stick around. They'll be up soon, and you can see them in action. When they're awake, kittens should be bright-eyed and bushy-tailed. Be concerned if a kitten seems tired or listless.

Healthy kittens are friendly and outgoing. They feel good, and given plenty of early socialization they like meeting people. Ask which kitten plays with the kids or prefers climbing into a lap instead of playing with his siblings. That one will be easy to handle and is likely to develop into a lap cat. The sad, shy kitten who hangs back in the corner might tug at your heartstrings, but she will probably be difficult to live with, always fearful of new people and places. Unless you don't mind having a cat who spends most of her life under the bed, pass this kitten by.

Healthy kittens have clean ears, white teeth, and pink gums. Peek inside the ears. No dark, waxy gunk? Good deal. Lift up the lip to check the teeth and gums. Besides being an indicator of good dental health, this quick little exam is a great way to see how amenable the kitten is to handling.

Take a good look at the eyes and nose. They should be clear and clean, not red or runny. Red eyes can be a sign of a bacterial eye infection called conjunctivitis—inflammation of the eyelids. A runny nose or coughing and sneezing are signs of infectious bacterial or viral respiratory diseases such as pneumonia or rhinotracheitis. Sometimes antibiotics can help, but often these upper respiratory infections hang on stubbornly and become chronic problems. Why start your adventure into cathood with a lot of veterinary bills?

Of course you want a cat with a nice coat. Soft, shiny fur? Check. No sores or bald patches? Check. Smooth skin with no scaly areas and no loose specks of what look like salt and pepper flakes, but are actually flea eggs and waste? Check. Fur and skin are some of the most obvious clues to a kitten's health. Don't ignore them!

A rounded, protruding tummy is a worrisome sign. A kitten with a potbelly hasn't been drinking too much of Mom's milk or not getting enough exercise. More likely, he has a load of intestinal worms that are feeding on his gut. Gastrointestinal parasites that affect kittens include roundworms and tapeworms, and a heavy load of them can kill a kitten.

Be concerned if a kitten is noticeably skinny. A healthy kitten's ribs don't stick out, even if he's really small.

Don't neglect the rear end. Lift up a kitten's tail to see if he has any signs of diarrhea or inflammation. Back away from a kitten with any kind of stinky discharge from his hind end.

Ask if the kitten has been tested for feline leukemia virus (FeLV), feline immunodeficiency virus (FIV), and intestinal worms, and whether he has been treated for fleas. If the kitten you've chosen is happy, active, and friendly, and appears to be disease and parasite free, he's good to go. Just to be on the safe side—and to meet common sales contract and adoption requirements—take him to your veterinarian for a once-over within forty-eight hours.

SHELTERS, RESCUES: HOW TO SPOT A GOOD ONE

If you're thinking of bringing a cat into your life, the idea of going to a shelter can be scary. All those sad kittens and cats needing homes! I know. You're worried you'll want to adopt all of them. But if you think about what you're looking for in a cat or kitten and go in with a plan, I bet you'll find that the adoption option is easier and more rewarding than you might think.

The first thing to know is that there are lots of advantages to adopting a kitten or cat from a shelter. Number one is health-care savings. The cats are almost always spayed or neutered before they're made available for adoption. That's a huge savings right there. The cats you see have already been vet-checked, vaccinated, and, in many progressive shelters, evaluated for temperament. Adoption counselors on staff are familiar with each cat's personality and can tell you which ones are lap-sitters, which are playful, which ones like kids and dogs, and which ones would rather live without them.

Another plus is the variety of cats you can find: long-haired, short-haired, tabby, calico, kittens, mature cats, sometimes even pedigreed cats, especially popular breeds such as Siamese and Persians. That's right. It's not unusual to find high-class cats who are down on their luck because of a death or divorce in the family. In fact, those are the reasons that many cats are in shelters, not through any fault of their own.

Want more reasons to adopt from a shelter? Most of these cats are already familiar with home life. They're cool around kids or dogs, and they know the litter box routine. I don't like declawing except as a last-chance alternative to losing a good home, but if you'd prefer to have a cat who is declawed, there's a good chance you can find one at a shelter. I'd much rather see you adopt a cat who has already been declawed than to get a kitten and have him declawed.

The best thing about adopting a cat from a shelter or rescue group?

That warm, fuzzy, tingly glow you get from giving a home to a cat in need and hearing him purr as he settles into his new digs.

So what's the process? First, think about what you want in a cat. Kitten or adult? Longhair or shorthair? Lap-sitter or lively? Cool with kids and dogs? Some shelters start with adoption counseling to help you narrow your options. The counselor is a trained matchmaker who takes your needs into account and can direct you toward the most suitable cats right from the beginning.

Others give you a chance to look the cats over and visit with them first, then help you choose the cat who's right for you. Adoption counselors often have information about each cat, such as whether he came from a home with children, how he gets along with dogs or other cats, and what his personality is like. When that information isn't available, shelter employees rely on their own observations. Keep in mind that the cat is in an artificial environment. Get him into a quiet room and see if he relaxes before you dismiss him as a fraidy-cat.

Old Shelters Get a New Look

Don't be surprised if you find a shelter environment that seems more like a home than a sterile kennel. More and more shelters recognize the benefits of group rooms with tall scratching posts, windows for sunning, and toys, televisions, and aquariums for entertainment. Cats who are relaxed and happy are more adoptable and adjust more easily to their new homes.

Some shelters are too small or too broke to have staff to help match pets with people. If you find yourself looking on your own, here's what to look for when you're choosing a kitten or cat.

Social cats and kittens who like people are up front and attentive. They're the ones asking for attention or petting.

Be concerned about choosing a cat who resists any handling at all. The ideal cat has a middle-of-the-road personality and enjoys being petted or held right from the get-go or after a short period of getting to know you.

The other cat you may want to think twice about is the one who's too bold. He charges the front of the cage, swats or hisses when you try to pet him, and squirms and struggles when he's held. Bossy cats can become demanding, controlling, and even aggressive, and that's no fun to live with.

Most important, look past appearance. Behind a plain-vanilla exterior you may discover a sweet cat with a calm, loving personality. That's a real instance of finding buried treasure!

SHOULD YOU BUY A CAT?

With the millions of beautiful, unique random-bred kittens and cats in the world, practically free for the taking from neighbors and animal shelters, why would anyone buy one? That's a good question, and there are a couple of good answers.

One reason is that you desire a cat with a particular personality, appearance, or size. (Cats don't vary as much as dogs when it comes to size and shape, but they do come in tiny, small, and not-so-small.) Because pedigreed cats are bred to a certain standard that outlines what they should look like and how they should act, it's easier to select one that suits your own lifestyle and personality. Making the right match is the first step in developing a beautiful relationship with a cat. That's not to say that a random-bred cat can't be just as great a friend, but you often have a better idea of what you're getting up front with a pedigreed cat.

People who breed pedigreed cats are committed to making each generation of cats better than the last. They work toward this by screening their cats for genetic disease and breeding the best to the best, with the result being bright, healthy kittens. They stay up-to-date on the latest news about cat health, genetics, and behavior. Believe it or not, there's a lot to know. By purchasing a pedigreed kitten from a blue-ribbon breeder, you have an increased chance of getting a cat who has a head start in the areas of health, nutrition, and socialization.

If you want a specific breed of cat, nothing is more important than finding the right breeder. Not availability, not price, not location. All of those are secondary to finding a breeder who is knowledgeable about and loves the type of cat you're interested in. If you pick right, she'll be a best friend to you and your new kitten throughout his life. With good care and a little luck, your cat will spend the next fifteen or more years with you. Don't you think it's worth investing a little time up front to make some phone calls, ask some questions, and take some field trips to cat shows and breeders' homes?

If you decide that a pedigreed cat is for you, the best place to start your search for a breeder is at a cat show. Hotshot breeders belong to cat clubs and show the cats that they've bred to earn points toward championships. A cat show in a major metropolitan area will have the greatest variety of cat breeds, but even a smaller show will have a good representation so you can see, touch, hear, smell, and just plain experience the breeds up close and personal. The cats are displayed in aisles by breed, and when they're not in the ring, you can see them lounging in their decorated cages. Sometimes breeders have kittens or cats for sale right there at the show, but don't buy until you've had a chance to learn more about the breed and get to know the breeder and visit her cattery.

If you see a cat who interests you, ask the breeder if she has time to talk. Most breeders are happy to visit with people about their breed, but if they're being called to the ring, they may have to rush off suddenly. Just come back later when they have more time.

A cat show is a great place to see cats and meet breeders in the flesh, but the Internet can also be a good resource. Searching for breeders on the Internet expands your choices around the country and even internationally. Proceed with caution, though. You'll find lots of great and not-so-great breeders. The trick is in learning how to tell them apart.

Good places to start your Internet search include the websites of the Cat Fanciers' Association, which has a breeder referral service, and the Fanciers and Breeders Referral List (see the Resources section of this book for contact information). Other cat registries, such as the International Cat Association and the American Cat Fanciers Association, also have breeder referral services. Just remember that not everyone who has a pretty website is a great breeder.

Don't be afraid to ask the tough questions that will separate the gold-standard breeders from those just out to make a quick buck. Here are some to get you started:

❧**Do you offer a health guarantee?** What does it cover and how long does it last? A one-year written guarantee against congenital health defects (those a kitten is born with) is a good start. If the Maine Coon kitten you purchase develops, say, hip dysplasia, the contract should guarantee you a new kitten without requiring you to give up the one you've fallen in love with.

❧**What genetic diseases are common in the breed?** Can you test for them to keep them out of the breeding program? Run away fast from any breeder who says that his breed doesn't have any health or genetic problems. They all do, and a breeder who tells you otherwise either is lying or doesn't know much about the breed. For instance, hypertrophic cardiomyopathy (a type of heart disease) can occur in Maine Coons and Ragdolls, and polycystic kidney disease can strike Persians and Exotics. Genetic tests are available that can identify the genes associated with HCM in Maine Coons and Ragdolls and PKD in Persians and Exotics.

❧**Which vaccinations are given and when?** Kittens need their first shots when they are six to eight weeks old, with booster shots every three to four weeks until they are four months old. That means your kitten should have had at least one set of core vaccinations for feline viral rhinotracheitis, calicivirus, and panleukopenia (FVRCP) by the time he's eight to twelve weeks old, when you take him home.

❧**Where are the kittens raised?** The best answer is underfoot in the home. Steer clear of breeders who isolate kittens in another building such as a barn or let them run wild outdoors. Kittens need lots of handling and exposure to home life from birth if they are going to be great companions. That's true whether you are buying a pedigreed kitten or one from your next-door neighbor.

Speaking of the home, that's the next thing to check when you're purchasing a kitten. When you walk in the door, put your nose to work. You might notice a hint of eau de feline, but overall the breeder's home should smell clean, not stinky. If her stud (male) cats are confined to separate quarters, as they often are, those too should be clean, comfortable, and large. Overcrowded, dirty living conditions are a recipe for unhealthy kittens. Walk away if a breeder doesn't want you visiting her kittens and cats at her home. It's likely she has something to hide. Top-notch breeders are proud to show off their beautiful, healthy cats and kittens.

Whether you've met a breeder at a show or online, conversed in person, by telephone or e-mail, don't go ahead with a kitten purchase unless you're satisfied that this is someone with whom you have a rapport and believe you can trust. A kitten's breeder can be a resource throughout the cat's life, so choose carefully.

WHAT ABOUT THE CAT/KITTEN WHO ADOPTS YOU?

Sometimes the best way to get a cat is to have one choose you. I can't tell you how many times I've acquired a cat because one wandered up to my front or back door and informed me that he would be moving in.

Sometimes these are kittens who have been dumped because the person whose cat had a litter couldn't find a home for them. Sometimes they are adult cats who simply decide they are ready for a new place and person. I'm not kidding! Cats are very opinionated about their living situations, and it's not unheard of for them to pick up and move when things aren't to their liking. There's a new baby in the home sucking up all the attention or a new spouse who doesn't give the cat his due. Or the cat simply decides the pickin's are better next door. It's not always easy to know what's going on in a cat's mind, after all.

If a cat chooses you, well, that's awfully flattering. Of course, you'll need to make every effort to talk to the cat's owner before claiming the animal as your own. And even if the cat's choice is agreeable to both parties, you'll want to find out from the current owner about the cat's health history and vaccination status.

If the owners don't want to give up the cat, well, sharing isn't uncommon where cats are involved. Many free-roaming pet cats "cat around" a lot and get fed in multiple locations.

Hello, Tabby

The tabby is the most common marking in cats. These tiger-striped markings are the original patterns of our cats' ancestors, and they can still be observed on some relatives of the domestic cat.

The name *tabby* comes from Atabi, a silk imported to England long ago that had a striped pattern similar to that of the domestic tiger cat.

Tabbies come in many colors, such as red (more commonly called "orange," "ginger," or "marmalade"), cream, brown, or gray. The tabby pattern is so dominant that even in solid-colored cats, if you squint a little you can often discern faint tabby markings, especially on the head, legs, and tail.

CAN YOU TAME A FORMERLY FERAL CAT?

At one time or another, I bet we've all had a cat show up in the yard, setting up camp and mooching food where he can. Sometimes these are stray cats who have left or lost their homes. After an initial period of skittishness, they warm up to your overtures and become willing to approach you and even be petted or scratched behind the ears. Former companion cats like these have experienced the comfort of home life and are often adoptable, happy to give up their wandering ways for two square meals a day, a warm bed, and all the love they can stand.

But not every stray cat strutting through your yard has a history with people. Some are feral, meaning that they have never become accustomed to the presence or touch of people. Feral cats are born from parents who are strays or whose family let them roam free without spaying or neutering them. If these kittens don't get that all-important early human contact, they become much like wild animals, living by their wits in urban, suburban, and rural areas. Just as cats have done for some nine thousand years, they often band together to live in loose-knit colonies near the places where people live and work, relying on the availability of food, water, and shelter that these areas provide. For all that time, up until the past one hundred years or so, cats and people had what's called a "commensal" relationship—a symbiotic association in which humans benefited from rodent control and cats benefited from an easy food source. You can tell the difference between a feral cat and a stray cat (stray being a cat who's lost, not born wild) by how willing the cat is to tolerate contact with people.

You may think that a feral cat will warm up to home life once he gets a taste of it, but that is almost never the case unless you take feral kittens in when they are four or five weeks old. At that age, just a couple of days of handling is enough to turn them from little hissing, scratching creatures to kittens that can become adoptable. By the time they are eight or ten weeks old, socializing them is much more difficult and time-consuming. And adult feral cats are well past the age where socialization can help. Even though they have adapted to live near people, they fear them and are unable to adapt to life as house cats.

That doesn't mean that they can't live a good life in their colony with the help of people. The best way to manage a feral colony is through a trap-neuter-return program, TNR for short (we've listed organizations that advocate TNR in our Resources section on page 294). This is a humane way to make sure the cats don't reproduce, stabilizing the size of the colony and reducing its effect on the environment, and it helps them live longer lives because they are less likely to fight over territory and females. Less feline sex, births, and fights mean that cats and people can coexist with fewer conflicts.

Another option, if these "community" cats must be relocated and you are near a rural area, is placing them as barn cats—with the permission of the property owner, of course. The cats get shelter, regular meals, and the chance to perform their natural work; property owners get great rodent control.

Cats don't need all that much in the way of equipment, but one kind of item that's overlooked as "extra" really isn't. Your cat needs toys to keep mind and body healthy.

Chapter 4

BASIC GEAR AND COOL CAT STUFF

You've finally chosen the perfect kitten or cat. You've read up on cat behavior and care, and your new pal has been vaccinated, dewormed, and spayed or neutered. All you need to do now is bring him home, right? Not yet. First, there's the little matter of a shopping spree to acquire everything you'll need to keep him happy, well-groomed, and entertained. Before you bring your new cat home, be sure you purchase the following supplies: litter box and litter, carrier for trips to the veterinarian and other car rides, food and water dishes, a collar, some basic grooming tools, a jug of enzymatic stain and odor remover, and a couple of toys. These essentials will help your kitten settle happily into his new digs. How do you know which ones to get? Here are a few tips to get you started.

LITTER BOX TYPES AND FILLERS

One of the many great things about cats is that they come already programmed to keep their living area clean. There's no training involved in teaching kittens to use a litter box; they are hardwired to dig in a soil-like substance before going to the bathroom, and most have already learned from their mother to hide feces and urine by burying them in a litter box.

Feline Fact

Cats are the ultimate predators, but they can also be prey, and they've got the self-protection racket down pat. Covering up feces and urine helps to conceal their presence from larger, more dangerous animals who might want to make a meal of them or simply kill them to eliminate a competitor.

Cats never "miss" the litter box. Cats can direct their urine very accurately, so the pee is where they want it to be, and it smells just how they want it to smell. It is a coping strategy and, as such, solves the cat's problems. If we could detect the pheromone that they leave with the pee, we would know if they're scared, frustrated, terrorized by neighboring cats, or in pain.

Choosing the right litter box and type of litter is the most important shopping decision you can make. House-soiling is the number one behavior problem people report in cats. When your cat doesn't like the location, smell, size, or any other aspect of his bathroom, he won't hesitate to let you know just what he thinks—by urinating and defecating outside the box. And don't think that maybe his aim was just a little off. Cats are precise when it comes to directing their urine and feces, and when it's out of the box, they are leaving a stinky but succinct message: I don't like the state of my bathroom. Here's how to keep your cat thinking inside the box. Cat pee is designed to stick on trees in all weather for three weeks, so it takes a lot of cleaning to get rid of the messages the cat is leaving outside the box (usually as a last resort).

You can find all kinds of litter boxes at pet supply stores and online. There's the basic rectangular, uncovered box; hooded boxes with hinged tops for easy scooping; boxes with sifters for lifting out solid waste; and even automated boxes that remove waste after every use. At least one, the CatGenie, hooks up to your water line and automatically cleans the box after every use. Now that's service! I prefer an inexpensive uncovered box myself, one that I can toss every six months and replace with a new one, but if you don't want your cat to scatter litter everywhere, a covered box may be a better choice for you.

It doesn't really matter, though, what I like or what you like. What's important is what your cat likes. People like covered boxes because they help contain odor and could be considered more attractive to look at. Cats, on the other hand, may or may not like covered boxes. Some appreciate them for the privacy aspect, while others prefer to have a 360-degree view so they can be aware of any approaching threats. Whose opinion matters most here? Not yours. If you want your cat to use the litter box on a regular basis, his wishes should take precedence.

Give your cat a choice—covered and uncovered—and watch how he approaches each box. If there's a lid, does he hesitate before entering? Try taking it off and see if he goes into the box more readily. If you absolutely must have a covered box, try adding a cover later, or purchase an open box that comes with a high, clear shield that fits around the sides. Your cat can still see out, but the litter mess is a whole lot less.

One more thing: when it comes to litter boxes, size matters. It should be big enough for your cat to stand up and turn around inside it. For a kitten, you don't want a box that is so large that it's difficult to get in and out of. For an older, arthritic cat, you don't want a box with high sides that's too painful and difficult to access. You might need to put a step in front of it to help the kitten get in. And as the kitten grows, you want to make sure the size of the box increases as needed, especially if you have one of the larger cats like a Maine Coon or a Bengal. You don't want him to have to scrunch up to use the box. If he does, he might just decide that it's easier to defecate outside the box. A good rule of paw is that a litter box should be one and a half times longer than the cat's body.

Whatever type of box you choose, you can't, can't, can't let it get dirty. Cats have a keen sense of smell—better than dogs! You know how you feel about using a filthy public restroom? Well, cats feel the same way about dirty litter boxes, times a thousand.

Scoop the box every time you see that it's been used. Every week, dump out the litter, clean the box with warm water and a mild, unscented dishwashing detergent, and fill it with new litter. Plastics retain odors, even when they're cleaned, so that's why I like to replace the box every six months. If you hate the thought of throwing plastic into the landfill twice a year, try using a large enameled turkey roasting pan instead. It's a good size, it's just as easy to clean, and smells won't cling to the metal. Wash it weekly, the same way you would a plastic litter box.

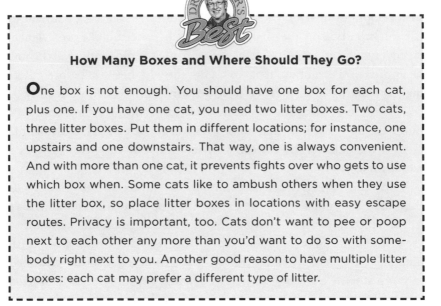

How Many Boxes and Where Should They Go?

One box is not enough. You should have one box for each cat, plus one. If you have one cat, you need two litter boxes. Two cats, three litter boxes. Put them in different locations; for instance, one upstairs and one downstairs. That way, one is always convenient. And with more than one cat, it prevents fights over who gets to use which box when. Some cats like to ambush others when they use the litter box, so place litter boxes in locations with easy escape routes. Privacy is important, too. Cats don't want to pee or poop next to each other any more than you'd want to do so with somebody right next to you. Another good reason to have multiple litter boxes: each cat may prefer a different type of litter.

What about what goes inside the box? There are all kinds of different cat litter, and they all have pros and cons. Most cats prefer clumping litter—one veterinary behaviorist I respect suggested cats have a preference for Fresh Step because of its soft, sandy feel. It's easy on the paws and easy to scoop. Other cats might like a fine-grained clay litter. Look for one that comes in a dust-free formula. Some cat litter is easier on the earth, made from recycled paper or natural substances like corn cobs or wheat.

Avoid scented litter. It might smell good to you, but that perfumey odor can be sensory overload for a cat. Using scented litter can be one of the quickest ways to teach your cat to go outside the litter box.

Start with what your kitten or cat is already used to, but if you plan to change litters, give him a choice. I like to get small containers of three different kinds of litter: clumping such as Fresh Step or World's

Best, nonclumping, and one of the alternative-type litters like Feline Pine, Yesterday's News, or Swheat Scoop. Fill each box a half inch deep with a different litter. Put them side by side so it's like *Let's Make a Deal*. It's usually obvious that the cat prefers one litter over the others. Donate the litter that's left over in the bag to your local humane society.

It's also a good idea to test what depth of litter your cat prefers: one-quarter inch, a half inch, or three-quarters of an inch full. Some cats like it mounded in the middle; others like it spread out. Some cats like to be able to scratch the bottom of the box, so the less litter the better as far as they're concerned. Others don't want their tootsies to touch anything but litter and prefer a deeply filled box. In a game we call "Pick Your Pot," the more personalized you can make your cat's litter box, the better he'll like it.

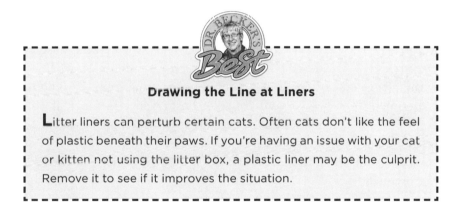

Drawing the Line at Liners

Litter liners can perturb certain cats. Often cats don't like the feel of plastic beneath their paws. If you're having an issue with your cat or kitten not using the litter box, a plastic liner may be the culprit. Remove it to see if it improves the situation.

When cats are good about using their litter box, they're very, very good. But when they're bad, well, let's just say it's not pleasant. Luckily, good management habits on your part can prevent or solve most problems and keep you and your cat living in sweet-smelling harmony.

If you're doing everything right and your cat is refusing to use the litter box, she may be trying to tell you something—namely, that she has a health problem such as a urinary tract infection. If you've ever had one yourself, you know how painful UTIs can be. Your cat may be trying to tell you in the only way she knows how that a visit to the vet is in order.

SCRATCHING POSTS, TREES, AND OTHER CLAW STUFF

Scratching is a natural, normal behavior for cats with a lot of important benefits. Activate your pet's cat scratch fever with scratching posts, cat trees, and other scratch-worthy paraphernalia.

Think creatively. A scratching post doesn't have to be vertical and it doesn't have to be store-bought, but generally the taller the better, as cats like to be up high (as predator to sight supper and as prey to be safe). In our horse barn, the cats are always bedded down on the uppermost bales of hay. Plenty of cats enjoy scratching on plain old logs placed on the floor as an alternative to their regular scratching post. Other options include rope scratchers that attach to corners of your wall and can be mounted at the appropriate height, or curved "chaises" made of recycled cardboard or rope. They resemble furniture and cats not only scratch on them, they also sleep on them, run across them, and tunnel beneath them. Models to look for include the Marmalade Pet Care Cheeky Chaise Cat Bed and the Petlinks System Dream Curl Curved Scratcher. Some cats like scratching trays lined with corrugated cardboard or scratching pads hung from doorknobs. Experiment to see what your cat likes best. And remember, if you don't provide them something you want them to scratch on and they want to scratch on, they'll find something they want to scratch on that you don't want them to touch. Like the side of the armoire or the arm of the couch.

Cats love to be up high, but we don't always want them on top of the wall unit or fireplace mantel. Provide climbing opportunities with a cat tree tall enough to make your cat feel like king of his own private jungle. Cat trees start at four feet and run as high as eight feet or more. Multiple perches, hammocks, rope ladders, dangling toys, and hidey holes are just a few of the amenities your cat can have in his sky-rise apartment. Just as you would with a scratching post, look for one that's wrapped in rope or sisal. Perches padded with faux fleece are a comfy touch. Want a more elegant look? You can purchase cat trees with a sleek, elegant design from companies such as Whisker Studio and the Refined Feline. They look more like contemporary sculpture than cat furniture. Some companies even allow you to customize the wood to match your furniture. Whichever one you choose, put the cat tree in a sunny spot with a view and watch the acrobatics and napping ensue. Veterinary behaviorists with feline specialties are recommending expanding the space in the home to reduce stress for cats. While precious few are going to enlarge the home's footprint to provide more room for the cat, it's easier, cheaper, and more welcomed by the cat to expand the vertical space. The easiest way to accomplish this is to put a series of small (big enough for one cat) shelves on the walls, so cats can bounce from one to another like a mountain climber.

BOWLS AND FOUNTAINS

Choosing food and water dishes for your cat should be pretty straightforward, right? I mean, how much is there to know? You just plop the food in a bowl or fill it with water, and you're good to go, right? If that's what you think, well, you probably haven't been in a pet supply store since Top Cat was a kitten. Dishes for cats can be made of serviceable stainless steel or attractive ceramic, and they come in more styles, colors, and shapes than you ever thought possible. Here's what to consider when making your choice.

Stainless steel. If your middle name is practical, there's no question: go for stainless steel. It's dishwasher safe, nonallergenic, and lasts forever. If you're worried that your kitten will bat a stainless-steel bowl around on the floor and spill food or water, look for one with a weighted or rubberized bottom.

Ceramic. Looking for dishes that match your décor? Ceramic is the way to go. It's heavy and won't tip over, and it's dishwasher- and microwave-safe. The drawback is that it's likely to shatter if you drop it on the floor or on your granite countertop.

Plastic. It's inexpensive, colorful, and easy to clean, but it has some drawbacks compared to stainless-steel or ceramic dishware. Plastic retains odors, which may repel some cats, and many cats are allergic to it, developing acne on the chin or face.

Throw Out Your Cat's Food Dish!

Yes, I just talked about dishes, because the fact is that most people will buy them anyway, and you'll need dishes for water, too. But here's what I'm really recommending these days: throw out your cat's food dish, or never get one at all.

Did you do a double-take? I bet you did, but here's the thing—my own cats don't have food bowls. They have food puzzles. These come from several companies, in a lot of different styles, but the basic premise is the same: you put kibble into a toy, and your cat has to work for her food, pawing and pushing at the toy to get pieces to tumble out. This is a great way to keep your cat active and thinking during the day, especially if you're not home to play with her. Think of it like this—it's far more rewarding to work for your food than to simply have it plopped at your feet.

Cats are predators, after all, and a food puzzle allows them to exercise their natural-born skills. The benefit is exercise for both mind and body, and our born-retired cats need plenty of both. My cats love going on the hunt for their meals, and I recommend this type of feeding to every cat owner I see.

Finding the right food puzzle for a cat is not quite as easy as finding one for dogs, but there are some good ones available. I like the Kong Wobbler for cats and Premier's Funkitty Egg-Cersizer. You can also just hide small stashes of food around the house for your cat to find: in the shower or bathtub, on a bathroom counter, in the closet on the floor with the door open, at the top or bottom of the stairs—you get the idea. I even do this for our barn cats, stashing small amounts of food up on hay bales or behind posts. The trick is to hide the food, but don't hide it so well that your cat can't find it or that it spills into the seat cushions and your cat disembowels the sofa to get to it. Once your cat gets the hang of the game, you'll get a kick out of seeing how much fun he has "hunting" for his food.

Cats instinctively know that drinking running water is a good survival strategy because it's more likely than standing water to be clean. If you've noticed that your cat prefers to drink dripping water from the faucet or shower, you can chalk it up to this sensible ancestral preference and get them a drinking fountain.

Water is the most important nutrient in a cat's diet. Your cat's body is approximately 70 percent water, and that life-giving liquid plays a vital role in cell and organ function. Cats are finicky about their drinking water, so keeping a clean, fresh supply on hand all the time is important to their good health. Change your cat's water a couple of times a day, and make sure the bowl is always clean, never slimy.

Or better yet, provide running water. Drinking fountains, which are available at pet supply stores or through pet supply websites and catalogs, make a steady supply of running water available to your cat, recycling and filtering it so it stays fresh. A couple of my favorites are the Drinkwell original dog and cat water fountains and the Deluxe Fresh Flow Fountain by Petmate. In fact, many cats, especially as they get older, are chronically dehydrated, and this can negatively affect their health. For that reason, I advise all of my clients to purchase drinking fountains, as cats can never drink too much water (unless they have a metabolic condition and excessive thirst is a sign of problems).

How Cats Drink

Did you know that until recently scientists weren't sure how cats lapped up liquids? It turns out to be an amazingly elegant process, one worthy of the graceful feline. Speed and gravity are the secrets behind the cat's delicate drinking process, as captured by high-speed photography. To take in liquids, cats curve the upper side of their tongue downward. As the tip of the tongue touches the water's surface, the cat rapidly pulls it upward, bringing up water that sticks to the bumpy surface of the tongue. Before

(Continued)

gravity can draw the water back down, the cat's jaws snap closed and swallow the water. A cat can lap water four times in a second—which just looks like a blur to the naked eye—and his tongue has been clocked at one meter per second.

TOYS AND ENTERTAINMENT

When we think of pets who need exercise and playtime, cats do not automatically spring to mind, but they should. They are predators, after all, and every predator has the excitement of the stalk and kill in his life. Our domestic cats don't need to hunt to survive, but they still have those natural instincts to chase and climb and hide. Play fulfills that predatory nature and is fun for them. More important, it gives cats something to look forward to besides food.

Toys, games, and other forms of activity enrich your cat's life and burn calories, keeping him happy and healthy. And kitty playtime takes only two or three minutes several times each day. Here are some of my favorite ways to keep cats active, both physically and mentally.

Feline Fact

Cats have many different eye colors as adults, but at birth they have but one color, and it's blue. Within a few weeks a kitten's eyes will start to darken as natural pigments are deposited in the iris. Cats with "points"—light body color and dark markings on the ears, face mask, legs, and tail—will keep those blue eyes. White cats will have blue, green, gold, or copper eyes—or a mixed set.

Other cats will have green, gold, or copper eyes, but those baby blues will go away as they leave infancy behind.

Get a move on! Cats are attracted by motion. Even the laziest of cats gets excited by the bouncing beam of a flashlight or laser pointer. Following the fast, erratic motion enhances a cat's ability to think and move quickly. To give your cat a real workout, direct the light beam up and down stairs or walls, encouraging the cat to run and jump. Be careful not to shine a laser pointer in your cat's eyes. Chasing a Ping-Pong ball down the hall will also get your cat moving. Some cats will even bring it back to you. You should note that cats like to play the least in the morning and the most in the early evening. If you take the time when you first come home from work—the time most people would most certainly not choose as the time to play with the cat—the reward will be a cat that is much more likely to sleep through the night.

Play Nicely, Kitty!

Kittens will pounce on anything that moves, including your fingers and toes. Teach them early on that your appendages are not playthings, or you'll suffer the bloody consequences when those sharp teeth and nails find their target. Talk about "shock and claw" tactics! If your kitten tries to play with your feet or hands, distract him with a real toy, and praise him for playing with it.

Gone cat fishin'. Other toys that arouse a cat's desire to chase are fishing-pole toys, which have flexible handles attached to lines with furry or feathery lures at the end. One that every cat loves is the original, the Galkie Kitty Tease. Dangle it over your cat's head or drag it in front of him and watch him become a silent stalker: ears forward, rear twitching, then pouncing on his prey, rolling and kicking to "kill" it. His amazing flips and spins in pursuit of the lure will keep your kitten—and you—entertained for hours, or at least until your cat is ready for another nap. Just remember to put it away when you're not around to supervise. You don't want your cat swallowing the string and developing a dangerous intestinal obstruction. The rule is: leave no kitten or cat with string unless he is supervised. Holidays like Christmas can be particularly tricky because lots of kittens get "tinselitis"—stringy décor gets stuck in their guts—resulting in a very expensive extraction process.

Live-action entertainment. A peaceful way to give your cat a taste of the hunt is to set a bird feeder into a window. Choose a feeder with a one-way mirror so your cat can see out, but the birds can't see in. The birds stay safely outdoors and get a meal out of the deal, while your cat's life is made more interesting on his side of the window. This is a great way to encourage your cat to do a little jumping—onto the windowsill—and to appeal to his birder nature.

Kitty brain candy. If a window box isn't possible, TV is the next best thing. The rapid movements of birds, meerkats, aquarium fish, and other prey animals are like crack for cats. Feed your cat's hunger for prey in a nonviolent way by turning on a nature show or popping in a DVD specially made for cats. Make sure your television set is securely placed so it won't fall over if your cat decides to leap at the screen in a vain attempt to score some fast food.

Will play for food. We've already talked about how food puzzles are a great way to feed and exercise cats at the same time. If you can't find a food puzzle that you and your cat like, try one of these home-made versions. Put dry food inside an empty paper towel roll, and let your cat figure out how to get at it. Or cut holes in a whiffle ball and insert pieces of kibble. They'll fall out when your cat bats the ball around.

Hide and seek. Not every toy has to be store-bought. Some are even free. Put an empty paper sack or a cardboard box with a little packing paper inside it on the floor and let your cat explore. He'll love the dark interiors and crinkly noises.

Teach your cat tricks. Cats are smart, and they can learn many of the same tricks as dogs: sit, come, jump up, give a paw, and so on. Teaching tricks is a great way to engage your cat's mind and deepen the relationship between you. The best time to teach a cat to have her nails clipped, take a pill, and have her feet/ears/skin examined is when she's a kitten.

SET UP A CAT PORCH OR ENCLOSURE

Hate the thought of keeping your cat indoors? A lot of us do. Cats still have a bit of the wild in them, and part of the pleasure in keeping one is watching him stalk a grasshopper, chatter excitedly at birds, or execute a death-defying leap. A safely covered outdoor enclosure gives your cat the chance to stretch out in the cool grass, sniff fresh air, watch the birds, and lie in the sun—all of the things that cats do best.

Depending on the size of your deck, balcony, patio, or yard, a cat enclosure can be as simple or as fancy as you wish. You can build it yourself or order a customizable system like the one from Cats on Deck. Some people create elaborate multilevel playgrounds with real trees, cat-safe plants such as catmint and catnip, perches galore, bridges, tunnels, fountains, and scratching posts. We jokingly call them "upscale cat houses," but the cats who live in them lead rich lives with lots of mental stimulation.

Whether you buy or build a cat enclosure, it should be sturdy with smooth edges. More important, it should be as secure as Fort Knox so that your acrobat of a cat can't escape and so that no dogs, coyotes, hawks, or owls can threaten him. A cement foundation and a covered top are your best weapons against escape or attack.

An alternative to building an enclosure is the installation of a cat-proof fence. At least two companies, Cat Fence-In and Purrfect Fence, make barriers that prevent cats from climbing over fences and gates or up trees. They work with any height and type of fence.

GROW YOUR OWN CATNIP

Most cats (including big ones) respond to catnip ecstatically, rolling around, rubbing against the floor or furniture, or exhibiting a dazed relaxation. The reaction to catnip is genetic, and approximately 30 percent of cats don't respond to it at all. But if yours is one who enjoys a catnip "high," you can grow him a little green and become his favorite supplier.

Catnip (*Nepeta cataria*) is an herb, a member of the mint family. It's one of the simplest plants to grow, so even if your thumb is nowhere near green, you should be successful. It does best in moderately rich soil, but you can also use soilless potting mix or grow it hydroponically. Catnip thrives in sun, which it prefers, but tolerates shade. You can also grow it indoors, beneath fluorescent plant grow lights. If grown indoors, it needs at least six hours of sunlight or artificial light daily. Be careful where you place catnip. Its scent has been described as a cross between peppermint and skunk. If it smells more like skunk to you, grow it someplace where the odor won't bother you.

To grow catnip from seed, sow it outdoors in late fall or start it indoors in early spring. When you move the seedlings outdoors, plant them twelve to fifteen inches apart. Water the plants regularly so they stay moist. Catnip that becomes dry will flower too soon. To help catnip grow, feed it a water-soluble fertilizer every three to four weeks.

As it grows, pinch off flowers to encourage leaf growth and to give your cat a sample of what's in store for him. Prune the plant for good air circulation, which helps to prevent mildew, a common problem when growing catnip. The plant can also be attacked by white fly and spider mites; if you see them, ask for advice at your garden-supply center.

Until the plant reaches its full size of three to four feet, protect it from your cat's affections or it will be destroyed before you can harvest it. Put it out of reach or cover it with a mesh screen. Of course, if you're growing it inside your cat's enclosure, let him sniff it, chew it, and roll in it to his heart's content. You can always plant more.

Begin harvesting the leaves when the plant is eight inches tall. Dry them by tying eight to twelve stems together with twine or string and hanging them upside down for seven to ten days. Make sure you hang the catnip in an area your cat can't access! Store the dried herb in an airtight jar or a plastic bag, or keep it in the freezer. It will maintain its strength and aroma for up to two years.

To tickle your cat's senses, throw fresh or dried catnip on the floor, make a simple ball or mouse out of cloth stuffed with dried catnip leaves, or give your cat a paper bag that once held harvested catnip leaves.

OTHER ESSENTIALS

Collars and Identification

That rhinestone collar might look perfect for your new royal companion—that is how cats think of themselves, after all—but cats need more than bling around their necks. Before you bring your kitten home, purchase a tag engraved with your name and telephone number (preferably a mobile number). Attach it to a breakaway collar—one that will slip safely off your kitten's head if it gets caught on something like a limb or fencing. It should be adjustable and designed to release under tension. These collars have saved cats' lives! They are usually made of nylon and come in many different colors and designs. If you don't like the sound of a jingling tag, look for a collar that can be embroidered or imprinted with your name and phone number. I'm a fan of Beastie Bands, which are made of soft, stretchy material and release easily if they're caught on anything. They are also comfortable enough that cats don't seem to mind wearing them.

Fit the collar and tag around your kitten's neck before you leave the shelter or the breeder's home. Check the collar frequently as your kitten grows to make sure it's not too tight, and adjust it as needed. You should be able to comfortably slip two fingers between the collar and the kitten's neck.

Because breakaway collars can, well, break away, your cat needs a backup form of identification, especially if you plan to let him go outside. An injectable microchip, about the size of a grain of rice, can be your cat's ticket home in case he gets lost and is missing his collar and ID tag. I've heard many happy stories of cats being returned to their families, sometimes months or years later, because they were microchipped.

Bird Protection

Will putting a bell on a cat's collar protect birds from being killed? Probably not. In fact, experts have observed that cats can learn to stalk their prey without making the bells on their collars move at all. A cat who's determined to hunt will probably keep hunting, given the opportunity to do so.

Groups such as the Audubon Society are very much against free-roaming cats, whether they're pets given access to the outside or former pets turned wild and living as best they can. Studies have shown that cats do take a fair amount of songbirds, but they also kill a lot of animals that are neither endangered nor wanted, such as mice and rats. People who advocate for humane handling of feral cat colonies argue that blaming songbird decline on cats is a bit of a "glass house" situation. The biggest threat to any endangered species is the destruction of habitat and pollution. Cats have nothing to do with either of those problems.

The debate will rage on, no doubt. In the meantime, if you want to keep your cat from hunting, keep him inside.

Carrier

Kittens are right up there with Columbus, Drake, and Magellan when it comes to being bold explorers, but the inside of a car is not the best place to let them roam free. For rides to the veterinarian or trips to your winter digs in Palm Springs, or even just to Grandma's house, your kitten or cat should ride safely contained in his very own transporter device. This can be a hard plastic carrier or a soft-sided model.

Plastic crates are tough, long-lasting, and easy to clean if Snowflake hacks up a hairball or lets loose with a spray of urine. They can be secured in a car by running the seat belt through the handle. Look for one with top-loading and front entries—two doors, in other words. Sometimes it's a heckuva lot easier to lift a cat out of a crate than it is to coax him out of the front of it. Note that airlines generally don't permit the use of crates with top openings, so if Snowflake will be traveling by air you'll need to select a different style.

Keeping Up with the Latest

Every year "Team Becker" heads to the world's largest trade show for the pet care industry, Global Pet Expo. The show draws companies from all over the world and is so big that the buyers would be well-advised to bring a GPS to help them navigate the twelve football fields' worth of products.

Every year with the help of my team of writers, editors, videographers, photographers, and producers, I pick Becker's Best: the products that I find the most innovative and useful, and that I most want pet lovers to know about. We shine the light on these great products through all my media platforms, including Vetstreet.com, YouTube, Facebook, and Twitter. If you want to keep up with the latest, come find me!

Soft-sided carriers are cozy for cats and easy to carry using a shoulder strap. They are usually made of nylon and can be wiped clean with little effort. If Snowflake will be living a globetrotter lifestyle, a soft-sided carrier fits easily beneath an airline seat, but it can't be used for cats traveling in the cargo area. Choose a soft-sided carrier with zippered top and end closures for ease of removal at your destination. Some soft-sided carriers roll along on wheels, but make sure you get one that's stable and won't tip over with your cat inside. That would be a CATastrophe! Whichever style you choose, go for high-quality construction, with sturdy latches and smooth edges.

LOOKING GOOD: CHOOSING GROOMING TOOLS

The earlier you accustom your kitten to being brushed and combed, the more she will enjoy it and the easier it will be to keep her clean. For the typical cat, a basic set of grooming tools includes a stainless-steel fine-tooth comb, a wire slicker brush or rubber grooming mitt, a nail trimmer, a finger brush for teeth, and some toothpaste specially made for cats. (Don't use your own toothpaste or your cat will be foaming at the mouth.)

Comb. The fine-tooth comb removes loose, dead hair. The more hair you remove with the comb and the slicker brush, the less hair you'll find on your clothes and furniture. That's also less hair that your cat will be taking in when she grooms herself, then hacking up as a hairball afterward. The comb is also a fine way to find and remove the little blood-sucking vampires that may be feeding on your cat: fleas! It won't get rid of them, but it will alert you to an infestation.

Brushes. Brushing keeps the skin healthy by distributing skin oils and getting the blood flowing. The wire slicker brush, which looks like a torture device but feels great to cats, removes dead hair and helps to prevent tangles from forming. A rubber mitt or curry brush also removes dead hair. One of my favorite grooming tools is a shedding rake with the dynamite name of the FURminator. It gets all the loose hair off cats, and that means less shedding.

Brush short-haired cats weekly. Depending on the length and texture of their coats, long-haired cats may need brushing daily or only two or three times a week. Remember, every cat hair that ends up in the comb or brush and into the trash is one less follicle that ends up on the carpet, the sofa, the bed, or you.

Many cats love a soft rubber grooming tool called the cat Zoom-Groom. It is the best for removing loose hair in a friendly way. It also stimulates the capillary circulation and the submusculature as well as activating the glands for the production and distribution of oils in the coat.

Many people consider cats to be untrainable, but that's not the case. Cats are very intelligent and take quickly to reward-based training.

Chapter 5

KITTEN- AND CAT-PROOFING YOUR HOME

You know that old saying, "Curiosity killed the cat"? There's a lot more truth to that than you might think. With their agile bodies and inquisitive nature, there's almost nothing that kittens and cats won't try to investigate, from the very back corners beneath your sofa or bed to the highest points in your home. Even the most experienced cat owners can find it difficult to kitten-proof a home. Be keen and vigilant when it comes to preparing your home for a kitten to take up residence. Here's what to watch out for.

Cats love string, thread, yarn, ribbons, and dental floss—in other words, anything that they can chase and pull. They're fun to play with but hazardous when swallowed, which happens all too often. Anything stringlike that goes down a cat's gullet and into the intestinal tract can cause a partial or complete obstruction. It can even saw through the wall of the intestinal tract and cause peritonitis, an inflammation of the membrane that lines the abdominal cavity.

Put all that stuff way up high, inside a container that can't be opened by a determined kitten. Stow your sewing basket behind closed doors when you're not using it, put used dental floss and string in a trash container with a secure lid, and don't use yarn or ribbons to decorate packages.

What else should you put out of reach?

- **Rubber bands, toys with tails or streamers, electrical cords, and drapery cords.** Put fishing-pole toys inside a closet with the door closed when you can't be around to supervise playtime.
- **Some kittens like to chew on electrical cords.** Protect them from electrical burns to the mouth by encasing the cords in sturdy covers available from hardware stores.
- **Tuck drapery cords out of reach.** Kittens can get caught in them and choke.
- **Certain medications are also lethal to kittens and cats.** Nonsteroidal anti-inflammatory drugs (NSAIDs) such as acetaminophen and ibuprofen are especially toxic. Be careful not to drop any kind of pill on the floor when your kitten is around to gulp it down before you can snatch it back up.

  Think your kitten can't open your pill bottles? Think again. Kittens might not be as good as puppies when it comes to breaking into childproof containers, but they are awfully dexterous and determined when they want something. I've seen a YouTube video that showed a cat unscrewing the lid of a jar to get the cat food inside it, so never assume that something is safe from a clever cat or kitten.
- **Plants are another concern.** Cats love to nibble on greenery, and they don't know what's poisonous and what's not. Lilies, sago palms, oleanders, rhododendrons, and castor beans are just a few of the harmful house and garden plants that don't have a place in a cat lover's home. Ask your veterinarian to help you figure out which plants in your home and yard might be toxic. If you aren't sure what plants are in your yard and home, take clippings to a garden center and ask for help in identifying them.
- **Other hazards to kittens include any small object that might be lying around your house.** I never cease to be amazed by the variety of items that kittens will chew on and swallow: coins, nutshells, the caps off the ends of doorstoppers, plastic wrap or aluminum foil that has been used to cover food, the plastic parts inside toys— you name it and a veterinarian has probably found it inside a kitten. Put away or throw away anything that might tempt a kitten to eat it. That includes potpourri scented with aromatic oils. It may smell wonderful, but those scented oils can be deadly if your cat eats them.

❖**Even household appliances and furniture can pose dangers to your kitten.** He'll explore, play, or nap in small, dark places like the washer or dryer, the sleeper sofa, or beneath the recliner. Always check inside your washer and dryer before you turn them on, and do a kitten search before folding up the sleeper sofa or Murphy bed or lowering the footrest of a recliner.

❖**Cats also like curling up inside a warm car engine.** If your kitten or cat has access to the garage or driveway, bang on the hood three times before starting the car. The noise should make her scamper out.

SOCIALIZATION AND BEHAVIOR TRAINING

Two of the most destructive myths about cats are that they are shy and standoffish, and that they can't be trained. Nothing could be further from the truth! Kittens who are handled and talked to by people from a young age grow up to be wonderfully social cats who enjoy being with their family, meeting guests, and going places. And kittens who have that kind of special relationship with their people learn quickly. With the right motivation—usually food—cats are highly trainable and enjoy the mental stimulation that training gives. They can be taught all kinds of behaviors, from a basic sit to giving a high five to running a feline agility course. Here's how to start your kitten off on the right paw.

Socialization

Between the ages of three weeks and twelve weeks, kittens are busy taking notes on everything they experience: the touch of a hand, the bark of a dog, the whir of a ceiling fan, the crinkle of a shopping bag, the feel of a carpet beneath their feet, the movement of a car as they ride to the veterinarian. The more they are exposed to, the more outgoing they will be. A well-socialized kitten is prepared for anything.

In the best of all possible worlds, your kitten will come from a home where he had good early socialization experiences starting when he was three or four weeks old. But even a kitten who doesn't start to get socialized until he is six or seven weeks old can still get the stimulation he needs to develop into a happy, outgoing cat. One of the best ways to provide him with new experiences is to sign him up for a kitten kindergarten class. Your veterinarian may offer these classes at her clinic, or she may be able to refer you to a class nearby. Kitten kindergarten is a new and important concept in kitten raising. Classes allow kittens and their people to get together in a fun and casual setting. Kittens play with one another and with different types of toys, and encounter items that they might not have seen before, while their owners get advice on dealing with potential behavior problems and tips on training their smart little kitties. This is such a great way to teach kittens that going places in the car and meeting other people and cats can be fun, not scary. It will pay off big time when your cat needs to go to the veterinarian or travel to your new home across town or across the country.

Gentling Techniques

You can also work on socializing your kitten at home. To help him get used to being handled, pet him briefly several times a day. Carry him around the house for a couple of minutes at a time, talking to him kindly as you go. Hold him close, so he can feel and hear your heart beating, but don't squeeze.

Gently run your hands over his body. Every cat should be comfortable with being examined, whether it's by you, your veterinarian, a groomer, or a cat show judge. A brief daily once-over will help him get used to this. Run your hands up and down his legs and over his belly. Lift up his lip and take a look at the teeth and gums. Handle his paws so he'll be used to it when you need to trim his nails. Look inside his ears and then give him a smooch on the head. Well, that last bit isn't really part of the exam, but how can you resist?

Part of gentling a kitten is letting him know when he's playing too rough. If he lays tooth or claw on you, set him down and walk away. Without yelling, you'll send the message that scratching and biting aren't ever rewarded with attention.

Increasing your kitten's knowledge of his environment is an important part of helping him to settle into it and become the confident cat he needs to be. Let him experience different textures underfoot: grass, gravel, concrete, carpet, hardwood. Brief periods of supervised play outdoors in a fenced yard is a great way to let him see, hear, smell, taste, and touch more of the world. Invite friends and neighbors over so he'll know who they are and get the chance to be petted and played with by more people. And train him, train him, train him!

Training

You're probably thinking that the phrase *cat training* is an oxymoron, but I promise it's not. Teaching your cat to come when you call, sit, play fetch, or jump through a hoop won't turn him into a dog and it won't affect his inherent "cattitude." It will deepen the relationship between the two of you and enhance your ability to communicate. We're not just talking about training a cat to come running when it hears the pop of the food can or the opening of the treat drawer or the rattle of the plastic sack. Training teaches your cat limits so that he doesn't completely run the household, and it makes interacting with him more interesting for you. It's also the best way to keep a cat mentally and physically agile throughout his life. That's all to the good when it comes to living with cats!

Kittens learn fastest, but even an adult cat can learn new tricks. Training a cat is simple. All you need are some tasty treats, a good sense of timing, and a little patience. The two behaviors every cat should know are sit and come. With these suggestions (you never want a cat to think he's being commanded) in his repertoire, your cat will sit politely instead of scratching at your legs or jumping onto your allergic neighbor's lap, and he'll be easy to find in case there's an emergency. Add walking on a leash, and you'll have a cat you can take anywhere. These behaviors, plus fun tricks like waving a paw or giving a high five, are perfect if you would enjoy doing therapy visits with your cat at children's hospitals, nursing homes, and other facilities. (More information on training is on pages 203–210 in Part Three.)

MISTAKES? WE'VE ALL MADE A FEW—AND HERE'S HOW TO AVOID THEM

You are already headed in the right direction by reading this book. The more you learn about caring for your kitten or cat, the more successful your relationship with him will be. I want to share with you the ten most important things you should do with your cat, in the hope that you will avoid grief and aggravation, and also save money.

The 10 Most Important Things to Do with Your Kitten

1. **Socialize your kitten.** An individual cat's personality is a unique blend of inherited traits and early experiences in life. There's not much you can do in the way of controlling your kitten's genetic influences, other than choosing one whose parents are both sociable and affectionate, but you absolutely can make a difference when it comes to his interactions with the world. Choose a kitten whose home life between two and eight weeks of age included plenty of contact with people and a stimulating home environment. That doesn't mean running wild in a backyard or barn. Young kittens need to meet, sniff, touch, and play with all kinds of people and other animals if they are going to grow up to be relaxed, friendly cats.

2. **Train your kitten.** Some cats are more trainable than others, but all are capable of learning basic behaviors, such as sit and come and using a scratching post. Why should you train your cat? The best reason is because it builds a strong relationship between the two of you. Training also gives your kitten's brain a workout, and some of the things you teach your cat will give him physical exercise, too. Cats like to have a good time, so always keep training sessions short, sweet, and upbeat.

3. **Set limits.** Kittens don't come programmed to know what behaviors you like and don't like. Like any other baby creature, they explore and try things out and see what happens. To help your kitten learn what's expected of him and how to live politely in your home, you need to set limits in a kind and intelligent way so he understands what is acceptable behavior and what is not. That means rewarding him when you see him doing things you like— scratching on his post, for instance—and redirecting him when he does things you don't like. If he's jumping on your kitchen counter, move him to his cat tree and reward him for playing there. Chewing on your shoelaces? Give him a toy instead and spend a couple of minutes playing with him. The best way to teach your kitten

what's what is to catch him doing something right and reward him for it.

4. **Kitten-proof your home.** Keeping kittens safe from household hazards can be an exhausting and demanding task. You've gotta look up, look down, and look all around to find all the things they could conceivably—and inconceivably—get into or get hurt by. That includes electrical cords, curtain cords, thread, string, needles, plastic bags, and hidey holes that you're sure they couldn't possibly squeeze through. Trust me. They can. If something has even the slightest potential of being dangerous to your kitten, put it behind closed doors.

5. **Play with your kitten.** It's easy to underestimate a cat's need for interactive play and exercise. Most people think that cats don't need exercise or play at all, and that's a huge mistake. Invest a few minutes a couple of times a day—especially in the early evening— letting your cat bat at a feather wand or chase a Ping-Pong or crinkle ball down the hall. Make sure he has some puzzle toys to challenge his brain and a tall, sturdy cat tree to encourage jumping and climbing. Rotate his toys so he always has something new and different to play with.

6. **Teach your kitten not to use his teeth and claws on people.** Lots of people with new kittens get caught up in all the cute and let the little furball bat at their hands with his claws extended or chew on their fingers until they bleed. You can usually spot these folks a mile away; they are the ones who look like they fished a fork out of the garbage disposal while it was still running. You need your hands for important things like eating and writing, so don't let your mini tiger shred them. Find an acceptable substitute like a laser pointer, feather cat toy, or your mother-in-law's expensive handmade doily.

7. **Leave your kitten's claws alone unless you have no other choice.** Some folks think declawing is just one of the "things you do" when you get a kitten, like buying a litter box or getting her spayed. Nothing could be further from the truth! We are not going to solve the contentious issue of declawing here, but it deserves some thought before you make a decision about it. Declawing involves removing some of the bones of the fingers as well as the claws, and I believe it should be reserved only for cases in which the cat's

life is in danger because of the damage he has caused, and only after you have exhausted every other option. Bored cats shred the couch, just like bored teenagers set fires. Give your cat plenty of acceptable things to shred, like a scratching post liberally treated with catnip, and keep him active and stimulated, and the chances of destruction go way down.

8. **Put collars and tags on, and microchip your kitten, too.** One out of every three pets becomes lost sometime in his life. When a kitten or cat gets lost, it's often for good because in many cases he's not wearing any form of identification. You can't get your kitten back if people don't know how to reach you. Put a breakaway collar on him with a tag that has your name and cell phone number on it. For added insurance, and in case he loses his collar, have your veterinarian microchip him. Most shelters and veterinary clinics these days have scanners that read microchips and reunite you quick.

9. **Alter your kitten.** Spaying and neutering improves a kitten's chances for good health throughout life and prevents the birth of kittens you might not want or be ready to care for. Female kittens can reach sexual maturity as early as three and a half to four months of age, and male kittens aren't far behind. Kittens can be altered when they are only eight weeks old, as long as they weigh more than two pounds. Neutering kittens this young is a safe and accepted procedure, and they bounce back more quickly than older kittens or cats.

10. **Buy pet health insurance.** It used to be the stuff of jokes, but pet health insurance is the real deal. It is available from more and more companies and can take the sting out of ever-growing vet bills. Veterinarians hate euthanizing cats who could be treated if only the owners could afford the therapy. Insurance helps to make sure this does not happen. Sometimes there are headaches regarding reimbursement; for instance, you usually have to pay the vet first and then submit your paperwork, but I know that many lives have been saved thanks to pet health insurance. Vet bills can run into the thousands for serious illnesses, and many folks don't have the savings to cover the unexpected.

The 10 Best Things to Do with Your Cat

1. **Learn about cat behavior and physical needs.** Cats are unique creatures, mysterious and even a little bit wild. Understanding your cat's physical and emotional needs can help you give him a stimulating environment that will enhance his life and prevent him from becoming bored and destructive. The most important thing you can know about cats? They never do things for spite or revenge. Cats definitely have emotions, but spite is a complex feeling that isn't within their range. There is always a good reason behind their behavior, but sometimes you have to be a cross between a detective and a psychologist to figure out what it is. Consider such possibilities as separation anxiety; not enough toys, playtime, exercise, or other enriching experiences; or territorial behavior caused by the presence of a new person or animal in the home.

2. **Scoop the litter box frequently.** How often should you scoop? Every time your cat uses the box. Think of your own bathroom. Would you be okay with flushing the toilet only once a day or, worse, once a week? If you hate scooping, and are a really dedicated cat owner, try out one of the new automated litter boxes or even consider teaching your cat to use the toilet. It can be done! And if your cat is really talented, you can even teach him to flush when he's finished.

3. **Wash the litter box regularly.** Yes, I said "wash" the litter box. One of the main reasons cats eliminate outside the litter box is because it stinks. A dirty litter box is also suspected of being a factor when cats develop idiopathic—meaning there's no known cause—cystitis, a painful urinary tract infection. Every two weeks, dump out the litter, clean the litter box using warm water and a mild dishwashing detergent, and then fill it with new litter. If that isn't good enough for your finicky feline, you may need to clean the box and change the litter weekly. You'll both be happier. And every six months replace the litter box and recycle the old one.

4. **Don't overfeed your cat.** Free-feeding cats—leaving dry food out for them all the time—is out of style. You must precisely measure out the amount of food you're going to feed. Cats are the original hunter-gatherers. Engage that hunting instinct by putting kibble

in a puzzle toy (see page 56) so they have to work for it, or hide small containers of food throughout the house to encourage them to move around and use their sense of smell to snare their "prey." Fat cats are funny in cartoons, but in real life they are like tubby time bombs ticking away their health. Obesity-related health problems include increased risk of Type II diabetes, arthritis, heart disease, asthma, skin problems, even cancer.

5. **Learn to read your cat's body language to recognize signs of illness or pain.** Cats, by nature, are self-sufficient and have an independent streak a mile wide. They don't typically come up to you and say, "Hey, Phil, I'm not feeling so keen today. Why don't you take me to the vet for a look-see?" Cats are masters of illusion, capable of looking totally normal while bad things brew beneath the surface. Behind that too-cool-for-school façade that proclaims, "I am doing perfectly fine, thanks very much," illnesses and injuries can go undetected for days. I constantly hear owners say, "But he was fine yesterday," when we know we are dealing with diseases that take weeks, if not months, to develop. Look at and touch your cat every day, or at least once a week, to make sure he is active, bright-eyed, and not losing weight. Pay attention to his water intake and litter box output. If you notice anything different, take him to your veterinarian for a physical and lab tests such as blood work, X-rays, or urinalysis, if necessary. This can help you spot problems early, when they are usually less expensive to fix. And if you've bought pet health insurance, it may help you cover the costs.

6. **Keep your cat inside.** I love the outdoors. I live on a horse ranch high in the mountains of northern Idaho. There's fresh air, sun, wind, and the sounds of nature. Things like that. Cats love the outdoors, too, where they can explore and climb trees and hunt mice and bugs. But along with all the positives for them come a handful of hazards: dogs, cars, infectious diseases spread by other cats, puddles of toxic antifreeze. The list could go on and on. I am not advocating for every cat to live a life of quiet introspection indoors—it just isn't possible with some cats—but if you do want to let your cat outside, consider supervised outings or building an enclosed playground for him in your yard. The average life span

for an outdoor cat is about one-quarter the average of an indoor cat.

7. **Watch out for toxic plants.** Lilies, for instance, are pretty…and pretty deadly. No one knows what toxin in lilies makes them deadly, but they can cause sudden kidney failure in cats after only a tiny nibble of a leaf or exposure to a dusting of pollen. All parts of the lily are toxic. Make sure your cat does not have access to lilies in your home or yard, and never send bouquets containing lilies to your cat-owning friends. Other toxic plants you should ban from your home include cycads, oleander, and sago palms. Ask your veterinarian for a complete list.

8. **Keep medications securely hidden.** You think you have a headache now? Wait until you get the vet bill for treating a case of feline acetaminophen toxicity! Acetaminophen, the active ingredient in Tylenol, is deadly to cats. I have treated many cases of this toxicity when well-intentioned but misguided people have given this medication to their cats. It causes anemia and severe liver failure. **Never, under any circumstances, give your cat acetaminophen or other NSAIDs made for people. A single capsule is more than enough to kill them.**

Pain specialist Dr. Robin Downing, a colleague and a friend, has reported about new feline NSAID guidelines for your veterinarian to follow. A thorough history, physical examination, and laboratory testing should be mandatory prior to NSAID therapy. To reduce the risk of adverse drug events, NSAID therapy should always be given with or after food. If the cat does not eat, therapy should be withheld. Cats are notorious in their ability to hide their pain, especially the slowly progressing, chronic pain of osteoarthritis.

As veterinarians have become sensitized to the presence of chronic pain in older cats, we want to do the right thing and relieve that pain. Previously, when veterinarians have reached for NSAIDs, we have been left wondering if we were truly doing the right thing or if, in fact, we were placing our feline patients in harm's way. Now, finally, we have consensus guidelines for the long-term use of NSAIDs in cats. This puts a map in our hands to craft a reasonable dosing, monitoring, and client education plan for painful cats who need and deserve our help.

9. **Vaccinate…just enough.** Vaccines are available for just about every ailment known to man, maybe with the exceptions of bad taste in curtains and a love of David Hasselhoff. Vaccines have prevented untold millions of illnesses and death in cats, but a growing body of evidence indicates that too many vaccinations can cause harm in the form of a type of cancer at the site of the injection. Young cats absolutely need vaccinations to prevent serious conditions like feline distemper and rabies, but have a conversation with your veterinarian about which ones your cat needs and which ones are optional, as well as how often they need to be given. The core diseases cats need to be vaccinated against are feline panleukopenia virus, feline herpesvirus-1, feline calicivirus, and rabies. The American Association of Feline Practitioners recommends a series of three to four vaccinations for kittens between the ages of six weeks and sixteen weeks, followed by a booster vaccination a year later. After that, vaccinations do not need to be given more often than once every three years. Noncore vaccines, meaning those that should be given only to cats at high risk, include feline leukemia virus, Bordetella, chlamydia, and feline immunodeficiency virus. Vaccines that are not generally recommended include those for feline giardia and feline infectious peritonitis (FIP).

10. **Practice preventive care.** Cats are taken to the veterinarian less frequently than dogs, and people are less likely to spend money on veterinary care for their cats. That's just not right. Cats need the same kinds of preventive-care programs and annual exams that dogs receive. Heartworm disease is seen more frequently in cats because people don't think to put them on preventive medications. Dental disease, feline asthma, and arthritis are just three of the conditions that are dramatically underdiagnosed in cats because they aren't examined on a regular basis. Annual exams will help ensure that any health problems your cat may be hiding from you are identified and treated before they become serious.

PART TWO

HOME CARE TO
KEEP PETS HEALTHY
AND SAFE

You've got a new cat or kitten. Congratulations! Your job now is to care for your cat's daily needs, and mine is to help you with that job by giving you the information you need. While your cat still needs regular attention from your veterinarian—yes, even healthy cats need their veterinarians!—the decisions you make for your cat's daily care will make a huge difference in making your cat's life the best it can possibly be...and the longest, too.

Cats are considered easy-care pets, and while that's true to a certain extent, they aren't the self-sufficient type most of them seem to want you to believe. Like those tough people who mutter "I'm fine" through teeth clenched with pain, your cat really wants and needs your help. (Hmmm, actually, having come from a background of tough farmers, I can say your cat wants and needs your help probably a lot more than those folks who mutter "I'm fine" through their teeth. But the fact that animals are generally less complicated than people is, after all, one of the reasons why I love being a veterinarian.)

The first thing you need to pay attention to in helping your cat not only survive, but thrive, is nutrition. It all starts at a momma cat's side, with simple, natural milk. After that, it gets a whole lot more complicated, with not only every brand trying to convince you what's best, but an entire Internet that sometimes seems devoted to confusing you. No worries. Let me break it down for you, so you can work with your veterinarian to give your cat the best.

And then, I'll help you figure out what's best in every other way, from cat trees to litter boxes, from toys to setting up your house. It's easy and it's fun. So let's go!

Your veterinarian should be your guide to choosing the right food for your cat or kitten. He can help you select a good variety no matter if you shop at a grocery store, a pet supply store, or your veterinary hospital.

Chapter 6

WHAT IS GREAT TO EAT AND WHERE TO FIND IT

Nearly everything about your cat's anatomy points to her genetic predestination to hunt, and hunt well. Her feet are designed for silent stalking; her claws can hook anything and won't let go; her teeth are long, pointed, and razor-sharp. And it all begs the question: what do you feed a creature who is so obviously designed to fend for herself? As holder of both the purse strings and the can opener, you get to choose what this natural hunter eats—at least, aside from the occasional "catch of the day."

Choosing a cat food should be simple business, but with so many options available, it can be tricky to find the right diet for your cat's best health. Even after thirty years of practicing veterinary medicine, I have to admit I sometimes find myself a little staggered by today's pet food aisle. When I was a kid, we fed our cats in the barn from a fifty-pound bag of generic, feed-store kibble. Now I go to the grocery store that sells my family's own food, and I see row upon row of dry, canned, and even refrigerated fresh foods for felines—something for every taste, dietary need, preference, and budget. The pet food industry has come a long way, baby. As a consumer, it's great to have choices. But you have to be able to sort through your options, weigh costs versus benefits, and know how to compare them to do your cat justice.

WHAT A CAT NEEDS

Knowing how your cat's nutritional needs differ from your own may help put his very distinctive dietary requirements in perspective:

- **Must have meat.** The feline system is designed to depend on the consumption of other animals to survive and thrive. Unlike humans and dogs, who are omnivores and can stay healthy on a variety of different kinds of diets, cats are "strict" or "obligate" carnivores. Just like their distant cousins the lion, the tiger, and the cheetah, house cats not only prefer meat, they can't maintain good health without it.

- **Pound for pound, cats need far more protein.** A cat needs more than double the amount of protein per pound of body weight that a person requires. And even though we omnivores can meet our protein requirements with nonmeat foods like dairy products, nuts, and beans, cats don't have that luxury—animal protein is the only kind that fulfills their nutritional needs. If a cat doesn't get enough protein in his diet, his body will actually break down its own muscle tissue to get the nutrients he needs.

- **Cats sponge vitamins and amino acids from their prey.** There are some nutrients that an omnivore can produce or convert from food, but cats have to get them ready-to-use from their diet. Among these are vitamin A, niacin, and the amino acids arginine and taurine. Each of these nutrients is essential for good health. Without usable vitamin A, for example, a cat can suffer vision problems and a weakened immune system. Taurine is critical for heart health and also for healthy eyes. Unless your cat is dining on fresh catch several days a week, you need to provide a diet that provides these nutrients in usable form.

- **Many cats don't get thirsty.** Cats are descended from desert hunters, and many scientists believe this is the reason they don't seem to have a strong thirst drive. In the wild, this isn't too much of an issue—any fresh prey a cat would catch is made mostly of water. In a world of indoor cats eating dry kibble, however, this can become a big problem. Cats need plenty of water, whether they drink it directly or get it from their food. Without enough water in their diets, cats are susceptible to urinary tract problems. Cats with dental disease have decreased water consumption that, combined with a cat's tendency to be dehydrated, can make for serious health problems.

To help prevent dehydration, make sure your cat absolutely always has fresh water available. Some cats prefer running water, leading owners to leave a faucet dripping. A better solution is a pet-sized water fountain (for more information, see page 57). There are many models of these inexpensive water-circulating fountains on the market, and you can easily recoup your cost on your water bills if you've been leaving the sink dripping for your cat. If necessary, you can also encourage your cat to drink by adding a small amount of flavoring to the water to make it more appealing. A bit of clam juice or a little broth will turn an ordinary dish of water into a lovely cocktail as far as your cat's concerned.

AN ENDLESS ARRAY OF FOOD CHOICES
FOR CATS AND THEIR OWNERS

The pet food aisle at your local big box store contains labels offering cuisine that's "fresh," "lean," "gourmet," "holistic," "natural," and "veterinary recommended." Regarding the latter, I often lament that putting "veterinary recommended" on a product is the easiest thing to do, but getting a "veterinary recommendation" may be the hardest. Honestly, every passed-over option can seem like a missed opportunity. Product descriptions seem to be written by the same folks who compose the menus at four-star restaurants, and the packaging photos are often worthy of the pages of *Bon* (not Bone!) *Appétit*. Whether you choose dry, canned, semimoist, freeze-dried, frozen, homemade, boutique brand, or generic food is a decision you should discuss with your cat's veterinarian. Here are a few guidelines, though, that can help you narrow things down substantially:

❧ **You don't have to choose just one.** In fact, it's better if you don't. Feeding a variety of cat foods offers multiple benefits. First, you can create a diet and schedule that suits both you and your cat. For example, kitty's hungry at two a.m., and you're not budging from the bed: a small dish of kibble set out just before lights-out fills the bill. In the morning, though, you can crack open a can of wet food to bring your cat to you, combining bonding and breakfast. Second, since cats are often finicky and resistant to new foods, keeping a few different flavors, brands, and formats in rotation will help ensure your cat never refuses to eat the food you have on hand because it looks or smells unfamiliar.

❧ **Choose a brand you know.** Large, brand-name pet food companies have very deep pockets for pet food research. They also have a great deal to lose if their products don't deliver. Most of these manufacturers have been around for decades, and though they are highly profitable, they are also committed to understanding pet nutrition, to long-term and multigenerational testing, and to quality control measures.

❧ **Buy the best you can afford.** Even though packaging and marketing are responsible for a significant chunk of the cost of pet food, cost *is* usually commensurate with quality. Premium pet foods are generally worth the price in their cost. This is one of the areas where your cat's veterinarian can most help you sort out the best value. Be honest about what you are willing to pay and what your limits are for inconvenience (driving to the vet office to purchase food, for example). Some midlevel brands are exceptionally good for their price point, and some high-enders are good, but not great. In general, though, the foods that fall at the bottom of the price spectrum have one thing in common—they are heavy on cheap fillers and light on quality proteins. Avoid them if you can.

❧ **Skim the label for two things.** First, choose a food specifically for cats that is labeled "complete and balanced" by the Association of American Feed Control Officials (AAFCO). All foods with this label have been proven to meet minimum quality standards. Second, look for meats—real meats with names you recognize—among the top ingredients. When a label says "meat by-products," for example, it may be referring to Kobe beef or beef hide. Rather than letting your imagination do the sorting, choose a label that gives you some idea of what you're getting.

❧ **Consult with a professional.** Veterinarians have the experience and training to look past tantalizing ads and competing food claims to know what food is best for each cat. You can ask them for a recommendation of a food that's best that they carry at the practice and one that's at the grocery store or the pet store. PETCO, for example, has certified nutrition counselors who are trained to help cat owners make intelligent choices in essential, advanced, and natural foods.

FORGET BRANDS FOR A MINUTE AND THINK ABOUT FOOD "FORMATS"

Since cat food comes in forms ranging from a forty-pound feed bag to single-portion homemade meals, you can pick and choose what best suits your cat's needs and your budget and lifestyle. As a veterinarian, I recommend combining a couple of different food formats. That way your cat has a varied diet and you have options for keeping her happy and healthy.

Kibble

Kibble is the convenience standard in pet food. It may seem odd that an animal naturally dependent on flesh and blood could manage on something that bears no resemblance to it, but many cats do just fine on nothing more than quality dry food and fresh water. There are veterinarians who express concern about the high percentages of plant-based starches in dry foods, and there are also cases where this kind of diet is not the best for a particular cat. The fact is, though, millions of cats are fed this economical diet choice and live long lives in excellent health.

I do recommend giving your cat hard treats regularly, even if they don't make up the lion's share of her diet, because dental treats like Feline Greenies help keep kitty's teeth clean and healthy.

Canned

While kibble is popular with many cat lovers, many veterinarians recommend feeding canned food over any other format. For starters, canned foods tend to have higher percentages of protein and fat than dry foods. Second, canned food has significantly higher water content than dry (about 70 percent versus 10 percent). That 70 percent water figure is coincidentally about the same water content your cat would get if he ate a small animal in the wild (or, heaven forbid, in the house). Lastly, canned foods seem to be more appetizing to finicky cats. They are an especially good option for older cats, cats with health issues, and cats with dental problems.

Dehydrated, Freeze-Dried, and Frozen

In an age when food markets like Fresh Market and Whole Foods are turning many shoppers' attention to the benefits of organic products and local produce, many pet owners are looking at their pets' food with a new perspective as well. In response, there's a growing segment of the pet food industry that now offers top-quality pet foods in dehydrated, freeze-dried, frozen, and even fresh forms. These companies are creating foods that are made to the same standards as human food, often using the same ingredients. The newest of these, Freshpet Select, has created a new wrinkle in the pet food industry by introducing refrigerated meals for dogs and cats in grocery stores coast to coast.

If your cat has a specific digestion problem, allergies, or another health condition, this kind of diet may also be worth a try. As with any major diet change, though, you should consult with a veterinarian before the big switch. There are many anecdotal cases of pet owners who believe their cats are healthier because of a nontraditional diet, but there is no evidence yet that cat foods in this category are any better for long-term health than good-quality canned food or kibble.

Homemade Diets—Raw or Cooked

Along with the trend toward pet foods that are organic and minimally processed comes a growing number of people who choose to feed their cat a homemade diet. There's peace of mind for some pet owners in knowing exactly what ingredients they are feeding their pets, where those foods came from, and what chemical additives are present. Home-preparing food for pets is nothing new—after all, people have been giving cats scraps from the table for as long as cats have been domesticated.

Some of the most popular homemade diets are comprised largely of raw meats, and many veterinarians and physicians have expressed concern that feeding this kind of food could put both cat and owner in danger of food-borne bacterial contamination. The jury is still out on this, as there are many pet owners who do successfully feed their cats raw diets, and not enough research has been done to prove or disprove the risks.

One thing is certain, though: if you choose to feed your cat a homemade diet, you can't just throw together a menu of raw meat and consider it done. It is far too easy to shortchange your cat critical nutrients without carefully planning and researching a diet. There are several good books and websites that share how-to information. I recommend Dr. Donald Strombeck's *Home-Prepared Dog & Cat Diets: The Healthful Alternative.*

For the majority of pet owners, a homemade diet for a cat is more trouble than it's worth: more expensive, more complicated, and more time-consuming than any commercial diet. For those willing to make a commitment to doing it properly, though, this kind of diet can be a viable, healthful alternative to more traditional options.

There are so many great options for feeding your cat—both from the pet food aisle and from your own kitchen. However, there are also some foods a cat should never eat. Ingestion of some of these foods can constitute an immediate veterinary emergency. In the case of others, health consequences may take time to emerge. Either way, steering your cat clear of the following foods will help keep him healthy, happy, and out of the veterinarian's office.

A word to the wise about these forbidden foods: Most of the cats we see in the veterinary ER were not deliberately given the foods that made them sick. Always remember that your cat is part acrobat, part stealth-reconnaissance expert, and ever curious. Foods and medications left on the counter, in an open wastebasket, or in the sink are all fair game as far as kitty is concerned, so store and dispose of any potentially dangerous foods accordingly.

Vitamins, supplements, and medications for people and dogs. Cats metabolize medications differently than you or your canine companion. A dropped tablet, a spoonful of medicine left on the counter, or even one of your dog's pain pills can be life-threatening for your cat. These substances are the number one cause of accidental poisonings in cats, and if your cat gets into one, please call her veterinarian right away for advice.

Xylitol. This artificial sweetener is commonly found in sugar-free candy and gum, as well as in some surprising products like mouthwash and toothpaste. Though cats don't crave sweets and aren't likely to seek these products out, it's important for you to keep them out of reach just in case. Even a small dose of this substance can cause extreme illness.

Chocolate. Chocolate has gained a reputation as being dangerous for dogs, but it holds as much or more potential harm for cats. Your cat's small size makes it easier for her to OD. An M&M or two is not going to cause a health crisis (though I recommend never giving a cat chocolate in any form), but as a general rule, the darker the chocolate, the more toxic it is for your pet.

Onions, onion powder, and garlic. Onions and, to a lesser extent, garlic are both potentially toxic for cats. These spices can damage your cat's red blood cells and lead to anemia. One of the big problems with onion and garlic powder is that both are commonplace in human diets, from boxed macaroni and cheese to jars of baby food. Check the label before you feed any people foods to your cat.

Dough. I don't know anyone who deliberately feeds uncooked yeast dough to their cat, but I've met a few cats in the veterinary office who have helped themselves to it anyway. Ingested dough can expand in your pet's stomach, leading to an intestinal blockage or, in severe cases, a rupture.

Feline Fact

Milk and dairy products are not toxic to cats, but they can cause intestinal upset. If your cat occasionally enjoys small amounts of dairy products without ill effects, it's fine to offer them once in a while. Many adult cats are actually lactose intolerant, though, and their owners unintentionally make them ill every time they offer a dairy product.

Dog food. An occasional mouthful (or bowlful) of dog food won't do your cat any harm. However, dog food is not an acceptable substitute for cat food as a regular diet. Dog foods are formulated with canine nutritional needs in mind, and they do not meet the basic dietary requirements of cats. Fed solely dog food, a cat can develop severe nutritional deficiencies.

Favorite foods. Like children who fill up on chips and won't eat their dinner, cats can definitely get too much of a good thing when it comes to foods. Cats fed so much fish, cheese, coldcuts, or any other favorite treat that it interferes with their consumption of a balanced diet can actually become malnourished and very sick kitties. I firmly believe there's a place for any cat's favorite foods in a healthy diet, but be sure you don't put the cart before the horse, so to speak, and give so many goodies that they get in the way of your cat's core nutrition.

Foods from your glass or plate. Cats should never have caffeinated beverages or alcohol—both can make them very ill. In addition, be very choosy about what you offer kitty from your own plate. An occasional bit of lean meat or fish will be much appreciated, but fatty meats can give your cat a nasty bellyache, and cooked bones from your table pose the danger of intestinal damage or blockage.

HOW TO KNOW WHEN A DIET IS RIGHT—AND WRONG

❧ **A healthy weight and body condition.** The single biggest feeding mistake cat owners make is simply giving too much. Most cats only need between 25 and 30 calories per pound of body weight each day to maintain a healthy weight. That's not a whole lot of food, no matter what diet you're feeding them. An extra pound or two on your cat's frame is very easy to overlook—after all, the cat's happy, you're happy. But a cat that should weigh 10 pounds and tips the scales at 12 is like an average human carrying around 30 extra pounds. The problem is that overweight cats are at risk for a whole host of health problems, including diabetes, heart conditions, and joint problems. If your cat doesn't appear to have a waist or a tuck to his tummy when you view him from the top or the side, hop on the scale with him and see if he's packing any new pounds.

❧ **Soft coat, shiny eyes.** You know the old saying that "the proof is in the pudding." Well, one of the clearest, most obvious proofs that a cat is eating a healthy diet is in the texture, shine, and softness of his coat. This is one of the first things your cat's veterinarian notices during any office visit. Dry or dull fur, greasy patches, and dull spots all indicate something wrong with your cat's general health, and often dental problems. In some cases, food allergies are the culprit when a cat has skin irritation.

❧ **Litter box tales.** The one place that holds the best clues as to whether your cat is eating the right diet is probably not among your favorites: it's the litter box. Veterinarians learn very quickly to get over any reservations about asking after and examining poop. There's just too much health information right there for us to observe. So what do you want to see in the litter box? Small, firm, formed stool with no mucus or blood. Also, the odor in the litter box should be consistent—any big change that doesn't correlate with a diet change is cause for concern. Cat poo should not stink when it's at room temperature. If it can be smelt two rooms away, or the smell "hangs in the curtains," then the cat (usually a kitten up to ten months old, but I've seen them older) needs treatment for a parasite called coccidia.

Pay Attention to Prospective Problems

In 2007, thousands of pets were sickened and killed when adulterated ingredients from rogue overseas suppliers got into many different brands of pet food. Anecdotal evidence suggests more cats were made sick or died than dogs.

Because there is no central reporting system for pet deaths, many of the sick and dead animals were considered to be isolated incidents, until routine product testing revealed the problem and veterinarians and public-health officials started putting the pieces together and revealed how widespread the problem was. Even today we're seeing cats whose kidneys were affected by tainted ingredients becoming sick—or dying—as the ravages of the toxic protein substitute and old age exacerbate each other. The unprecedented recalls of affected products went on for weeks as companies scrambled to find out the problem and pull affected food off the shelves.

Pet food comes from the same food-supply system as human food, and that means you must be aware of recalls for your entire family. Be sure to pay attention to any news about recalls. You can get recall information straight from the US Food and Drug Administration by signing up for notices at FDA.gov. If a product you've bought turns up in a recall, stop feeding it to your cat, but save the food. And call your veterinarian for information.

If you routinely store pet food in containers, always save the part of the package with the manufacturer's contact information and lot number.

Treats

As both an animal lover and a veterinarian, I'm a firm believer in the power of treats. You can use them to build your relationship with your cat, to teach her to trust and listen to you, and just to make her happy.

With my own pets, I try to cultivate the vibe that being around me is like playing a very generous slot machine—they just never know when I'm going to pay out or how much, but they know I'm good for at least the occasional jackpot!

There's room for treats in every cat's diet, even those who are overweight or have food restrictions. The key to giving away the goodies without giving up your cat's good health is that treats should comprise no more than 10 percent of her daily diet. If your cat has weight or health issues, choose treats that are different from her regular food but still within her dietary restrictions. For example, tiny dices of lean chicken or cheese or low-calorie commercial treats are fine for most cats on a weight-loss program. Think small, with treats the size of the nail on your pinky finger, or less. You can offer more treats—equating to more warm feelings and bonding moments—if you feed tidbits instead of chunks. And don't forget to amplify the power of any treat by using the "happy voice" and warming body language your cat loves.

One last note about cat treats: when you choose for your cat, skip the sweets. Cats' taste buds aren't calibrated to appreciate sweets, and sugar has no redeeming nutritional value. Instead, offer savory (but not salty) options from your pet pantry and your own fridge.

Fat Cats Are Not Funny

Your tubby tabby is lovable and huggable. I know. I feel the same unconditional love for my own pets: feline, canine, equine, and otherwise. But as both pet owner and veterinarian, I've seen firsthand that letting our furry friends pack on the pounds is a huge, and potentially costly, mistake.

Think of it this way: a single pound doesn't sound like much extra weight to a human, but you can appreciate what a burden it is on a cat if you imagine strapping a can of soup on his back and expecting him to carry it around day and night. At first, that pound would just be uncomfortable, but over time it would strain your cat's bones and joints, causing him to be achy and slow. If the pound were actual fat, it would also put a heavy burden on his lungs, heart, liver, and kidneys, asking each system to do more work than nature intended. Over time, the extra strain will cause damage that shortens a cat's life by months or, more likely, years.

Rather than thinking of excess weight as part of your cat's charm, ask the veterinarian how to help get him in shape. Being fit will add years to his life, and life to his years—and you'll both be better off for the effort.

EATING ISSUES

Some cats are prone to a variety of eating issues that can make simple feeding a difficult or even health-threatening issue. Sometimes our feline friends lose their appetites and need our help to "find" them again. Sometimes they won't get near—let alone eat—a new diet. And some cats—well, their problem is that they've never met a food they didn't like. Actually, you'd rather have the latter problem than the former, and one way to prevent the "finicky" in cats is to feed a wide variety of foods to them when they're kittens—different shapes, tastes, etc.—so they don't get fixated on any one kind of food.

Refusing food. If your cat is simply off food for a day or so, there's no reason to worry. A simple stomach upset, a stressful change in his environment, or just a weary day could be the culprit. If a lack of appetite persists for more than a day, though, please take it seriously. A human can outlast any dog in a food duel—sooner or later, they'll eat just about anything. A cat, however, can stop eating completely and literally starve himself to death with a dangerous and often fatal condition called hepatic lipidosis. I don't know a single veterinarian who has not seen this in practice multiple times, and it can be very dangerous. Try these suggestions to help your cat work through a finicky phase, but if he's still not eating after two days, touch base with his veterinarian.

❧**Fresh is best.** Cats may be the original food snobs. In addition to having strong likes and dislikes, they often turn their noses up at food that's been sitting around too long. This can be especially true of canned food, which does get pretty unpleasant when left uneaten. Instead of leaving food out for long periods, offer your cat a small meal, fresh from the packaging. If he doesn't eat it after thirty minutes, take it away and try again in a couple of hours.

❧**Serve warm.** Warming your cat's food amps up its flavor and aroma, and can be the simplest way to bring him back to the dinner bowl. A few seconds in the microwave will do the trick.

❧**Break out the good stuff.** Over the years, some of my veterinary clients have had a simple "Is Fluffy sick?" test they rely on at home. If the cat won't eat a regular meal, they chalk it up to a fussy day; but if kitty rejects her favorite treat, like a bit of canned tuna or a smidge of liverwurst, then they assume she is sick. No one knows your cat better than you do, and if she suddenly rejects a food she's been willing to beg and barter for all her life, you'll know she's got troubles worth taking seriously.

Losing weight. It's one thing to be finicky, but something else entirely when your cat starts losing weight. One of the problems is that while weight change is typically easy to spot in a dog, too often cats can gain or lose weight and the hair hides the changes like a curtain. Many times I'll have a cat come in that is like a fur-covered skeleton and the owner didn't even know that the cat had lost weight. The kidneys had almost turned to stone before their unseeing eyes. One of the reasons we want to see cats at least yearly in the veterinary hospital is to track weight change. If lack of appetite is an ongoing concern with your cat and he's lost a half pound or more, ask his veterinarian about the possibility of a medication to stimulate his appetite. Some antidepressant and anti-anxiety meds, including Valium and Xanax, can help switch a cat's appetite from the "off" position back to "on."

Rejecting a diet change. Cats are notorious for becoming very attached to a single food, flavor, or even kibble shape. If you need to introduce a new food for any reason—perhaps the manufacturer is changing your kitty's standard fare, or the veterinarian has recommended a prescription diet—you can quickly find that a switch is easier said than done. The way to avoid this problem is to feed your cat plenty of different foods throughout her life, but especially as a kitten. If you're having this problem, though, it's likely too late to go this route. Instead, try these suggestions:

- **Offer a choice.** When you want something from your cat, the best way to get it is usually by asking, not telling. Rather than simply plopping down the new food instead of the old one, try setting out small portions side by side. Some cats respond better to a new diet if they are given a choice. Offer a half portion of the old food and a half portion of the new food for him to try.
- **Jazz it up.** If the side-by-side route doesn't pan out, raise the stakes by flavoring the new food—still served next to the old one—with a bit of liquid from canned tuna, baby shrimp, or another favorite. Or try clam juice.

Overeating. You can keep kibble out 24/7 for some cats and never see any resulting problems. But that's just some cats. For others, food on the floor day in and day out is like living at the all you-can-eat buffet. If your cat is overworking her food dish and showing the extra ounces that prove it, start feeding her on a schedule instead. The average cat needs only between 250 and 300 calories a day to maintain her weight. Divide her allotment into portions and divvy them out over the course of the day; this will make feeding more like "hunting" than "finding."

The trick to providing care for your cat is to make the experience pleasurable. A love of grooming comes naturally to cats, who can learn to share the pleasant times with you.

Chapter 7

HEALTHY CATS ARE BUSY CATS

In nature, all creatures great and small go about the business of seeking and storing food, staying out of the way of predators, propagating their species, and raising their young. There are natural rhythms of work and rest, but there are no couch potatoes. None of Mother Nature's animals lounge about, staring out at a world they are not part of, waiting for the timely delivery of their next meal. That wouldn't be healthy—physically or mentally.

In domestication, our pets often find themselves with none of these jobs to do, and even though there are great advantages to living the cushy indoor life, there are a few drawbacks as well. The greatest dangers to your well-fed, well-cared-for indoor cat are probably obesity and boredom. Overweight cats are susceptible to a host of health problems, including joint disease, heart conditions, asthma, skin problems, diabetes, even cancer. Plus fat cats are frequently ill-tempered. And bored cats, well, they're often the ones who develop behavioral problems—including bad habits like shredding your curtains, yowling in the wee hours, or piddling on your bedding or in your suitcase.

Evolutionarily cats were amazingly efficient hunters, and as such the day didn't require much time for hunting but did require a lot of time for napping. In fact cats can spend 80 percent of their waking hours napping. Modern house cats come from a long line of ancestors who know the value of a good nap, so having a cat who sleeps for much of the day is nothing to worry about. However, every cat needs a job to do, a game to play, an adventure in his day, to be happy and healthy. Physical and mental exercise are the keys to vitality for cats—for all of us, really. It takes only a few minutes a day of your time to help your cat stay busy enough to maintain physical and mental health.

EXERCISING THE BODY AND THE MIND: GAMES THAT WORK OUT BOTH

If you've ever walked a dog, you know that there's one domesticated species that's easy as pie to exercise—self-motivated, enthusiastic, eager to a fault—and that species is not the cat. As in all things, cat owners must offer a little subtlety and enticement if we want to get our feline friends to shake a leg. Here are a few uniquely feline approaches to exercise and mental stimulation to get things started:

Short bursts are best. All the members of the cat family share a highly efficient operating system: they rest a great deal, and when it comes time to hunt, they perform at an amazing physical peak for a short period of time. That's why they're such fantastic hunters. When you think about exercise and activities for your own tiny tiger, set a five- or ten-minute goal for keeping your cat engaged. Two or three short exercise sessions sprinkled throughout the day are likely to be more pleasant experiences for both you and your cat than any attempt at a thirty-minute "workout." If all those play sessions add up to thirty minutes or so, you're doing a great job of getting your cat moving.

Pay attention to your cat's body language, and you'll see when she's had enough. Of course, if she takes off and leaves you, the sign is perfectly clear. More subtle indicators to note are a low crouch with the ears back, hair standing on end, and ears that are lowered. All of these postures are signs that your cat isn't having fun anymore but feeling stressed, which could lead to aggression.

Attention, please. Even if your goal is to help your cat lose an extra pound or two through exercise, you'll find your best success when you choose activities that are mentally engaging as well as requiring physical effort. Simply put, you can buy every kitty toy on the market or build the world's best climbing gym, but unless your cat's interest is piqued and he's mentally on board, you'll be the only one getting any exercise for your effort. The key to getting a lock on your cat's attention is almost always in presenting a scenario that lets him act like a hunter. Prey drive is so hardwired in most felines that they can't resist a good invitation to exercise it.

Step it up. One of the best ways to help your cat get some exercise is to use his natural inclination to climb. Most cats love getting a little height—whether it's the top of your fridge or the peak perch in a floor-to-ceiling cat tree. Being high up gives cats a sense of safety and, as a bonus, the opportunity to look down on you and your world while they're elevated. The stairs, the furniture, tiered cat shelves (book shelves just large enough for a single cat and covered in a nonskid surface), or any other height challenge available not only appeals to your cat's natural instinct to seek out high spots, but also lets him expend more energy during exercise time.

Creative Crate Training

I'm all for any kind of multitasking that gets two good jobs done at once. Here's one of my favorites: as long as you're playing with your cat, why not teach her to go in her crate while you're at it? I can't tell you how often I see cat owners who have been scratched, and cats who are traumatized by the simple act of going into a carrier for a trip to the veterinary office. This is an avoidable and fixable problem by incorporating your cat's carrier into playtimes and mealtimes until she learns it's a safe, happy place.

The key is to make a carrier appealing so your cat will want to go in it. Start slow, by setting the crate out, with an open door (or with the door removed), and with a soft blanket on the bottom and a

(Continued)

toy in the doorway. Don't press the issue by forcing your cat inside. Just let her get used to having it around for a day or two.

When your cat seems to be comfortable with having the carrier around, toss a treat inside, say "in," and let her take it and leave. It may take a few tries before your cat will venture in after a treat, but in time she'll do it. When kitty is happy to go in and out of the carrier, start closing the door briefly, then opening it back up and giving her a treat. Over time, your cat can come to think of the carrier as a favorite, and a secure place. Once you've accomplished that change of attitude, you'll never have to show up at the veterinary office with scratched-up arms and a freaked-out kitty again.

Consider fresh air and sunshine. If you have an indoor cat, you can use his natural curiosity about the outdoors to provide mental and physical inspiration. There are several ways to accomplish this:

- ❧ **Walking with a harness.** Some cats love getting outdoors enough to tolerate a harness; some don't. You know which camp your cat belongs in. If your kitty will tolerate the harness and leash, you can let her walk you (because you surely won't be walking her) through the yard or the neighborhood. The outdoor experience is a revelation for indoor cats, and most are eager to go again soon.
- ❧ **Strolling.** One of my colleagues, a brilliant cat behaviorist, tells me her cats live for the opportunity to go for a ride in a stroller. Any stroller, whether designed for a cat or a kid, with a zip-close seating area, makes a perfect place for a cat to safely see the world while you get in a walk.
- ❧ **Enclosed spaces.** A safe outdoor space for your cat is a gift that keeps on giving—it's the ideal compromise between the safety of an indoor-only lifestyle and the joy of nature for your cat. A screened patio or sunroom can be paradise for a kitty. If you want to go an extra mile, cat-safe fencing can make any outdoor space a cat sanctuary. There are companies that build cat-safe fences, or if you're more the DIY type, you can find plans online to build one yourself.

*   *   *

Hide and seek. Cats love hiding places, and if you can incorporate these "secret" spots in your playtime, you may hold his interest. Tunnels, both homemade cardboard versions and colorful, creative ones manufactured for kitties (or for toddlers), are big enticements, especially if you use them in conjunction with your cat's toys.

High-up hiding spaces are a big hit with most cats, too. Giving your cat a covered perch atop a carpeted cat tree or a safe nook on a wide, secure shelf will appeal to both her natural inclination to climb and the pleasure of a good hiding place.

Use food! Cats are like teenagers: they're gone all the time, or hiding away in their rooms, and you're wondering where the heck they could be. But when it comes time to eat, they always show up. If there is one development in the care and feeding of pets that has literally changed our lives at Almost Heaven Ranch in the past decade, it's the advent of the food puzzle. We don't even use food bowls anymore. Why bother when our pets can get so much mental stimulation and physical exercise just by working for their food?

Instead of putting a measure of kibble in the cat's bowl in the morning, try putting it inside a basic food puzzle, like a Kong Wobbler, a Funkitty Egg-Cersizer, or a tennis ball with a small hole cut to allow you to place food inside. Offer it to your cat with a quick demonstration to show her there's food in there, and then observe. Suddenly your cat is thinking, examining, and working for her breakfast. There are a million ways to make mealtimes interesting for your cat by making her work for her food. The best way to ensure enthusiasm for these games is to not offer free feed between meals. Where's the fun in that?

HERE ARE 5 EASY FEEDING GAMES TO TRY AT HOME

1. Sprinkle a portion of kibble up and down a staircase, then let your cat work the steps to gather it.
2. Broadcast the food a few pieces at a time down a hallway, and watch the kitty workout that ensues.

3. Close the door to one room and hide a portion of kibble in all the nooks and corners. Call your cat in, then turn her loose to find it. (Remember your own hiding places in case any pieces get left behind!)

4. Play a game of Hansel and Gretel. Take a walk around your home as you carry your cat's kibble with you, dropping pieces as you go. This is especially fun for your cat if you mix in a few extra special treats with her normal food, so she's not sure what you might drop next.

5. Take a few pieces of diced lean meat and freeze them in small ice cubes. On a hot day, give your cat the ice cubes to play with (on a floor that won't mind the damp spot) and let her work her way down to the treats frozen inside.

Next to the occasional midnight crazy run, playtime with you and her toys is probably the best exercise your cat gets. Thinking in terms of getting kitty up and really moving will help you choose toys and games. Most of all, though, remember that hunting is the job your cat instinctively wants to do, and toys and games that play on this instinct are almost always going to be the ones she responds to best.

No matter how great a toy is, your cat will get tired of it after a while. The best way to keep toys "fresh" is to put them away when you're not using them so your cat will be happy to see them on their next appearance. Rotate a couple of different toys into view each day, and be creative in their placement. For example, a toy dangling from a doorknob will be more interesting to kitty than one laying on the floor. A few Ping-Pong balls on the carpet may not be exciting, but placed in an empty bathtub, they're an adventure waiting to happen.

Toys for kitty don't have to be pricey. In many cases, a homemade item is just as good as a store-bought one. Think prey, prey, prey, and you'll find yourself on the right track. Here are a few suggestions:

Irregular rollers. Balls that roll in unpredictable patterns catch a cat's eye and make her want to start a chase. Ping-Pong balls with an added dimple or two to change their roll, homemade balls from aluminum foil or paper, plastic waffle balls, and corks are all cat favorites. If you want to raise the stakes, rub the ball with a bit of catnip, a dice of bologna, or a bit of cheese before putting it into play to pique your cat's interest.

Fishing toys. Fishing-pole toys may be the gold standard of cat toys. Few of my own feline friends can resist them. Retail successes like Da Bird (which has interchangeable feather ends) and the Cat Dancer (which has an obscenely simple design but is a favorite of cats everywhere) are inexpensive to buy, easy to use, and versatile enough for you to tempt your cat to play in dozens of different ways. You can make a cat fishing-pole toy at home, too, if you don't want to shell out for one.

One note about these toys and any toy that involves string: always put them away after play. Veterinarians see cats nearly every day because they have swallowed string, tinsel, or ribbon and are suffering from resulting problems in their intestines. These toys are fine while you are supervising, but don't leave your cat alone with them, lest he decides to stop playing and start snacking.

Squeaky Fun Without the Ick Factor

Runs like a mouse, hides like a mouse, even sounds like a mouse.

When I play with my own pets and interact with pets at the animal hospital, I figure I might as well give them my best effort. The best effort you can give your cat is to make her preylike toys come to life. Make that remote-control mouse skitter like a real mouse. Would a real mouse just lay there on the floor in the kitchen waiting to be caught? Heck no. It would hide, and peek out at your cat, and make things interesting. There are even toys from OurPet's that have the real mouse sound. When you use a toy that's supposed to look like a bird, make it act like a bird—not swinging in loop-the-loops, but lighting from one surface to another, trying to stay up high and out of reach. Have fun. Cats are adept at reading your mood and body language, and if you are feeling relaxed and playful, your cat can loosen up and feel that way, too.

*   *   *

Puzzles and treasure boxes. You can buy a great puzzle box for your cat, or you can get creative and make one yourself. These really simple devices keep cats occupied and active. For example: Take a shoebox and cut a few half-dollar-size holes in the sides. The holes should be big enough for a cat's paw to get in and out, but not big enough to slip a Ping-Pong ball through. Put a few Ping-Pong balls in the box, then securely tape the top shut. Now drop a few bits of kibble into the box and give it a shake to get your cat's interest.

Another fun, easy play box can be made by taking a large cardboard box and cutting a couple of small holes in the top. Poke one or two cat toys through these holes and secure them to the top of the box. Toss a treat in the box to get your cat's attention, and then let her discover her toys suspended from the "ceiling" inside.

A word about laser pointers: Some cats love chasing a laser light—and heaven knows playtime with kitty couldn't get any easier for you than waving one around from the comfort of the couch. Surprisingly, though, some cats have developed compulsive disorders from this kind of play. Behaviorists aren't sure why, but one theory is that because there's nothing to touch or grab in this game, cats get frustrated and stressed out by it.

What's Good for the Dog—Is Dangerous for the Cat

There are certain things healthy cats just do not do. And one of those, unfortunately, is easily mistaken for a normal, healthy behavior because it's perfectly common and fine for dogs. Openmouthed breathing, or panting, is a sign a dog is getting tired from exercise, or overly warm and trying to cool down. Panting in cats is an indication that something is wrong. Sometimes extreme anxiety or stress can cause panting. But it can also be an indication of a respiratory or cardiovascular problem. Openmouthed panting warrants a call to your cat's vet.

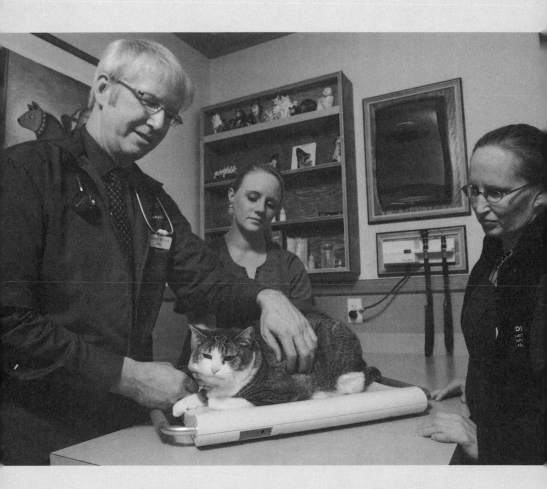

More than half of all cats are overweight or obese. Fat cats aren't funny: their lives are shorter, sicker, and more painful.

Chapter 8

ESSENTIAL HOMEWORK
FOR GOOD HEALTH

There's no substitute for a good veterinarian in your cat's life. At home, though, Dr. Mom (or Dad) rules. Your cat depends on you to be a good steward of his health, and his veterinarian counts on you to be an astute observer of any concerns or changes. Without Dr. Mom, vets like me would have to start every office visit at square one—a daunting task at best. Instead, we're blessed with cat owners who come to the office prepared with concerns, status updates, and reports of anything that might be a little off at home. This information is critically important, especially for cats. They don't exactly wear their hearts on their sleeves. This instinct to appear normal and healthy would be useful in the wild, but for a house cat it can get in the way of early detection and treatment of illness.

Having a hands-on relationship with your cat, starting with a basic grooming routine, is the best way to stay in tune and aware of his health. I realize that there are some cats who will happily submit themselves to rituals like tub bathing, tooth brushing, and nail trimming; and there are other cats who will make it clear you can fuhgeddaboudit. Only you know what your cat will tolerate. I encourage you, though, to take small steps toward good home care, even with cats who are going to make you earn their trust one brushstroke, bath, ear check, and tooth wiping at a time.

What's normal for your cat?

VITALS SIGNS AND HOW TO TAKE THEM

You don't need a veterinary degree to take your cat's vital signs at home—just a watch with a second hand, your powers of observation, and a little practice. To check your cat's pulse, put your hand on her ribcage, behind her front left leg. Be still, and you'll feel the heartbeat beneath your fingers. Count your cat's heartbeats for fifteen seconds, then multiply that number by four to find the beats per minute. Normally, a cat's heart beats between 140 and 220 times per minute, with kitties who are stressed out or sick coming in on the high end and those who are relaxed and restful on the low end. Taking your cat's pulse at home will give you a more reliable baseline than taking it at the veterinary office—many cats run an unusually high heart rate when they're away from home.

Checking your cat's respiration rate is even simpler. Observe her when she's relaxed and still, counting the number of times her chest wall expands and contracts in one minute. The norm for most cats is between fifteen and twenty-five breaths per minute.

Normal feline body temperature runs between 100 and 102.5 degrees Fahrenheit. Alas, this measurement cannot be achieved with your powers of observation. You'll have to use a rectal thermometer with a little petroleum jelly and check your cat's temp the old-fashioned way. Despite the slightly unpleasant nature of this job, every cat owner should own a thermometer and be able to take a simple temp. This information can be vital if you and your cat's veterinarian ever have to make a decision about whether your cat is experiencing a health emergency. If you really don't want to take your cat's temperature this way, check out new thermometers on the market that take temps by the ear. They're more expensive, but likely easier on you both.

APPEARANCE: EARS, EYES, MOUTH, COAT

Eyes. Cats' eyes should always appear bright and moist, with no discharge, no tearing, and no redness, cloudiness, or irritation. Both eyes should appear identical, with neither bulging or appearing swollen.

When you change the lighting, both pupils should react in unison. Cats have a unique, protective "extra" eyelid that's normally not visible when you look at them. If this lid is ever observable when you look into your cat's eyes, something's up. If either one or both of your cat's eyes appear red, swollen, or irritated, have him checked by the veterinarian. Eye disorders are sometimes just as they appear—and often easily treatable. However, they can also be the first outward sign when a cat has a more serious health problem, such as dehydration, a virus, an infection, or cancer.

Ears. A healthy cat's ears should look clean, both inside and out. The outer part of the earflap should have a light covering of fur, with no bald spots, no debris, and no caked ear gunk. The inside of a healthy ear is pink and clean. You may see a little wax, but any significant accumulation of discharge of any color is a sign of trouble. One of a veterinarian's simplest, and most telling, tools is an acute sense of smell. If you notice an unpleasant odor coming from your cat's ears, she may have an infection that requires treatment. If one ear is warmer than the other or feels swollen by comparison, that can also indicate an infection. Black flakes or sticky gunk in ears is not always ear mites. Cats are increasingly getting environmental allergies in the same way dogs do.

Mouth. Your cat's teeth should be clean, with no visible buildup or stains, and her gums should be pink (not red or white) and moist. Use your finger to push gently on your cat's gum and watch the color change to white, then quickly back to pink. A quick return to normal color indicates her circulation is normal and healthy. Your cat's breath may never be minty fresh, and that's fine, but if her scent is strongly offensive, she may have a gastrointestinal upset or a problem with tooth decay. If her mouth smells unusually sweet, she should be screened for diabetes.

Coat. Your cat's coat should be soft and shiny, with no mats, clumps, or bald spots. Healthy cats take scrupulously good care of their own coats, and if yours is not taking care of herself, it may be an indication that something else is wrong with her health, such as arthritis, dental disease, or a metabolic disease.

WEIGHT AND BODY CONDITION

Overweight cats are prone to a host of health problems, so keeping an eye on your cat's weight at home is always wise. It's very easy for a pound to sneak up on kitty between veterinary visits, and the sooner you notice a change, the easier it'll be to help him get back to a healthy weight. The easiest way to get a weight for your cat is to stand on the scale, first without your cat and then with him, then subtract the difference. In general, a healthy cat weighs around ten pounds, with some breeds running a little smaller and others ranging slightly larger.

A quick observation of body condition isn't a substitute for the occasional weigh-in, but it will keep you cognizant of your cat's current pudge factor. First, feel his ribs. If individual ribs are prominent on sight or to your touch, your cat is likely too thin. If you have to poke or prod to feel ribs through layers of fat—or can't seem to find them at all—he's too tubby for his own good. The goal is to feel the ribs through a light layer of fat.

For a second assessment, look at your cat from above while he's standing. A healthy shape is long and sleek, like a lean oval with your cat's head at one end and rump at the other. Ideally, he should have a small tuck at the waist. If he's looking more like a circle (or one very lumpy oval) with a shape that bulges in the middle, it's time to talk with the veterinarian about a gentle weight-loss program.

You can also look at your cat from the side. An ideal shape has a tucked abdomen that looks like a wasp, not a furry cylinder or, worse yet, rolls of fat that hang down in the abdominal area like fatty side bags.

STRESS

A recent study bore out a fact nearly every veterinarian and cat owner has seen in practice: cats who are stressed or depressed can exhibit the exact same symptoms as cats who are actually suffering from a specific ailment. Being aware of your cat's stress level is just as important as keeping up with his physical health. Cats like things to stay the same,

same, same. Anytime there's a change in your cat's environment, he may react with behavior changes that reflect his anxiety.

If you notice a decrease in appetite, lax self-grooming, a varied sleep schedule, or—most noticeably—sudden litter box issues, ask yourself what has changed. Sometimes a new household routine is the culprit, or friction between members of a multicat household, or a change in food or litter brands. If you can put your finger on a reason your cat might be stressed, you may be able to help rectify the problem your-self. Since stress and sickness are so intimately linked for cats, though, don't hesitate to check in with the veterinarian if your cat goes from being a little out of sorts to acting like he might be genuinely sick.

HEALTHY MOUTH, HEALTHY CAT

Nearly 70 percent of cats age three and older have symptoms of dental disease. Many of those cats will never receive any home dental care, and the condition of their teeth will worsen every year for the rest of their lives. Over the years, I've seen countless feline patients with severe and painful mouth conditions, and let me tell you, they are a sorry lot. Some drool constantly. Some can barely manage to eat. Most suffer from mouth pain all the time. Think of yourself. Have you ever had a cold sore in your mouth, let alone an infected tooth, and you thought to yourself, *This is nothing to worry about, no big deal?* Of course not! Dental disease is incredibly painful, as well as detrimental to overall health and happiness.

I can honestly tell you that this is the one area of home care where more pet owners are failing their pets than any other. Teeth—even cat's teeth—are not all that difficult to care for. But left untended, they quickly accumulate plaque buildup, which causes the gums to recede and bacteria to take up lodging in your cat's mouth. And oral bacteria don't stay put. Over time, they cause infections that will enter the bloodstream by way of a cat's mouth and spread throughout his body. These bacteria can damage your cat's heart, liver, and kid-neys, and compromise nearly every aspect of his health. This process sounds like it should be a rare occurrence, but it is incredibly common.

There are two keys to ensuring this doesn't happen to your cat. First, make sure your cat gets her yearly dental exam with her veterinarian, and schedule an appointment to have her teeth cleaned and scaled so you have a clean slate. Second, start a program of home care. A lot of cat owners don't think their cats will stand for tooth brushing—and some of them are darned right. You know your cat's temperament better than anyone, so don't force the issue. Instead, try these steps:

- **Work up to brushing.** Don't get all carried away and launch at your adult cat with toothbrush and toothpaste in a single day. Work up to it. Start by touching your cat around the mouth while you cuddle him. Gently pull up his lip to look at his teeth. Touch a tooth. You may be surprised to find that when things are calm and your cat is happy, he doesn't mind this kind of contact. If you can work up to tooth brushing once, twice, or, ideally, three times a week, that's excellent.
- **Alternative to brushing.** If a toothbrush scares your cat, you can get nearly the same results by wiping his teeth with a gauze pad or a dental wipe from the pet supply store. Use a toothpaste formulated for cats if you can, but even a regular swipe with a gauze dipped in water is much better than no tooth care at all.
- **Provide useful treats.** Choose dental toys and treats for your cat—especially if she's not going to let you clean her teeth. Regular use of products like Greenies and C.E.T. Dental Chews for cats will help keep your kitty's teeth in good shape.
- **Try cat mouth wash.** One of the most recent innovations in home dental care is an oral rinse that kills bacteria in your cat's mouth. Ask your cat's veterinarian if this might be helpful for your cat—especially if she's not willing to let you directly clean her teeth.

A FRONT-TO-BACK GROOMING GUIDE

It's hard to imagine improving on the grooming system your cat has for herself. A healthy cat is fastidious and completely faithful to her grooming routine, regularly cleaning herself from the tops of her ears to the tip of her tail. Have you ever felt a cat's tongue? It's been described as being caressed by a caterpillar wearing golf shoes and is certainly a really raspy tool for grooming. Cats groom themselves for a number of reasons: to make sure their scent is well distributed over their bodies, to clean themselves of parasites and debris, and to distribute the natural oils on their skin.

Even though cats are impressively self-sufficient on the grooming front, they can still use your help to stay in good health. A well-groomed cat will shed less, have fewer hairballs, and do less destructive scratching than one who is left to her own devices. As a bonus, with a little patience and a lot of treats, the time you spend grooming your cat can become a calming, bonding time for both of you.

What's in a Hairball?

Cats spend 30 percent of their waking hours grooming themselves, and their raspy tongues can pull free a lot of hair, especially if the cat is long-haired or a fastidious groomer. Swallowed hair is indigestible, and when it's in a cat's stomach it has two ways it can go: down and out or up and out. When it comes up—to the accompaniment of the middle-of-the-night hacking noise every cat lover knows so well—it's a hairball.

If you want to impress your friends, the scientific name for what you step in on your way to the bathroom at two a.m. is *trichobezoars*, and they truly are made of the excess hair your cat swallowed. The hair is held together with a sticky mucus...but you knew that from cleaning it off your bare feet, didn't you?

Hairballs usually don't cause problems, but if you see anything else in the mix, take the cat and the hairball (the former in a carrier, the latter in a plastic bag or tub) to your veterinarian. And if your cat's hacking without producing a hairball, that trip is likewise warranted. Chronic coughing can be a symptom of many health problems, from heartworms to heart disease to asthma. Occasionally, hairballs can cause an obstruction that will require veterinary attention to resolve.

(Continued)

For cats who seem to have a chronic problem with hairballs, additional fiber in the diet may help. Special diets are available from your veterinarian; milder cases may be resolved by adding a little canned pumpkin (not pumpkin pie filling mix) to a cat's wet food. Regular brushing will also help keep your cat from chowing too much loose hair.

One caution: While over-the-counter hairball remedies do exist, don't let your cat get hooked on them to the point where you're always giving him hairball remedy, and do work with your veterinarian while using them. Overuse of such products can hurt your cat's ability to absorb some essential vitamins.

Choosing the Right Tools

Brushes and combs. If your cat has thin, fine fur and doesn't shed much, a simple stainless-steel comb with narrowly spaced teeth will do the job of keeping his coat clean of debris and mat-free. You can alternate the comb with a grooming glove, which may feel more like a massage than a comb-out to your kitty.

Cats with long or thick coats require more, and better, tools to keep them manageable. A comb and a pin brush will do the trick, but a deshedding brush like the FURminator may be the best tool for you. If you haven't used a deshedding brush yet, you (and your vacuum cleaner) are in for a treat. These brushes remove fur on the surface of your cat's coat, but also rake away loose hair from the undercoat at the same time. FURminators are a little on the pricey side for cat brushes, but if you have a shedder, the dramatic difference in how much hair you can remove by grooming may well be worth the expense.

Shampoo, conditioner. Choose a shampoo designed specifically for cats. In a pinch, baby shampoo will do. If your cat has a long or thick coat, choose a conditioning shampoo or a separate conditioner. Never, ever use a flea shampoo formulated for dogs on a cat. The concentration of insecticide in dog flea products is toxic for felines.

How to Bathe a Cat

In my line of work, I get to see a lot of photos and videos of people's pets. I have to tell you, there are few quite as funny as the ones of bath time for cats. There's just something inherently amusing about a wet cat—let alone a wet cat and a well-meaning cat owner with intentions of offering a shampoo, rinse, and repeat. For a little helpful instruction about giving your cat a bath, read on. If you'd benefit from a good laugh first, log on to YouTube and watch a few of the hundreds of videos of other people giving their cats baths.

Home videos of cat baths provide us with a few helpful tips as to what NOT to do. For example:

❀ Don't force. Many cats are far more tolerant of bathing than you'd expect, but one ugly experience can set up a lot of future cases of a disappearing kitty when the water starts to run. Start with small steps. Reward your cat with treats and praise for letting herself be carried to the sink. When she's okay with that, reward for being by the sink with water in it, then in the water a little, and so on. This is far easier with kittens than with cats, by the way, but not all cats will tolerate bathing. If yours won't, you'll have to give in, and if a bath is absolutely necessary (because of a health reason) let your veterinarian's staff or a good groomer handle it.

❀ Don't raise your voice and stress out your cat.

❀ Don't squeeze, although it is okay to "scruff" your cat, firmly holding her by the loose skin on the back of her neck. Do not lift your cat this way. If cats came with handles, this whole bathing thing would be a heck of a lot easier.

❀ Don't forget to clear the counter, pull up the blinds, and stow anything valuable or breakable away from the sink or tub.

With a clear handle on the Don'ts of bathing, move on to the Dos:

❀ Do have all supplies and tools on hand before you add either the water or the cat to your bathing area. I recommend using a sink rather than the tub. You'll have the advantages of a smaller basin of water and a comfortable working height.

(Continued)

- Do fill the sink before placing the cat in it, as opposed to filling it while the cat sits there.

- Do dress for success. Your cat may quickly start looking for something to hold on to if she gets nervous, and it may as well be your shirt instead of your arm, so wear an old shirt you don't care about. If you're not sure how she's going to react, a pair of long dishwashing gloves for a trial run isn't a bad idea, either.

- Do comb or brush your cat ahead of time. Getting out tangles and mats before a bath will save you having to cut them out later. The more excess fur you remove prebath, the easier it will be to get what remains nice and clean.

- Do make sure the water is warm. Even a cat who's a good sport about getting wet will not appreciate cold water or cold air on his wet behind.

- Do be ready with towels. Line the bottom of the sink with one towel before adding the water. It will give your cat better footing and help make him feel safe. Towel-dry your cat as much as possible after the bath to keep him from getting chilly.

- Do rely on a sprayer to help you do the work. Some cats who won't stand for being submerged will go along with a spray bath instead.

- Do be sure to rinse thoroughly. Shampoo residue can irritate kitty's skin and make him itchy.

- Do know when to call it a day. If a bath starts to go bad, wrap things up quickly and let your cat go with a treat. In general, keep bath time cheerful, short, and generously peppered with your cat's favorite goodies, in the hopes that the process will get easier after a couple of test runs.

Clipnosis

No veterinarian wants to sedate an uncooperative cat for simple procedures like nail trimming, ear cleaning, veterinary exams, or even giving medication. But none of us wants to go home with our hands raked to shreds, either. One new advancement in keeping pets calm has vets like me feeling very hopeful about a coming trend in accomplishing these routine procedures. Clipnosis is the simple use of specially designed clips to calm a cat the way her momma would—by firmly holding the skin on the back of her neck when carrying her from nest to nest.

Veterinarians and veterinary technicians do this all the time by hand: scruffing a cat is one of the most effective ways to get him to be still. The problem is that scruffing means having one of your two hands occupied at all times, making things like nail clipping pretty much impossible in a one-person operation.

The Clipnosis tool may look awful, but it doesn't hurt the cat. Clipnosis clips are a fairly new product that's still being tested in veterinary clinics. The early results, though, are promising. Nearly 80 percent of vets and techs using Clipnosis reported it as being "very" or "somewhat" effective. If these clips, which are inexpensive and easy to use, make it possible to work with even a fraction of that percentage of cats without requiring sedation or risking injury, Clipnosis may well be the next big thing not only in veterinary care, but in grooming cats at home as well.

CLIPPING CAT NAILS

I can give you at least a dozen good reasons to clip your cat's nails regularly, but here's the one most people appreciate most: saving your furniture from scratching. Cats' nails are always growing, and if they don't keep them under control, they'll get overly long and eventually cause crippling pain. So cats scratch, primarily to wear down their claws, and partly because it spreads their scent and feels good to them. You can't take away a cat's desire to scent-mark her environment, but you can take away her need to scrape and abrade her nails to control their length by keeping them trimmed yourself.

Some cats are easily convinced it's time for a monthly mani-pedi, and others, well, they're never gonna let that happen to them. Most cats are somewhere in between. If you gradually work up from handling the paws, to pushing down on the pads of the feet to expose the nail, to clipping one nail at a time, you may find your cat who didn't seem like a mani-pedi kind of guy really doesn't mind it so much.

Nail Tools

Cats' nails can be trimmed with a guillotine-type clipper or small nail scissors. Some cats are more tolerant of a nail grinder. These Dremel-type tools have a small opening for your cat's toes and grind down a little bit of the nail at a time.

To clip your cat's nails, choose an area with bright light and sit comfortably. Gently push down on each of your cat's pawpads to expose the nail. Under each nail there's a vein, called the quick, which will bleed profusely if you cut it. In good light, you can see where the quick is pink under the nail and where the rest of the nail is transparent. You don't have to cut all the way to the quick to do a good job of trimming. Rather than get too close, focus on trimming the curved end of your cat's nail. Removing these hooks should cut down not only on how much your cat scratches but also on how effective she is when she does it. It is far better to leave a cat's nails a little long than to trim them too short and hurt her.

Some owners have success gently wrapping the cat in a towel for this procedure—it's commonly called a "kitty burrito"—then drawing out one foot at a time for clipping. There are cats who respond well to being wrapped up, and others who just get freaked out and struggle. Your cat will be happy to tell you which camp he belongs to the first time you try this at home.

As your cat gets older, he may need more help from you to keep his claws trimmed. Less active cats sometimes have a hard time doing this job themselves.

Ambling, Cat-Style

If you've ever carefully watched a dog walk, you may have noticed that they step forward with one front paw and the back paw from the opposite side at the same time. For example, the front right paw reaches forward at the same time the rear left paw does. When moving at a faster clip, this gait is known as a trot.

Cats move differently than dogs. They step with both left legs, then both right legs. Their natural gait, in other words, is what's known as a pace.

One thing cats and dogs do have in common: they walk on what in human terms would be fingers and toes. Most cats have five toes on their front paws, but only four of them hit the ground. The fifth toe is called a "dew claw" and is found on the inside of the front paw.

The dew claw is the feline equivalent of our thumb, and it's used for grasping prey or climbing trees. A normal feline back paw, by the way, has four toes that are all called into service.

Any number of toes over the norm, usually an extra one or two but occasionally as many as three or four, makes a cat what is termed a *polydactyl*, which means "many fingers." These cats are also some-times known as "Hemingway cats." That's because the famous writer Ernest Hemingway became a fan of these cats after being given a six-toed cat by a ship's captain. Legend has it that sailors once valued polydactyl cats for their extraordinary climbing and hunting abilities.

Descendants of Hemingway's cat remain popular tourist attrac-tions at the author's former residence (now a museum or dare we say cat house) in Key West, Florida. Around sixty cats share the grounds, and about half are polydactyls.

GROOMERS CAN BE GODSENDS

Some cats simply won't stand for bathing, trimming, and the like at home, and it takes a professional to get the job done. Other cats can benefit from occasional grooming as well. If you have a long-haired cat, a pro can restore her coat from time to time so you can keep it under control. When kitty gets matted beyond the help of a good brush or comb, a groomer can clip her down so she can start fresh. This kind of clipping is scary for your cat, and potentially traumatic if you clip her skin.

If you do decide to use a groomer, choose one who specializes in cats—or, better yet, a mobile cat groomer who will come to you. Ask your veterinarian for a recommendation. If the groomer wants to sedate your cat, ask her veterinarian first. I'm not a big fan of any heavy sedation outside the animal hospital, but it is possible to prescribe a small dose of an anti-anxiety medication to take the edge off for a cat who doesn't groom easily.

PARASITE PREVENTION: CARE AND CAUTIONS

If you have an indoor-only cat, you've substantially lowered your cat's risk of getting parasites. The more outdoor access your cat has—anything from afternoons on the patio to in-and-out privileges all the time—the greater the chances she'll bring home bugs and/or worms sooner or later.

Fortunately, we live in a day and age when no pet should have to suffer from parasites. The emergence of preventive medications to keep fleas, ticks, mites, and roundworms away means your cat can be protected from these scourges that were his ancestors' cross to bear.

Fleas, Ticks, and Ear Mites

I strongly recommend putting your cat on a monthly parasite preventive. These treatments put pet owners at ease about infestations. I can't stress enough, though, that you need to consult with your cat's veterinarian about the right medication and dose. Misuse of flea and tick products is one of the biggest causes of accidental poisoning in cats. Once again, *never, ever* use a flea or tick product designed for dogs on your cat. The concentration of insecticide in dog products is toxic, and sometimes fatal, to cats. Two products I recommend are Assurity from Elanco Companion Animal Health and Revolution from Pfizer Animal Health.

Heartworm? Really? Really!

I know, we all tend to think of heartworm as a dog's problem. One of the reasons for this perception is that it's easier to diagnose heartworm in dogs than it is in cats—so we hear a lot more about it. In recent years, though, veterinarians are increasingly discovering heartworm disease in cats who were diagnosed with other maladies, like asthma and bronchial infections. The statistics are pretty wide ranging, with estimates from 5 percent to nearly 30 percent of cats infected. One of the reasons statistics vary so much is because heartworms are much more prevalent in some parts of the country than others, so the numbers are vastly different from state to state. Ask your veterinarian, and if heartworm is a problem you'll need a preventive medicine, typically Heartgard, Revolution (which also treats fleas, ticks, and ear mites), or Advantage Multi.

If you live in an area with a heartworm problem, keeping your cat indoors is not enough prevention. Mosquitoes are the carriers for this disease, and we all know how good they are at getting inside the house. Instead, ask your cat's veterinarian about preventive medication. Heartworm is completely preventable with a monthly pill, but once a cat who was not protected has it, it's not treatable. One recent study found that less than 5 percent of all cats were taking heartworm prevention meds, compared to more than 50 percent of dogs. It's high time we start protecting cats from heartworm disease, too.

More cats are living indoors these days, both for their own protection and for the protection of native birds and animals. Keeping cats indoors does require working to keep them from being bored or overweight, both of which can lead to health problems.

Chapter 9

AVOIDING PREVENTABLE *CATA*STROPHES

We all enter into cat ownership with hopes of smooth sailing—a simple, happy life for our new companion, one that isn't marred by disease or discomfort, accidents or illness. Every time Teresa and I add a new member to our "fur family," we wish for all this and more: that the new pet will find a way to fit in with the "old" ones; that he or she will learn our house rules quickly and easily; that we'll be able to build a strong bond of trust and affection.

I'm sure every newly adopted pet's life begins with the same kinds of high hopes. Unfortunately, wishin' and hopin' aren't always enough. Life is full of surprises, both the kind that delight us and the kind that stop us cold. And while no one can ever plan for everything, as good cat owners we need to do our best to anticipate the dangers and be prepared. Many common CATastrophes are avoidable if you think ahead and practice prevention right from the start.

THE INDOOR-OUTDOOR DECISION

In a perfect world, your cat would be just as safe and happy outdoors as he is in your home. He'd be able to experience nature every day on his own terms, and you wouldn't have to worry a bit. In the real world, though, there are countless dangers associated with allowing your cat outdoors, and those risks must be weighed carefully before you make a decision about what's best for your cat.

Let's just look at the facts. The average life span of an indoor-only cat is somewhere between fifteen and eighteen years. Average span for an outdoor cat? Less than five years. A cat who divides his time between indoor living and outdoor freedom may split the difference, but chances are all too good that the price of freedom will be paid in years off his life.

I'm not going to ramble on about this, because the numbers speak for themselves. But please remember when you make this lifestyle decision that outdoor cats have exponentially higher risk not only for all the obvious dangers—cars, other cats, predators, poisons, and bad people—but also for dreaded diseases like feline immunodeficiency virus, feline leukemia, parasites, and infections.

If you do have an outdoor cat, the kindest thing you can do for him is to lock him in at night. The old saying that nothing good happens after midnight applies to cats just as aptly as it does to people. Predators, neighborhood hoodlums, drivers with limited visibility—they're all a greater risk to your cat from dusk to dawn than during daylight hours.

Other Special Precautions for Outdoor Cats

- **Thump three times on the hood if you love me.** Every year, outdoor cats are accidentally killed when they climb into a warm car motor from below and settle in. If you park your vehicle outside in winter, make it a habit to give the hood a solid thump before starting the engine. Even if you don't have an outdoor cat of your own, do this to prevent injury to someone else's pet.
- **Take care with chemicals.** Outdoor cats can easily get into poisons in the neighborhood and in your own yard. Carefully read and observe the precautions on any lawn products you use, including fertilizers and pesticides.
- **Ramp up parasite prevention.** Be honest with your cat's veterinarian about his outdoor adventures and completely faithful to the regimen of parasite prevention you are given. Your outdoor cat is at increased risk for bringing home the bugs and other crea-

tures that can not only make him miserable—I call them heinous hitchhikers—but possibly spread to you and your house.

COLLARS, HARNESSES, CHIPS, AND TAGS

Your cat absolutely, positively, needs to be identifiable as a member of your family at all times. The first step in accomplishing this goal is fitting her with a comfortable collar. Don't let anybody tell you that cats can't or won't wear collars. They can, and they will, and they need to. A collar around her neck tells anyone who sees your cat that she is loved and cared for, and has a home where she belongs. Lost cats are forever being "adopted" by well-meaning good Samaritans who assume they don't already have a home—but a collar is a clear indication that kitty has an owner somewhere.

I recommend choosing an elastic collar like the Beastie Band, a soft collar with an elastic insert or a collar with a breakaway fastener. These collars come in lots of colors and patterns, but they will all allow your cat to escape if too much pressure is applied—an important feature for cats who have a habit of getting themselves into tight squeezes and high-climbing feats. Better to lose a collar than risk choking or even strangulation.

Your cat should have an identification tag attached to his collar with his name and your phone numbers. Cell phone is best because then you can be reached anywhere. Since ID tags sometimes come detached, the best option is a slide-on style tag that won't dangle. You can also purchase safety collars that are permanently printed with your cat's name and phone number.

Perhaps more important than an outward label is a permanently implanted microchip that will identify your cat anywhere in the world, even if he gets lost with no collar at all. If your cat has not been chipped—and it's not expensive—ask your veterinarian to perform this two-second, nearly painless procedure. The microchip—the size of a grain of rice and with antimigration features—is inserted between your cat's shoulder blades and is no more painful than a routine vaccination. Once it's been implanted, if your cat is picked up by animal control, or taken to a veterinarian or an animal shelter, he can be scanned for the chip and your contact information retrieved from it. Consider this: one wide-reaching study found the return-to-owner rate for cats with microchips to be twenty times higher than the rate for all strays that entered the shelters. You can't argue against those vastly improved odds, my friend.

How to Find a Lost Cat

If your cat does get lost, you need to launch a quick, effective search.

* Act fast. Only a small percentage of lost cats are recovered, and the single best way to boost your chances of success is to get started the minute you discover your cat is missing. The vast majority of lost pets stay close to home, so that's where to concentrate your initial search. Call your neighbors, distribute flyers, and enlist the help of family or friends.

* Have pictures on hand. It only takes a few seconds to take a couple of good pictures of your cat. You could do it right now. Put one in a frame on your desk, and know you'll have a critical tool in hand if you ever need it for a search.

* Make signs that work. The most effective "Lost Cat" sign is simple, eye-catching, clear, and legible. Make your sign extra large (buy a poster board at any pharmacy or superstore), extra bright (choose a neon color), and clear (use ten words or less, all in large-print letters, to ask for help). Enlarge a photo of your cat and display a copy on every poster. Blanket your neighborhood with flyers at every intersection and have a friend hand-deliver them to every veterinary office, animal shelter, convenience store, and post office in the area. Also, ask your mail carrier and the local UPS and FedEx drivers to keep a lookout. Don't be shy about ramping up the emotion, such as putting "My child wants her cat back!" on the poster.

* Think like a cat. Cats are strongly territorial, and so they rarely run away—at least not far. It's very common for a lost cat to be found hiding near home. As you search, keep in mind that just

because you call your cat's name doesn't mean she will answer or come out of hiding. If your outdoor cat is missing, she may be sick, injured, or inadvertently locked inside a neighbor's garage or shed. If your indoor cat is missing, her first act of self-preservation in the unfamiliar outdoors may be to find a spot to conceal herself. Either way, there's a good chance that she's on your property or that of someone nearby. Ask your neighbors for their permission (or better yet, their help) to search for your cat in their landscaping, under porches—in short, any spot that might have seemed like a safe hideout for your missing kitty.

GPS for Pets?

When the technology to microchip pets came along, it became a great white hope for shelters—a way to quickly identify collarless dogs and reunite as many as possible with their owners. In the last couple of years, the amazing, mysterious world of gadgetry has taken one giant step beyond the microchip: inventing GPS for cats and dogs. A microchip gives information up if scanned, but a GPS collar can actually help you track down your missing pet. Look for these devices to improve and fall in price in the years to come. The ability to simply activate a tracker in your cat's collar and find him yourself may one day make the "lost pet" poster a thing of the past.

MORE POTENTIAL DANGERS AT HOME

Poisoning. A cat's liver is less effective at eliminating toxins than that of a human or a dog. Tylenol, aspirin, essential oils, mothballs, and cleaning products are all common causes of poisoning. Choose nontoxic cleaning supplies whenever you can. Keep your medications closed and behind a cabinet door. If possible, assign your toxic household products to a single cupboard, and secure that latch with a child- (and kitty-) proof lock.

Tinselitis. Ingestion of string, ribbon, or yarn is an everyday cause of emergency clinic visits for cats. What starts as a cute playtime between your cat and a bit of string can turn into a situation that's unnerving (ever gone to pull something from your cat's mouth only to realize it is simultaneously residing in her intestines?) and potentially very dangerous, causing intestinal blockage and even permanent damage. This one is easy to prevent, simply by keeping strings and things out of reach of your cat, except when you are supervising.

High-rise syndrome. If only it were true that a cat always lands on his feet, things would be a little quieter at the veterinary emergency room. Even though cats are inarguably blessed with great grace and agility, they do get injured in falls, all the time. In many cases, falls from single- or two-story buildings are the ones that result in harm. While no one can say for sure why this happens, the theory is that the farther a fall, the better a cat is able to position himself for the landing, making shorter falls more dangerous than long ones. Over a certain height, of course, no fall is survivable, and no one can say exactly what that height is—although more than a half-dozen stories up is increasingly more deadly.

To prevent injury in your home, test screens to make sure your cat can't push them through and fall out. If a particular climbing spot in your home seems to pose a danger—a wobbly shelf, for example, or a ledge that's too narrow for kitty to get good footing, block it sooner rather than later to keep your cat off it. When your cat is outdoors, remember that cats are great at climbing—their claws dig in perfectly for the task—but are far less adept at coming down. Don't rush to get the ladder if your cat gets stuck. Most of them are able to figure out how to get back down on their own.

Dryer danger. Cats love to be warm and snug and love to hide. What place offers more warm, snug hidden-ness than your clothes dryer?

Unfortunately, the dryer is a very dangerous place indeed for a kitty. If she goes unnoticed and the dryer gets turned on, she can be gravely injured or killed. You can prevent this kind of tragedy by (1) always keeping the dryer door closed when you're not loading or unloading; and (2) making a habit of checking inside the machine before you hit the start button.

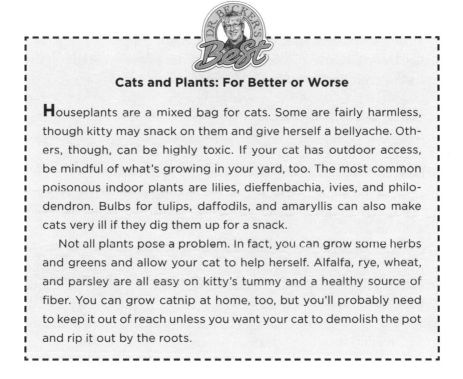

Cats and Plants: For Better or Worse

Houseplants are a mixed bag for cats. Some are fairly harmless, though kitty may snack on them and give herself a bellyache. Others, though, can be highly toxic. If your cat has outdoor access, be mindful of what's growing in your yard, too. The most common poisonous indoor plants are lilies, dieffenbachia, ivies, and philodendron. Bulbs for tulips, daffodils, and amaryllis can also make cats very ill if they dig them up for a snack.

Not all plants pose a problem. In fact, you can grow some herbs and greens and allow your cat to help herself. Alfalfa, rye, wheat, and parsley are all easy on kitty's tummy and a healthy source of fiber. You can grow catnip at home, too, but you'll probably need to keep it out of reach unless you want your cat to demolish the pot and rip it out by the roots.

KEEP FROM BEING BITTEN OR SCRATCHED

Here's one preventable danger that's a threat not to your cat, but to you. The average house cat weighs about ten pounds, but boy, can she pack a punch when she needs to. Believe me, a lot more veterinarians are injured by cats than by dogs. We do get dog bites from time to time, but dogs don't have those little bacteria-tipped hypodermic needle-claws on the ends of their paws, and their teeth are not all razor-sharp like the ones your cat's got. A cat can shred your arm or do hieroglyphics on your face in a second, and she won't hesitate if she thinks she's in danger. Your cat doesn't do this to be mean; it's just that she's scared.

Because cat bites need to be taken seriously, there are a couple of rules every cat owner should always follow:

- **Respect your cat's limits.** Many cat bites are simply the result of an owner pushing an interaction just a minute or two too long. Cats almost always give body language warnings before they attack. You need to know what to look for, so yours doesn't have to tell you the hard way when she's had enough. Signs a cat is getting edgy include tail swishing, crouching, ears rotated back or lowered, dilated pupils, hair standing on end, a low growl. Tuning in and ending an interaction before your cat reaches her breaking point will be a vast improvement for both of you.

- **Freeze!** If your cat does go after you, you need to think fast to prevent serious injury. First, if you are holding him, let go. Second, don't move a muscle. Your cat's instincts are to fight until she wins, and your lack of movement tells her you're not a threat anymore.

- **Never, ever get in the middle of a cat fight.** If you have more than one cat, the possibility of a fight is always real, even if it's a remote one. If a fight breaks out, the last thing you want to do is put your hand in the mess—it's like reaching into a blender to try to fish something out: maybe you get it, maybe you don't, but you darn well might lose a finger. Instead of reaching between fighting cats, do something to startle them and redirect their attention. Throw a blanket over them, make a loud noise, or spray them with water to break their focus.

- **Wash, wash, wash.** If a veterinarian or veterinary team member gets scratched or bitten, they immediately head for the sink for a lot of soap and water to wash off any bacteria the cat may have had on his nails or teeth. Keep the lather and rinsing coming for about three minutes.

DISEASE SHOULD NOT BE SHARED

In some people's minds, zoonotic diseases are the dark secret of pet ownership. Let me tell you, there are folks out there who truly believe kissing the cat or letting her sleep on your bed will result in a dreaded disease you'll suffer for the rest of your life. The facts are as follows: Yes, there are diseases you can get from your cat. No, it's not likely that you will get them. Taking the simple steps of keeping your cat's vaccinations and routine checkups up to date, maintaining a parasite prevention program, and using care when cleaning the litter box will keep most potential problems far away from you and your home.

These are the conditions that can be passed between cats and people:

Cat scratch disease. Around twenty-five thousand people in the United States are diagnosed with cat scratch disease every year—and those are just the ones who went to the trouble to visit a doctor and be documented. Despite its name, this bacterial infection can be contracted when a person is bitten as easily as through a scratch. Also known as bartonellosis, cat scratch disease is far and away the most common condition transferred from cats to people. Symptoms include swollen lymph nodes, fever, aches, and fatigue. Since as many as 80 percent of cat-inflicted wounds may become infected, your best bet is to see your doctor for a course of antibiotics anytime you are injured by a cat.

Salmonella poisoning. Most cases of salmonella poisoning are caused by eating contaminated food, but it's also possible to contract salmonella after coming in contact with feline fecal matter that harbors the bacteria. Thorough hand washing after cleaning the litter box and after handling your cat will help prevent this infection. Wearing disposable gloves while you tend to the litter box is even better.

Toxoplasmosis. This disease is caused by a parasite and affects almost all mammal species, including humans. It is possible, though not likely, for a person to become infected by coming in contact with cat feces. Even though cats often get the blame for spreading toxoplas-mosis, Americans are actually more likely to get it by improperly han-dling raw meat than we are in the course of daily cat ownership duties.

Many, if not most, people who contract the disease never even know they have it. Symptoms are generally mild to nil. The real threat of toxoplasmosis lies in its potential dangers for pregnant women and for individuals with compromised immune systems, like AIDS patients and those undergoing chemotherapy. In these cases, the disease can cause severe illness or even be fatal. If a fetus is exposed during the first trimester, toxoplasmosis can cause birth defects.

Because of the slight risk of exposure to toxoplasmosis when clean-ing the litter box, you should always scrub your hands with soap and hot water after doing the job. Better yet, wear disposable gloves. Preg-nant women and people with low immunity should simply not do this task. The potential of the illness is too worrisome to take the risk.

Rabies. Rabies is kind of the granddaddy of zoonotic disease. Most people are familiar with it and know enough to understand it can be deadly. Because of the very serious nature of rabies, all cats, whether they live indoors, outdoors, or both, need to be vaccinated for it. In many states, it's the law. But even where it's not, ask your cat's vet-erinarian to administer this shot to protect your cat, and your whole family, from rabies.

Ringworm. Ringworm really isn't a worm at all, but rather a skin infec-tion caused by a fungus. It can be transmitted by contact between individuals of the same species or between species. It is most common in puppies, kittens, and—sometimes—children. Each species is very capable of picking up this fungus without any help from the others, but ringworm is the most common contagious skin infection in cats. Regardless of who contracts it, ringworm can usually be treated with a topical ointment. The best way to prevent ringworm is simply to limit your cat's exposure to other cats. Ringworm is often brought from a kennel or into your home on the skin of a new addition.

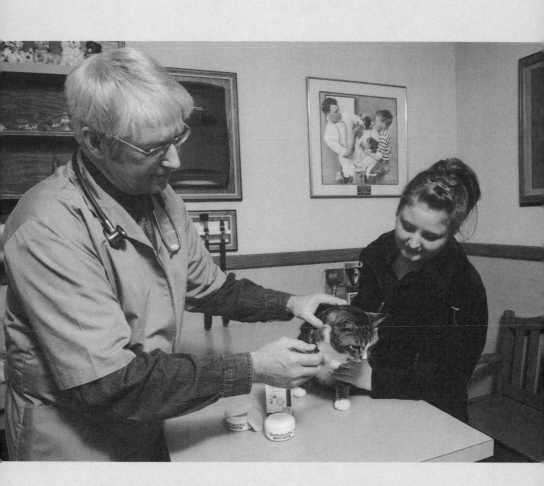

Since cats are good at hiding illness, it's essential to focus on preventive care, working with your veterinarian to avoid illness or to catch it early before it becomes a serious problem.

Chapter 10

TIME, MONEY, AND CAT CARE

The price of owning a pet is never a fixed one: that free kitten from the shelter will require food, litter, toys, beds, veterinary exams, and your time and attention. She might need to have a bone set one day, or a blood transfusion, or daily insulin injections. She may scratch the guts out of your favorite chair, and cost you tears or sleep if she gets sick or lost. No matter how you look at it, your kitten will definitely not really be free.

In return for your expenses, your kitten will make you laugh, keep you company, and curl up by your side when you're sick or tired. If you take care of her, she may be a friend and companion for the next fifteen, eighteen, or even twenty years. Even though she'd be a loner in the wild, your kitten will learn that you are her family and your home is her safe place.

Every pet owner has to make sacrifices and compromises to be a good guardian. That said, we all have to be careful not to waste time, money, or energy, too. Managing your pet-related spending and keeping order and cleanliness in your home are important priorities. With forethought and care, you can keep both under control and still enjoy a good life with your "free" cat.

FINANCIAL PLANNING FOR PET CARE

Americans spent more than $10 billion a year on veterinary care for their pets, and that number continues to increase. The good news is that nearly every major advancement in human medicine of the past two decades has found its way to veterinary care—and those that haven't, will soon. These improvements in diagnostic tools, surgical techniques, and pharmaceuticals are healing and saving pets' lives every day.

The downside of all that advancement is that someone has to pay for it. Veterinary care, once a small part of the price of pet ownership, gets more expensive every year. There's no stopping this trend—not for pet owners or for veterinarians, either. As a result, more and more people are faced with veterinary bills that are hard to handle, or, worse yet, effective treatment options they cannot afford to choose.

Veterinarians call the point where a sick pet and the inability or unwillingness to pay for treatment meet "economic euthanasia"—the owner's choice is to put the pet to sleep to spare the animal suffering rather than to treat the illness or injury. In most cases, these situations are heartbreaking conditions for both pet owners and veterinary professionals who do everything they can to serve their clients and keep costs under control.

Planning ahead for your cat's future veterinary care makes good financial and emotional sense. The last place you ever want to be is standing in an urgent pet care clinic, turning down a lifesaving procedure for your cat because you can't swing the expense. With a little luck, your cat will live a long, happy, emergency-free existence, but just in case, consider these options to be prepared:

Pet health insurance. Fewer than 5 percent of Americans have health insurance for their pets. And that's astonishing, considering the cost of veterinary care and the grim options for those who cannot afford care at any level.

But the industry is growing and changing, with more choices and options, and pet health insurance is picking up steam as people realize its benefits. When consumer advocacy groups look at pet health insurance, they inevitably point out that most people won't "make" money on the insurance plans—that paying cash for care is less expensive over a pet's life than paying insurance premiums. While that's true, it's also the way insurance is supposed to work. It's not designed to make you money—it's there to cover you if you ever do have a crisis.

In a way, it's helpful to think of pet health insurance more like car insurance than human health insurance. If you have health insurance, you are generally covered for everything, after you shell out for your co-pays. Your "maintenance" and your "accidents" are both covered. By contrast, when you choose car insurance, you're not looking for someone to pick up the cost of your oil changes and tire rotations. Instead, you want some peace of mind that if you ever do wreck your vehicle, you won't have to go into debt to deal with the consequences.

Many veterinary health insurance companies offer both kinds of policies: the ones that cover everything under the sun, and the one that is just there in case your cat has a severe illness or injury. The latter is less expensive, especially if you choose a higher deductible, a cost you can plan for with the use of a savings account.

No matter which plans or companies you consider, I hope you will consider one of them for your cat. Because having to euthanize a pet we could have saved is the worst part of what veterinarians do. Help us help you and your pet.

Savings accounts. My wife and I both come from families of savers, and savers we have always been. It takes commitment, discipline, and the ability to turn down temptation to make this work. Every cat owner should have a savings account for emergencies. Everyone. There is simply no downside to this strategy.

One option is to open a dedicated savings account, and have your bank put whatever amount you want into it, at any interval you choose. Easiest plan? If your employer offers direct deposit, have part of your paycheck routed to your pet's emergency account. What you don't see, you won't spend.

Since few veterinarians take pet health insurance as payment, a savings account can complement insurance perfectly. You can pay your pet's veterinary bill, put in your insurance claim, and then put the money back in your account when you get the check.

*   *   *

Give me credit. It's safe to say the era of easy credit and a mailbox full of great deals on credit cards is long gone, and probably just as well. So, too, is the idea of using your home like an ATM machine— those people who had equity credit often find those lines disappeared along with their equity. That doesn't mean you can't use credit to help in a pinch, although it's probably not the best of your options, especially not traditional credit cards or putting your home on the line.

There's also CareCredit, which may work for you. This company partners with veterinary offices to offer short-term, low-interest credit for veterinary costs. The time frames for these arrangements vary, but generally clients have six to twelve months to pay back the cost of treatment, and as long as you make your payments and beat the payoff deadline, you don't have to pay any interest. Of course, if you do miss a payment or the payoff, interest rates are punitive, so be sure you can see this kind of plan through before you agree to it. Your veterinarian's office may also have its own version of this line-of-credit financing. Ask about it at your cat's next visit, so you know what might be available if you ever need it.

Bottom line: ask now. Make a discussion on the what-if a part of your pet's next wellness exam so you are not caught making decisions that are based on your lack of money, not your pet's lack of options for care.

Veterinarians Need to Make a Living, Too

At the risk of sounding overly biased on behalf of my profession, I think it's important to share a glimpse of the challenges today's veterinarians face.

Your veterinarian lives in the same world you do and is well aware of what it costs to make mortgage or rent payments, keep clothes on children, keep the car repaired, and, yes, take care of pets, because we all have them, too. What a lot of veterinarians have that you may not, though, is a crushing level of debt they signed on to so they could get through school. Many veterinarians spend up to 25 percent of their salaries every month just to pay off student loans. That's typical of younger veterinarians, who often are working for the practice you go to—they don't own it. Those who own practices are dealing with the same issues all businesses do: employees' salaries and benefits, insurance, taxes, loans on the property and equipment, inventory, and much more.

Almost every client wants all the most modern care for a pet, but they want it at 1972 prices. Unfortunately, that's just not possible. Your veterinarian usually cannot donate goods and services, or carry patients while they make payments. Veterinarians will always work with you on options or solutions, but giving away care isn't an option. They simply cannot stay in business, and that's why I urge you to plan now for emergencies, so you have more options if and when something happens to your pet.

SAVING MONEY: WHAT CORNERS CAN BE CUT?

Everyone loves saving money—and we all should be doing more of it. But there are two areas where you shouldn't try to trim expenses, since it'll catch up with your cat, and your wallet, sooner or later:

❧ **Don't skip your regular wellness exams and preventive care.** The cost of a checkup, even with basic diagnostics, is a fraction of the cost of treating any major health problem. And consider: the vast majority of health problems that are identified in their early stages are far cheaper and easier to treat than those that are left to fester and worsen before they're discovered.

❧ **Don't lower the quality of your cat's food.** Good nutrition keeps your cat healthy and strong. I even have a saying: "Nutrition is therapy." Please don't mess with his diet to save a buck or two. In general, pets need larger portions of low-quality foods anyway, so any savings is a wash once your cat's been fed.

Some Other Tips

🐾 **Work with your vet to cut costs.** If your cat is sick, ask the veterinarian for suggestions on treatment options that are less expensive, even if they are not the "gold standard" of care. Surprisingly, there are often options.

🐾 **If your cat requires medication, shop around for the best price.** Most veterinarians are used to being asked to write prescriptions, and you may find considerable savings at a pharmacy. If you choose to use a catalog or an Internet pharmacy for pet-specific medications such as heartworm preventive, check into the reputation of the company and choose one that requires a written prescription (in other words, not one that spams you with e-mail promising brand-name drugs for next to nothing). Once you've found the best price, you should ask your veterinarian to match it—you may be able to get the lowest price point and the convenience of picking up your cat's meds in your neighborhood. Your veterinarian may even offer competitive online order fulfillment through an increasingly popular web service for veterinary practices such as Vetstreet.com (for which I'm the spokesman, I must add).

🐾 **Don't let your cat get fat.** Obesity is the cause of a host of health complications—all miserable for your pet, inconvenient for you, and expensive to treat. It's not that difficult to keep your cat at a healthy weight by monitoring his food and helping him stay active. Your efforts may save you a fortune in veterinary expenses down the road.

🐾 **Cat grooming, tooth brushing, nail trimming:** If you're on a tight budget and not already doing these things yourself, now's the time to start. Most people can learn to handle any basic grooming task at home. If your cat really needs professional maintenance, try stretching the time between appointments by a week or two to thin the costs.

🐾 **Make a deal.** Why not trade pet-sitting time with a friend whose cat you love? Or, if you have a skill or product others need, barter! Bartering with your time or special skills for the goods and services you need is a tradition as old as human history, so why not make it work for you and your cat? If you have a business or trade, you might be able to trade for pet supplies or even veterinary care.

❧**Shop smart.** If you feed your cat kibble, buy in bulk and store it in an airtight container, preserving the label with contact information and lot number in case there's ever a problem. Work with other cat owners to buy in bulk at a lower price and split the expense. And don't forget that you don't need to buy everything new. Whatever you need, you can often find it used at a greatly reduced price at garage sales or through online classifieds.

KEEPING CLEAN SAVES MONEY, TOO

There's a reason why real-estate agents ask clients to send their pets to live with friends and relatives when a house is for sale: because pets bring down the value and the perception of a home—and often cause greater wear and tear on a property than a coat of paint can hide. Of course, you wouldn't be reading this book if you hadn't already made peace with your cat putting her stamp on your home in some way. Even the most doting pet owner, though, doesn't want to live in an animal house. You don't want your carpet to be the color of fur, to replace or reupholster damaged furniture, to see your favorite arm-chair turned into a scratching post, or to spend your free time mopping up messes. Some tips:

Keep it covered. One sure way to keep your house neat is to choose washable surfaces whenever possible. If you're making big choices—like for furniture or flooring—pick surfaces that are scratch-resistant and easy to wipe clean. Tile is super stuff, as are leather and microfiber furniture. Steer clear of natural fabrics in furniture, decorations, and rugs. Nothing soaks up the scent of a cat and holds it better or longer than wool or cotton. Synthetic fabrics repel scents and stains much better.

No matter what flooring or furniture you have, it'll stay cleaner and last longer if you make use of covers. Throws and slipcovers are terrific tools. Choose washable materials only, and put them through the laundry once a week or so. This is far easier than trying to clean the surface of a chair or a couch.

Brush, comb, and clip. Your cat is going to shed X amount of fur in an average day, week, month, or year. The portion of that fur that ends up on your furniture and floors pretty much depends on how much of it you comb, brush, and wash off somewhere else. A five-minute daily brushing for heavy-shedding cats can save you hours of housework.

Use an electrostatic sheet to mop and dust. The advent of products like the Swiffer is a gift to cat owners everywhere. These sheets attract lint and dust and hold on to them. By quickly picking up all those small particles, you not only keep a cleaner house, but you keep that debris off your cat. And don't forget the benefits of a powerful vacuum. Some companies—notably Dyson, Bissell, and Dirt Devil—are so aware of the need for pet mess cleanups that they have models designed for and marketed to pet owners.

Keep cat toys and dishes clean. Many dishes (especially durable stainless steel) and toys (such as hard plastic or Kongs) can be run right through the dishwasher. Hot water and soap works on most everything else, and soft toys can go through the washer and dryer.

Provide a great scratching post. Cats scratch. There's no way around it, short of the declawing extreme. Unfortunately, cats sometimes choose to scratch objects we'd like to keep unmangled. Like that antique armoire. Or your favorite recliner. Or that carpet on the staircase that seems to have become a favorite. Choosing, or building, the right scratching post and teaching your cat to use it exclusively can save you a fortune in damaged goods and property value.

What makes a great scratching post? It has to be sturdy, so your cat can dig in comfortably. It has to be tall, so she can stretch to her full length while she scratches. It has to have just the right feel to it—and what that is you probably know from the surfaces your cat scratches already. It has to be placed front and center where your cat spends her time. And it has to seem like the best spot to scratch in your cat's whole environment. (For much more about scratching posts and pre-venting inappropriate scratching, see page 54.)

Mess be gone. Of course, no matter what you do, there will be messes, from one end of the cat or the other. Products specially designed for cleaning up pet-made messes contain enzymes that remove odors and break down organic wastes. These products are perfect for cleaning up house-soiling accidents and fur balls, and often yield better results than all-purpose cleaners.

Products that contain ammonia are never a good idea for cleaning up after your cat. Ammonia smells too much like urine to be a safe scrubbing agent. Left to deduce this particular chemical smell on his own, your cat might come to the unfortunate conclusion that he's discovered a convenient new potty place. You'll need an enzymatic cleaner, such as Anti-Icky-Poo, Nature's Miracle, or others, and might even consider an appliance made just to get to pet stains, such as the Bissell SpotBot Pet. And remember: the size of the spot is typically the tip of the iceberg—the entire "plume of stain" is often deep and wide, so you'll want to apply the enzymatic cleaner that covers the surrounding area as well. (But do follow directions, especially with regard to testing for colorfastness—you don't want a pet stain replaced by a light spot where color had been.)

Whatever you do, don't procrastinate. If your cat has a house-soiling incident, or a fur ball, or if he manages to dump a houseplant and get dirt on the floor, don't wait to start the cleanup. Carpets get first priority, as they can be permanently stained by almost any soiling agent that's left sitting around. Even wood and tile floors, though, fare better if you clean them up right away. Keep cleaning supplies stocked and ready, and be sure to jump on any pet mess before it can set.

PART THREE
THE SOCIAL ANIMAL: TEACHING GOOD BEHAVIOR

Cats have shared our lives since the days when our ancestors figured out that farming produced a more steady means of support than living off the land. As hunters and gatherers became farmers, our new ways attracted vermin—rats and mice who wanted a share of our grain supplies. Fortunately, these opportunists were quickly followed by others, as cats chose to domesticate themselves and live alongside us.

But unlike dogs, whose instinctive skills we broke down and separated into components—herding dogs, coursing hounds, guard dogs—and then refined into the many breed types we know today, cats came to us as a complete package. They hunted on the periphery of human existence, and for the most part, we left them alone. Oh sure, some of us enjoyed their company, while others of us decided their ability to survive without our guidance meant they followed the lead of the devil.

Cats didn't change what they were doing no matter what we thought of it. For countless generations nothing much changed, until we changed so much that we demanded more of them, bringing them into our homes for good and asking them to adjust to a life they weren't really meant to live.

For the most part, they've done what we've asked of them, and done it well. We've asked them to give up their free-roaming ways, where the world was their privy and every vertical surface could be a potential scratching area, and use a small box as a potty and a small tree to keep their claws sharp. We've asked them to give up the hunting that defined them and to eat the processed food we offer them. We've asked them to share territory with a competing carnivore—the dog—and with smaller pets that look for all the world like lunch to them.

And they've done it, but it hasn't always been easy. To make it easier, this section is all about what you can do to help your cat cope, and to offer a life as stimulating as the wild one you've asked your pet to give up.

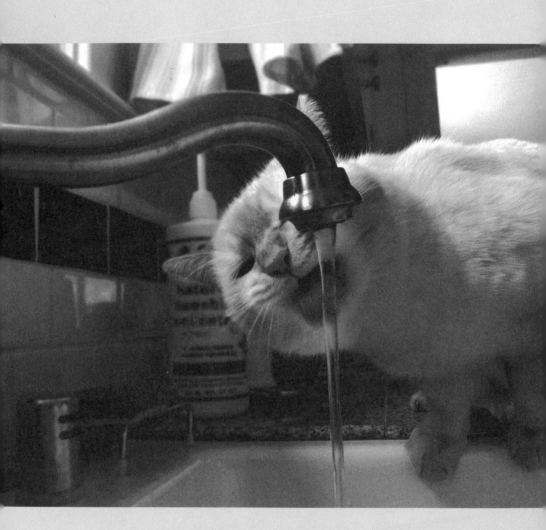

Cats enjoy their water fresh, and many teach themselves how to drink from the faucet. Instead of punishing a cat for being on the counter, encourage good hydration by getting a cat fountain.

Chapter 11

SHAPING AND TRAINING GOOD BEHAVIOR

Can you imagine letting a puppy, or a toddler, for that matter, just do his own thing as he grows up without ever teaching him how to behave around people and animals, and what the rules are for living in your home, not to mention the world at large? No? I didn't think so. But every day, people take kittens home and seem to expect them to raise themselves and turn into well-behaved cats overnight. I hate to break it to you, but that's just not gonna happen. Sure, kittens already know how to use a litter box when they go to their new homes, but there's a lot more than that to being a great cat. That cute little kitten is just waiting for you to teach him how to be successful in life, and that means showing him what you want and rewarding him when he makes you happy.

Cats live differently now than they ever have before. It wasn't that long ago that most people kept cats outdoors and valued them mainly for their skill as mousers. Hunting for food, fending for themselves, and bringing up kittens was a full-time job for cats. Now they've moved indoors, have all their meals provided for them, and are spayed or neutered for health reasons. Their only "job" is being America's most popular pet. Basically, they're born retired.

Our perceptions and expectations of cats have changed, too. Because we live so much more intimately with them, we know now that cats have a much greater ability to learn and a greater capacity for affection and desire for human companionship than we gave them credit for in the past. Cats today need us to be more than two-legged food dispensers. Now that we have them living an indoor lifestyle, they need us to deliver not only that challenging, action-packed lifestyle that is the birthright of every cat but also our company and our appreciation of their essential catness.

Teaching a cat how to live in a human world takes a special approach. Cats *can* learn and they enjoy learning, but they can never be forced to learn. Cats do things to please themselves, so the best approach is one that understands and respects the basic nature of cats. Take the time to learn why they do things and what motivates them. Think of it as an ongoing process of learning how to relate to a cat. With cats, discipline is not harsh punishment; it's simply good communication. When you make the effort to build a strong relationship with a cat, he will respond to your efforts to communicate—and that's all training is, really: an interspecies communications system.

Does that mean that every cat will respond exactly the same way to your efforts to train him? It would be nice if it were that easy, wouldn't it? But cats are individuals, and how receptive they are to training depends on what kind of kittenhood they had, how they were raised, their current environment, and the type of relationship they have with their person. Sounds a lot like the same things you discuss with your therapist, huh?

With cats, there's a period of time during kittenhood, when they are two weeks to seven weeks old, that is sort of the character-building stage of life. Behaviorists call it the sensitive period, a time when kittens learn rapidly and are most open to new experiences. How cats behave later in life is based in large part on how they are treated during the sensitive period. Kittens who get lots of handling and talking to by many different people, plus exposure to lots of different sights and sounds, are more friendly and outgoing and just plain braver than kittens without those advantages. They are more advanced in other ways, too. They open their eyes earlier, start exploring earlier, and approach unfamiliar items and people more willingly. So we can change the way cats behave just by the way we treat kittens during those crucial early weeks. Isn't that amazing? The good news is that even older kittens can learn to become more friendly if they receive increasing amounts of daily handling when they are seven to fourteen weeks old.

Feline Fact

One of the really interesting things about kitten personality development is the genetic contributions of the father. Even though the kittens may never see him, his personality has a big effect on how they respond to people. People-friendly males are more likely to produce people-friendly kittens.

Even before they are born, kittens are affected by their environment. Kittens whose mothers don't get enough to eat are less likely to be sociable, more likely to be fearful or aggressive, and don't learn as well as kittens with well-nourished mothers. Sometimes their development of motor skills is delayed or diminished.

Now most of these aspects of early life we can't influence because we aren't the ones raising the kittens during those first two months, but by knowing some of these things about kitten behavior, you can get a head start in understanding where he's coming from when he does —or doesn't do—certain things.

Of course, not everything can be influenced by environment or socialization. Take something as simple as sitting in a lap. We all love a cat who will do that, don't we? Turns out it's a genetically influenced behavior. Not every cat will be a lap cat, and that's not something you can change through socialization or training. But if you know that for some cats, sitting close to you—within eighteen inches—is their version of being friendly, then you might feel better about not having a cat who will sit in your lap.

Even if he won't cuddle with you, you can encourage your cat to be more affectionate by communicating with him through touch and body language. It's tempting to stare into his beautiful eyes, but to a cat that's rude beyond belief. A stare is a threat, so direct your gaze elsewhere when you're talking to him. Speak in a soft, gentle voice. Cats have superb hearing—better than dogs!—so you don't need to yell for them to hear you loud and clear. Spend time grooming your cat. Being brushed is very relaxing, as you probably know from visiting your own hairstylist. The act of grooming him can be therapeutic for both of you and is a wonderful way to build a bond of trust. Talk to him softly and give him a treat when you're done. Bonus: less hair on your clothes and furniture and fewer hairballs hacked up!

Cats are also particular about the amount and type of petting they'll tolerate. It's soothing for us to run our hands across their fur, again and again, but for a cat, not so much. Too much petting can irritate a cat, and the next thing you know, he's swiping at you with his claws or trying to take a bite out of your hand. Don't you sometimes want to do the same thing when someone endlessly strokes your hair or rubs your arm? Cats are no different. They each have a specific tolerance level, influenced by genetics and socialization, for the amount of petting they'll allow before they express their displeasure. To save your skin, learn to read your cat's body language. A twitchy tail, a forward flick of the whiskers, pulled-back ears, and rippling fur are all signs that your cat has had enough. Stop! Cats go from delight to bite in the blink of an eye.

How to Speak Felinese

When you're visiting a foreign country, you probably try to learn some words and phrases in the native language to help you get around; magic words like *please, thank you,* and, most important, *Where is the bathroom?* It's smart to do the same thing when you get a cat. The ability to understand your cat's body language and vocalizations will help you communicate with him. As a bonus, your cat will think you're a genius. Here's a short feline phrasebook to get you started.

Head butt: "I like you."

Face rub: "You belong to me."

Whiskers forward: "I'm feeling friendly or curious."

Whiskers moving during a nap: "I'm dreaming about chasing mice."

Ears up, whiskers straight to the side, staring intently: "I'm on guard here."

> Arched back with tail bushed out: "Back off."
>
> Crouching, ears low, whiskers back, pupils wide: "I'm ready to defend myself."
>
> Narrowed pupils: "I'm feeling aggressive."
>
> Tail swishing rapidly: "Leave me alone!"
>
> Tail low, twitching erratically: "I'm on the prowl!"
>
> Tail moving languidly: "Keep petting me."
>
> Tail upright: "I'm happy."

Cats who have a short fuse may never enjoy hours of petting, but you can take some steps to try to increase their tolerance for it. Start by stroking those really pleasurable areas: beneath the chin, between the ears, that sweet spot between the eyes, and the base of the tail. (Most cats get a rise out of being scratched there, a phenomenon I like to call "elevator butt.") Avoid belly rubs unless you just like to live dangerously. Reaching for that vulnerable area triggers most cats to respond instinctively with a punishingly painful "rabbit kick" or even a bite. Remember cats are both predator and prey. (When an animal is prey, being on his back with something grabbing his belly is about the last thing that happens before he is disemboweled and killed.)

Watch your cat closely for any sign that she's becoming overstimulated and stop immediately before she nails you. Literally *nails* you. Try to gradually increase the length of time she'll allow you to pet her before she's had too much. Giving her a treat while you pet her may also sweeten her attitude. When she signals that you're becoming annoying, stop and let her leave if she wants. If none of that works, try a nice massage instead. Firmer, deeper massage strokes are often less irritating than the butterfly kiss of a stroke down the back.

COMMUNICATING WITH CATS

If cats were granted the power of speech, probably the first thing they would say is "So what part of *meow* don't you understand?"

Cats have an extensive vocabulary that goes far beyond *meow*. With other cats, they rely on scent and body language to get their message across, but their communications with people involve a number of different sounds that include chirping and chattering in addition to the well-known meow in all its infinite variety. Those vocalizations develop and vary from cat to cat based on which ones get the best response from the people they live with. One study showed that cats motivate people to fill the food bowl by combining an urgent cry or meowing sound with the comforting sound of a purr. The result is a noise that's annoying, endearing, and difficult to ignore, all rolled up into one. If your cat's demand for food has a particularly whiny tone, it's because he learned from your response that it was the best way to get you out of bed and into the kitchen.

How did cats get so smart? Well, first of all, it's not true that they are aliens who have enslaved us to do their bidding, although it sure seems that way a lot of the time. I don't really buy the old joke that "dogs have owners and cats have servants." What is true is that when cats aren't sleeping they are watching us very closely. Cats are great observers and one of the things they have learned over millennia of living with people is that humans aren't very good at reading body language. We are more verbal and cats have learned to communicate with us vocally rather than with the body language that works with other animals. In evolutionary terms, animals who can use signals to manipulate others have an advantage. It's easy to see that cats have been highly successful in this area.

While "feed me" might be the best-known or most obvious feline command, cats have a lot more to say and many ways of expressing their demands. They chirp for petting, let loose a string of chirps when they want to play, emit an urgent cry for treats, purr both in pleasure and in pain, and chatter in excitement when they look out the window and see a bird or a squirrel. If we can learn to associate a cat's vocalizations with his body language—ear position, tail position, over-all posture—and the events surrounding those actions and sounds, we can crack the code of feline communication. If you really want to meet a cat at a richer, deeper level, you've got to listen for the sound, look for the body language, and then look for an overarching event that's happening. You'll almost always see vocalizations matched up with a change in body language. When you can do that, it's the equivalent of graduating from a Berlitz course in feline lingo.

Not every feline vocalization is a demand for food, attention, or play. Sometimes, a change in voice is the only way a cat has to let us know that he doesn't feel right. It might be subtle, but when you notice a change, you should have your cat checked out by the veterinarian, even if he appears healthy on the surface. He might have a painfully infected tooth or some other problem that isn't obvious.

Now that you know a little something about the development of cat behavior and the ways cats communicate, let's take a look at the ways you can build a solid relationship with your cat through training and other interactions. First, let's get rid of the notion that cats can't be trained. They absolutely can, but they don't work for free. The cat union frowns on that. To get the behaviors you want, you have to offer cats something in exchange. Luckily, they favor treats and catnip toys over cold, hard cash. Find your cat's motivation and be prepared to pay up for his efforts. Who knows? You might have the next feline agility star or Las Vegas performer.

Cats, Agile on Command

Agility cat? You read that right. Feline agility is a fun new sport in which cats run an obstacle course that includes jumps, tunnels, and platforms, competing against one another for the best time. It's a popular spectator event at cat shows, and any cat can play, pedigreed or not.

Even if you don't compete with your cat to earn titles, you can use furniture and other objects in your home to teach your cat an agility routine that will hone his physical and mental dexterity. Playing with your cat like this is easy to do, doesn't cost much, and is a great way to interact with him beyond feeding and petting.

Second, opportunity has to knock more than once for cats. In fact, it practically has to beat down the door. You not only have to give your cat opportunities to learn new things; you very often have to offer them more than once before your cat will take you up on them. Cats are inherently conservative and can be suspicious of anything new or different. They have to experience something several times before they decide it's not going to kill them and, heck, they even kind of like it. That goes double for things like walking on a leash or riding in a carrier in the car. People try it once, the cat pitches a hissy fit, and the people think, "Well, I'm not going to do that again!" But doing it again, and again, and again, is exactly what you have to do. Patience and repetition are essential when it comes to doing anything with cats and persuading them that it's really not so bad.

Try some tough love. Expose your cat to a little adversity every day, especially when he's young. This can be something as simple as getting him used to having his nails trimmed. Just clip a couple of claws and then let him go and give him a treat. Trim a couple more the next day, followed by a treat. Pretty soon, he learns that even though he might have been uncomfortable with the process at first, it doesn't really hurt. With repetition, it becomes a ho-hum experience. Do the same thing with car rides. Put him in the car in his carrier, back out of the driveway, then drive back in. Trip over. The next day, drive down the street a little way, then come back. The next trip can be around the block. When cats experience something every day that's a little disturbing to them—and almost anything new is disturbing to a cat—and then they get over it, their confidence increases and they start to remember that the scary thing isn't so bad after all. And I've mentioned it before, but it's really important to remember that pheromones—smells that cats themselves manufacture and put on people and things they love to mark them as their own—can really help a cat stay calm. When I'm working as a veterinarian in practice I go through so much Feliway—a synthetic version of those feline-friendly smells—that it's practically aftershave for me.

Take your cat places. If he only gets in the car to go to the veterinarian, and that happens only once or twice a year, your cat is probably not going to be a fan of car rides. But if you take him with you to make a deposit at the drive-through teller or to pick up a fast-food meal, he's going to experience car rides in a whole new way. Get a cat stroller and take him to the park where he can see birds and squirrels. When your cat is used to going different places, he will be easy to travel with whether you are going across town to the veterinarian or across the country to a new home. Don't let him get set in his ways.

Build on skills your cat already has. Does he like to jump? Teach him to jump through a hoop (flames optional) or over an obstacle. Does he like to roll over onto his back? Clicker-train him to play dead when you say, "Bang!" Cats have tremendous memories. Once you teach them something, they can do it at any time. Try teaching your cat different behaviors and see which ones he likes to do or shows interest in. Then you can build on those actions to teach new things. In other words, accentuate the positive.

Follow the KISS principle: Keep It Simple, Samantha. Use simple words or directions to tell your cat what you want. Sit, down, off, up, in, place: those are all great one-syllable words that are easy to say and get across exactly what you want. Even if your cat doesn't know exactly what they mean, he'll get the picture when you pair them with an action.

Be upbeat. If you and your cat aren't having a good time, you're not doing something right. Serve tasty but tiny treats that are easy to swallow, and train only when you're in a good mood.

Keep kitty training sessions short and sweet. Your cat's attention span probably has a range of two to ten minutes. Any more than that and he's *cat*atonic. Always end training when the cat has done something right. The adage "Quit while you're ahead" comes to mind.

All of these things will help you and your cat learn to communicate with and develop trust in each other. That's critical to building a relationship. When your cat is used to communicating with you and trusts that you will never do anything to hurt him, he will be willing to try new things for you and with you.

Many problems people attribute to their cat's bad attitude are caused by improper handling. Never play rough with your kitten or you'll be rewarding the animal for biting and clawing you.

Chapter 12
HOUSE RULES FOR GOOD CATS

R ules? For cats? Really?

Really. Like teenagers, cats are happiest when they know what you expect, even if they deny it to your face. Laying down some rules when you first get your kitten or cat will help make life easier for both of you. Teaching your cat where it's okay to scratch, not to jump up on the kitchen counter or dining room table, and how to welcome guests and play with kids in a way that's dignified, not deranged, is all part of being the best cat caretaker you can be.

And following the rules goes both ways. If you expect your cat to have nice manners, you need to provide an environment in which he can not just survive, but thrive. That means providing comfortable, appropriate places where he can do his catly things. Resting, sleeping, observing, and scratching make up the bulk of a cat's activity during the day, so think elevated perches (cats like to be high up so they can see everything going on) and sturdy scratching posts where he can get his groove on. Here's what you need to know about giving your cat a structured yet satisfying home life.

PLAYTIME

Cats are predators. They like to lurk and prowl and chase and pounce. Your indoor cat doesn't have the opportunity to go after real prey, but he still has strong hunting instincts. They don't disappear just because he lives a royal lifestyle in your home and has his Mice-A-Roni delivered on a silver platter. When a cat's need to hunt isn't fulfilled with live action, he turns to the next best thing: feet moving beneath the covers, hands dangling at an owner's sides, arms, legs, you name it. Instead of letting a kitten believe your body parts are fair game, provide him with toys that will satisfy his urge to hunt as well as save your skin. Cats like toys they can stalk, chase, pounce on, and bite.

The good news is that you don't have to release crickets, mice, or birds in your home to protect your skin from getting flayed or your fingers and toes bitten. Turn your home into an indoor hunting ground with perches for watching the outdoor world go by (consider installing a windowbox bird feeder), scratching posts for paw marking and nail maintenance, cat trees for climbing, resting, and observing, and an ever-changing assortment of toys. Puzzle toys are particularly good for giving your cat an outlet for his hunting instincts and ensuring that he keeps his sleek, sinewy physique. Wands with feathers or other dangly bits and wind-up or battery-operated toys that move on their own excite a cat's chase instinct. Balls inside a track let him paw for "prey," just as if he were exploring a mousehole. The fast, erratic motion of laser pointers and flashlights increase a cat's ability to think and move quickly. (Direct the beam up and down the stairs to give him a real workout, but make sure your cat reacts well, as some do not.) And don't forget the classic catnip-filled mice for rolling and rabbit-kicking (which is the name for the action when cats kick with their back leg at something they're hugging in their front paws) under the influence.

Teach Your Kitten to Play Nicely

It's all too easy to accidentally encourage kittens to bite or scratch in play, but this type of aggressive behavior can turn into a big, painful problem as the kitten gets bigger. Never "arm-wrestle" with a young cat, and keep some distance between you through play with toys that don't involve direct contact with the kitten. When a kitten tooth or claw touches human skin, screech loudly and immediately walk away. Kittens learn fast that playing rough ends the game.

USE OF SCRATCHING TOOLS

It's a fact of life that cats scratch. When they do, they can destroy furniture, wallpaper, and carpet in just minutes. But you don't have to live with shredded furniture or ratty-looking walls and flooring. It's easy to teach a cat to use a scratching post as long as you understand what he's looking for in the way of communication, claw conditioning, and fulfillment of his need to stretch and exercise.

That's right. Cats don't scratch to sharpen their claws, as is so often believed; at least, that's not the only reason or even the main reason. It's first and foremost a means of communication. Your cat is saying "I, Purrcy, was here. Look how big I am, how high up I can scratch." That's why cats like to scratch in places that will be seen by other cats; think of it as feline gang signs. Scratching leaves traces of scent, undetectable by people but perceptible to other cats, deposited from glands on the paws. We don't know exactly what message they're sending, but it's obviously important. So scratching on a post stuck off in a dark corner makes no sense to a cat. He's going to look for an object to scratch that has a much more prominent place in his living area, and that may well be the arm of your sofa.

What's Mine Is Not Yours

If you already have a cat and are bringing home a new member of the feline team, plan on bringing home more cat stuff as well. Cats

(Continued)

do not learn to share in kittygarten. They like to have their own things, and plenty of them. That goes for toys, litter boxes, beds, places to perch, scratching posts, and food and water dishes. And don't think you can get away with clustering them all together. To a cat, four scratching posts lined up next to one another are all just one big scratching post—his scratching post. Distribute the booty throughout the house so that each cat can choose his own space with his own stuff.

Scratching also keeps claws and paws in shape. It sheds the dead keratin that sheathes the claws, making way for a new covering, and exercises the muscles in the legs and paws that are so important to a cat's agility. Stretching is a big part of scratching, and we all know how good that feels. So instead of trying to stop your cat from scratching, encourage him to scratch on objects that are convenient for you and attractive to him.

The best scratching post is tall enough for your cat to extend his body full-length when he scratches. A little one-footer might be okay for a kitten, but a full-grown cat needs a post that is at least three feet high to allow him to perform the stretches that are part of his scratching enjoyment. The post can be upright or angled as long as it's an appropriate length.

You also need to think about what's covering the post. Forget carpet! For one thing, cats don't see why the carpet on the post is okay to scratch but not the carpet on the floor. For another, materials like rope, sisal, hemp, and burlap offer a lot more texture and shreddability, making them more pleasurable for the cat to scratch. You want him to think that the post, the cat tree, and other acceptable scratching items—hemp mats, for instance—are so great that he doesn't even want to scratch anywhere else.

Choose a sturdy post. The fastest way to turn your cat off using a scratching post is to buy one that falls over on him while he's climbing or scratching on it.

Provide more than one post. And don't hide them away. Remember that cats like to show off their scratching prowess. If your cat is making his mark on a certain piece of furniture or pair of drapes, place the scratching post nearby so he'll have a better option for giving his claws a workout. Put one in front of a window so your cat can check out the birds and squirrels while he's scratching.

Wean Your Cat from the Furniture

Encourage your cat to use the post by running your fingers up and down it or brushing a feather along the side of it. The motion will attract your cat and entice him to scratch. A little catnip, judiciously placed on top of the post and rubbed into the rope or sisal, may also gain his attention. Spraying Feliway, a synthetic pheromone, on the object you want scratched really encourages its use.

Never punish or frighten your cat when he's using the post. If he has even one bad experience while using it, he may never go near it again.

Praise your cat or give him a treat every time you see him using the post. Using a clicker to mark the behavior you like—scratching the post—and following up with a treat can be a very quick way to teach your cat that scratching in the right place has rewards.

TEACHING TOLERANCE OF OTHER CATS AND PEOPLE

Cats have a lot of different reputations, not all of them good. People often think they are unfriendly, shy, fearful, independent, or just plain crazy. If you've ever seen a cat go off like a hairy hand grenade when you try to approach him, you know what I'm talking about. A cat's personality is partly written in his genes and that can't be changed, but his early environment and experiences are important, too. If you can plan ahead, or simply get lucky in your kitten source, you can create a kitten who is friendly toward people and enjoys new experiences.

If you plan to buy a kitten from a breeder, choose one who is familiar with the needs of kittens during their early development and can provide them with the safe, moderate stimulation they need to become great feline companions. You can take on this role yourself if you'll be getting your kitten from, say, your neighbor or coworker whose cat just had kittens. Visit them frequently and handle them so they'll become accustomed to your touch and scent. In a controlled situation, let them see and hear your dog. Make sure they're raised indoors so that they hear vacuum cleaners and blenders and kids shouting after school. All of these experiences will help your future cat stay cool, calm, and collected in the face of anything new.

Now, if you can do those things, you'll be way ahead of the game, but most people don't have the opportunity to mold a kitten from such an early age. Does that mean you're out of luck and just have to take what you get in the way of your cat's personality? Nope! There are still things you can do to help him adjust to new situations, people, or places.

With an older kitten or adult cat, the best way to start is with gradual exposure combined with treats or other rewards, like play with a favorite toy. The key word here is *gradual*. You want your cat to feel in control anytime you're introducing him to a new person or experience. When you try to rush things is when your cat's prey side is likely to "explode," and the cat will disappear in a frenzy of fast-vanishing fur.

Preventing Cat Spats After Vet Visits

Have you ever taken one cat to the veterinarian, only to discover when you bring him home that your other cat treats him as a deadly enemy? What's up with that? Is a cat's memory really that short?

Cats are all about smell. They identify one another more through scent than appearance. So when one of them goes away and comes back smelling of alcohol, disinfectants, mystery cat—or worse yet, dog—their fellow cat may go ballistic because he doesn't recognize his buddy. Not every cat does this, but if you have one who does, consider taking both cats to the veterinarian at the same time so they'll come back smelling alike. An alternative is to put a dab of rubbing alcohol on each cat's head. The strong odor will briefly shut down their sense of smell and make them look at each other instead. You can also rub the "preauricular area"—the oily, less hairy area in front of the ears—on each cat and swap scents between them. (Do this when the cats are separated by a solid door and let them sniff each other beneath the door first. You can open it when there is no hissing or nasty body language.) For cats, the oils from that particular spot are always "happy" smells. "Unhappy" messages come from the anal glands and other areas.

Never force your cat to be touched or held, and never put him in a position where he feels cornered. That's the best way I know to get scratched or bitten and to turn your cat off ever wanting to meet your friends or do anything different. In fact, you don't want to try to hold a cat who wants to get away.

The real secret to getting a cat to pay positive attention to someone is a bit of reverse psychology. When you bring someone new into your home, tell her beforehand to ignore the cat. The two most important things to know about becoming best buds with a cat is that cats like to make the first move in any relationship and, deep down, no matter how aloof they might seem, they are innately inquisitive. If people are quiet and don't pay attention to the cat, his curiosity will get the better of him and he will come closer to investigate. Once the cat gives a nudge with his head or rubs up against the new person, she can stretch out a hand to let him sniff or maybe give him a nice head scratch. Another trick is to sit on the floor and calmly toss treats toward the cat or dangle an interactive toy—one that gives the cat plenty of space between himself and whoever is holding the toy. Few cats can resist either of those invitations!

SPECIAL GUIDELINES FOR KIDS AND
CATS (HOLDING PROPERLY, ETC.)

The relationship between a cat and a child can be a wonderful thing. A cat's unconditional love and patient listening skills are sometimes the only things that help when a child has had a bad day and needs someone to talk to about it, someone who will only purr and never scold. A cat is the perfect friend to hang out with, read or watch TV with, and sleep with at night.

To help children build that special relationship, teach them from a very early age how to pet cats gently. Toddlers don't have good motor skills, so hold their hand and help them stroke the cat nicely. A good way to let them practice is with a stuffed cat or a Pat the Cat book, neither of which can be injured by too vigorous patting or accidental bops on the head.

A cat can provide a child's first lessons in personal space and treating others the way we'd like to be treated. Young children don't know how to recognize that the cat is uncomfortable or unhappy, so they need help to understand that they might be hurting the cat or making him angry. Always supervise when a young child is interacting with a cat, and never allow him to chase the cat, pull his fur, ears, or tail, or bother him while he's eating, drinking, or using the litter box. All too often, a harassed cat stops using the litter box because that's the one place the child has been able to catch him, so it's to your benefit not to let that happen. If you can't supervise them, separate them or make sure that the cat has a place he can go that's out of reach of the child.

For happy interactions, teach your child how and where it's okay to hold the cat. Grasping the cat beneath the front legs and letting the rest of the body hang down just isn't the way to go. A two-year-old isn't able to pick up a cat and support his body weight, at least not comfortably for the cat, so don't let that happen. Instead, have your child sit on the floor or on the sofa with the cat next to him. Cats don't like having people stand over them, so petting works best when cat and child are on the same level. Many cats are then satisfied to sit close to the child or even climb right onto her lap. And don't forget that cats like to take the lead when it comes to making friends. Tell your child to let the kitty come to him to be petted. When children know how to treat cats respectfully, a cat will recognize that and come to them with confidence.

Which Breeds Are Good with Kids?

How cats react to children depends on the individual, but some breeds have a reputation for being especially kid-friendly. They include the Abyssinian, the Burmese, the Cornish Rex, the Maine Coon, the Persian, and the Siamese. The Aby and the Cornish Rex are bold, fast, high-energy cats, perfect for older children who want to teach a cat tricks or take him for walks on leash. They are also fast enough to get out of the way of younger children who are trying to grab them. Siamese also enjoy walking on leash, and as a bonus they are talkative. Children often love to carry on conversations with them. I mean, how cool is that, to have a cat who will talk back to you? It's not unusual to find that three or four generations of a family have all had Siamese as children and then get the cats for their own children. Maine Coons are big, kindly lugs, patient enough to put up with the child who wants to push them around in a baby buggy. Burmese and Persians are popular with quiet older children because they like to cuddle and sit on laps. A laid-back Persian cat and a child who likes to play hairdresser can be a match made in kitty heaven.

Children who are old enough to pick up and carry cats around can learn through experience which method works best with the individual cat. Some cats like to be held over the shoulder, some snuggled up against the chest, and some on their back like a baby. Whichever way a cat likes to be held, there's only one good way to pick him up. First, get his attention so he isn't startled when you reach for him. Place one arm beneath his front legs and use the other to support his rear end. Hold him firmly against your chest, but don't squeeze tight. You don't want to squish his guts. The cat will settle down more quickly in a warm, dry towel with Feliway on it.

A kitten or cat who doesn't like how he's being held will squirm and try to readjust himself. Help your child figure out which position is most comfortable for the cat. Bear in mind that some cats don't like being held at all. Your child may need to settle for interacting with the cat in other ways.

Speaking of kids interacting with cats, should you let your child dress the kitten or cat up in doll clothes? Kids and kittens and tea parties and baby buggies go together like peanut butter and jelly—sometimes. Cats can occasionally be willing participants in these activities, but it's important to make sure they aren't helpless victims. Clothing shouldn't constrict the cat, especially around the neck. Check for elastic that might be too tight. Lay down some ground rules and enforce them. If the cat doesn't like the game and walks away, that's his choice. If he is hissing, his tail is switching, and his ears go back, he's not having a good time at all, and play needs to take a different form before someone is scratched or bitten.

KEEPING CATS OFF THE COUNTER

Cats are natural explorers, and it's normal for them to want to check out the place where meals are prepared. Even better, the kitchen counter is up off the ground, always a cat's preferred position in life. However, it's just as natural for you to want to keep little cat feet off your food preparation surfaces. Cats tracking across the counter does pose a health risk, albeit small, that still should be minimized.

Experienced cat owners laugh at the thought of keeping cats off the kitchen counter, the dining room table, the top of the refrigerator, or any other place they want to go. Most consider that goal an exercise in futility. With their athletic build and jumping skills, cats tend to go where they want with impunity. You can sometimes win the battle, if not the war, if you have patience, ingenuity, and a little stick-to-it-iveness.

Be firm and consistent. Every time you see the cat jump on the counter, pick him up and put him back on the floor. Every time. You can't let him get away with it, or he'll never stop.

Enlist a weapon of cat destruction, er, dissuasion. Water. Fill a squirt gun or spray bottle with water and aim it at your feline counter insurgent when he makes a move to take the high ground. Try to do this from a distance so your cat doesn't associate the spray of water with you.

Does Punishment Work?

Punishment is something that most cat owners try at some point, but it's very difficult to do it effectively. Punishment can be yelling, squirting the cat with water, or flicking the cat on the nose. Certain types of punishment such as hitting the cat are inhumane and dangerous, not only in a physical way but also to your relationship with your cat. Something that seems minor, like flicking the cat on the nose, may not inflict serious physical harm, but it can cause your cat to become suspicious or fearful of you. The next time you reach for him, even if it's in a friendly way, he may react defensively by biting or scratching you or fearfully by running away.

Punishment works only when it's immediate (within one or two seconds of the undesirable behavior), consistent (every time the behavior happens), and effective (strong enough to inhibit the behavior but not so strong that it injures the cat or damages the relationship with the cat). Achieving all of that is really hard to do. When punishment is administered inconsistently, the result is that the cat simply learns to do the behavior when no one's looking. That might satisfy you—until you notice the imprint of his tongue on the butter or the bite marks in the chicken. The bottom line is that punishment never changes a cat's behavior for the better. Even remote punishments like water squirters and loud noises make cats think of us as unreliable and strange, which is not really the best basis for forging a close relationship. Better to teach the cat using more positive methods and to remove temptation altogether.

Stick it to your cat. Literally. A product called Sticky Paws—which is like a large sheet of masking tape applied sticky side out—will help deter your cat from jumping up where you don't want him. It won't hurt your cat, but he will dislike the sticky feeling beneath his feet. You can't cover the entire counter with it because then you can't work on it, but if you can find the area where your cat is most likely to jump and put Sticky Paws there, he may give up his high-altitude excursions. Of course, more persistent cats will simply find another place to jump that drives you crazy. You could also try the Whoa Buddy blanket, one of the new products that caught my eye at the Global Pet Expo trade show. An old trick for keeping cats off horizontal surfaces is putting foil out, and that's what the Whoa Buddy builds on: one side is soft so it doesn't skid off upholstery, and the top side is Mylar, which feels like foil and keeps cats off.

Teach your cat to go to his cat tree or some other place where he can see what you're doing yet not be on the counter. The action could be cued by placing food or dishes on the counter. This is a complex trick, but it's not beyond the abilities of many cats. Consider getting the help of a trainer if it's beyond your ability to teach it.

Compromise. Put a counter-height stool or a scratching post with a small perch on top next to or near the counter. From there your cat can supervise all kitchen activities without getting in the way or setting paw on the counter.

Now, does any of this mean that your cat will always stay off the kitchen counter? Nope. If you've left something irresistible out, like roast beef or an uncovered butter dish, and you're not around to guard it, I can guarantee you that your cat is going to take advantage of the situation. And who could blame him? If I left out a million dollars and you knew you could take it without any consequences, well, you probably would. Your cat is the same way, only more so. If you're not around to correct him 90 percent of the time and he gets caught and yelled at only 10 percent of the time, the average cat is going to yawn and think, *Whatever.* For the feline equivalent of a million bucks, he's going to go for it. So lead him not into temptation.

GET YOUR CAT TO SLEEP AT NIGHT

One of the most comforting feelings in the world is drifting off to sleep snuggled close to a warm, purring cat. That is, until the cat drapes himself over your head, wakes up for a two a.m. play session and wants you to join in, or takes his paw and bops you on the nose in the hope that you'll get up and feed him when it's still 0-dark-thirty. Cats who believe nighttime is the right time to play can be the source of considerable insomnia for their people.

Cats can sleep as much as twenty hours a day, so it might seem as if it should be easy to get a good night's shut-eye. Alas, cats are wired by nature to nap intermittently throughout the day, then hunt between twilight and dawn's early light. You're likely to see this behavior in action round about bedtime. Cat lovers call it the ten o'clock crazies, that time in the evening when cats suddenly run wild through the house, as if hunting unseen mice.

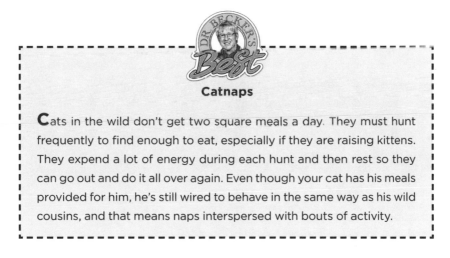

Catnaps

Cats in the wild don't get two square meals a day. They must hunt frequently to find enough to eat, especially if they are raising kittens. They expend a lot of energy during each hunt and then rest so they can go out and do it all over again. Even though your cat has his meals provided for him, he's still wired to behave in the same way as his wild cousins, and that means naps interspersed with bouts of activity.

Take advantage of that bedtime burst of energy and institute a high-energy kitty playtime just before you get ready to go to bed. Toss a Ping-Pong ball down the hall to initiate a feline hockey game. Don't stop until you wear your cat out. That should take at least five to ten minutes. Pull out the fishing-pole toy and put your cat through his acrobatic paces, encouraging him to turn flips and chase the line through the house, up on the sofa, and back again. The goal is to tire him out enough that he'll sleep peacefully through the night.

There are other ways to change your cat's sleeping habits. If you see him sleeping during the day, wake him up and play with him for a few minutes. Do that several times throughout the day, and he'll be more likely to sleep through the night. Increase his activity level by placing food bowls up high so he must jump up to eat. One of the perches on his cat tree might be a good place for this. If you have stairs, toss toys or treats up them for him to chase.

Sweaters with No Holes

Some cats chew holes in sweaters, blankets, or even plastic bags. No one's really sure what causes it. It probably hasn't anything to do with a dietary deficiency but rather is one of those habits (like people who chew fingernails, pop knuckles, chew gum) that relieves stress and brings them comfort. There's probably a genetic link as well, since Siamese cats are more likely to chew. The best we can offer are some "might help, can't hurt" suggestions.

You should definitely put away anything that's too nice to be damaged, like Great-Grandma's quilt that won first place at the 1908 Iowa County Fair. Keep bedrooms off-limits by closing the doors to protect the blankets on the beds.

Set out some "decoy" blankets, and apply a deterrent such as Bitter Apple, Tabasco, hot pepper oil, etc. This may break the habit, but maybe not. Spraying fabrics lightly with perfume is also a common recommendation.

Some experts believe that increasing the fiber in the cat's diet may also help. You can do that by adding a little canned pumpkin on a regular basis—it's also good for hairballs—or feed one of the premium quality high-fiber diets sold as hairball formulas. More activity is also recommended, such as playing with your cat regularly with a fishing-pole toy or other lure object.

When exercise and interrupted naps don't work to keep your cat from bothering you at night, try water power. Keep a squirt gun or spray bottle at hand, and aim a spray of water at your cat anytime he disturbs you during the night. Often, the hiss of the water and the spatter of wetness on his fur are enough to send a cat skulking away, although a determined few persist. When they do, you might consider closing the cat out of the room at night. Be prepared for a few nights of yowling until your cat accedes to the new routine. A good set of earplugs or your airplane noise cancellation headphones can help drown out the noise.

Does your cat keep you awake because he's scratching himself throughout the night? That can be a major annoyance. Cats who scratch frequently or frantically often have external parasites such as fleas or suffer from bacterial or yeast infections or some type of allergy (environmental or food). If you want to sleep soundly, take them to the veterinarian for an accurate diagnosis and appropriate treatment.

A more serious reason for a cat's inability to sleep, or at least to sleep comfortably through the night, is the aches and pains of old age. Older cats with arthritis may have difficulty getting comfortable in bed or even getting onto the bed at all. If your cat is overweight, putting him on a weight-loss plan will help assuage the pain. Other remedies to ease discomfort and help your cat sleep include a ramp or steps to help him get onto the bed, supplements that help with joint function, and veterinary-prescribed pain medications. (No cat has to suffer: your veterinarian has several powerful weapons at his disposal for joint problems ranging from anti-inflammatory drugs to lasers, even stem cell therapy.)

Some cats sleep just fine throughout the night but like to rise with the sun. That would be fine except they usually want you to get up with them. Their methods of persuasion include insistently patting you on the cheek, using a paw to bop you upside the head, that thrumming purr that tickles your ear, sitting on your chest and staring intently at you, and worst of all, that unrelenting call that says, *I'm so hungry. Feed me NOW!*

You can't hit the snooze button on an insistent cat, but if you can keep from giggling, pretending to be asleep helps. Pull the covers over your head and lie still. Whatever you do, don't yell at the cat when he wakes you. That simply reinforces the behavior by giving him attention. It's best to ignore him. Cats who never—and I mean never—get a response will eventually give up and leave you alone.

To help train your cat to sleep beyond sunrise, invest in blackout shades. They will keep the room dark and may encourage him to sleep a little longer. Cats have their own internal alarm clock, but without the trigger of sunlight you may be able to "set it" to go off a little later in the morning.

To satisfy a cat's hunger pangs without having to leave the bed, leave a loaded puzzle toy out or purchase a timed feeder (I like the Petmate LeBistro) that you can set to open at whatever unholy hour your cat usually likes to wake you. Place a little dry food in it to tide him over until you're ready to get up and feed him. If you are starting out with a kitten, teach him that breakfast doesn't come until you leave for work in the morning. Putting him on a schedule can help prevent those early morning wake-up calls. As a bonus, it teaches your cat that good things happen when you leave the house, which is one of the best ways to deter the development of separation anxiety.

Want Your Cat to Sleep in the Bedroom, but Not on the Bed?

That's tricky. Cats enjoy the intimacy of sleeping with us (and they're great bed warmers!), but if that closeness interferes with your ability to get enough sleep or sets off your allergies, you may need to encourage your cat to sleep elsewhere. Appeal to his love of high places with a floor-to-ceiling cat condo, giving him the opportunity to sleep in a "tree" like his wild relatives. Scent it with catnip or pheromones to make it even more appealing. If your cat has a canine roommate, a high perch like this can give him a feeling of security.

Cats like dark, cavelike areas. Look for a cozy, tentlike cat bed that you can situate near your own bed. If your cat likes sleeping on your pillow, place a pillow like yours—with your scent on it or pheromones—in the cat's bed or on the floor.

If nothing else works, it can't hurt to try a little bedtime snack. Turkey contains tryptophan, an essential amino acid that's said to have sleep-inducing qualities. Thanksgiving naps aside, evidence suggests there's not really enough tryptophan in turkey to serve as a sedative, but it can't hurt to give your cat a small amount of fat-free or low-fat turkey just before you turn in for the night. Try a little yourself. Maybe you'll both have sweet dreams.

A cat who avoids the litter box often has a medical condition that must be treated before retraining can begin. In retraining, pheromones can help reduce stress triggers that make litter box training difficult.

Chapter 13

SOLVING LITTER BOX PROBLEMS

Refusing to use the litter box is the number one reason cats are given up to animal shelters. That's a tragedy because when the cause of the house soiling can be determined and a targeted treatment plan is put into place, the success rate is 80 to 90 percent. That's a much better treatment response than for most diseases or conditions!

If your cat is urinating or defecating outside the litter box, you can take steps to figure out his motivation—and I can assure you that revenge is not it—and deal with the problem. There is always a reason when a cat starts avoiding the litter box. Most often, litter box problems develop when a cat doesn't like the litter being used, the cleanliness of the box, the size of the box, or the number of boxes.

Take the number of boxes. Cats don't really like to share, especially not something as personal as a litter box. Free-roaming cats avoid eliminating in a spot another cat has used. They also don't like to urinate and defecate in the same place. If your cat had his way, he'd probably like to have a separate litter box for each of those functions.

Other times, the cat associates the litter box with a bad experience, such as painful urination because of a urinary tract infection or because he was punished for going outside the litter box and then placed back in it. Being disturbed in the box by another cat, a dog, or a child can turn your cat off using it, too. For cats with medical problems, urinating outside the litter box is the only way they have of saying, "Hey, I don't feel good. Take me to the veterinarian." It's not always possible to meet all of a cat's desires regarding the litter box, but if you are able to discover the underlying cause for his dissatisfaction and change the situation, you are likely to get the improvement that you're hoping for.

DEALING WITH LITTER BOX ISSUES

The first step is to take your cat to the veterinarian to rule out a physical problem. Sixty percent of house-soiling cases can be traced to medical issues. And they're not always what you might think. Senior cats—golden oldies, I like to call 'em—often begin avoiding the litter box because they have arthritis in their hips or knees, making it difficult to get in and out of the box or to crouch down comfortably. Old cats with cognitive problems may have trouble remembering where the litter box is or that they're supposed to use it. Diabetic cats have a need to urinate frequently, and sometimes they can't make it to the box in time.

Other times cats may be suffering from some type of bladder disease, which can make it painful to urinate. Cats associate that pain with the litter box and go around trying to find places where it will hurt less to pee. Sometimes they choose a sink or bathtub because the porcelain feels cool and soothing. (On the upside, it's easy to clean up after cats who pee in the sink or tub, and it's also easy to see if there's blood in the urine, which could indicate an infection.) Those are just a few of the health-related possibilities that could be causing your cat to think outside the box.

Don't Give Up on an Achy Cat

If your cat's litter box issues are caused by the aches and pains of arthritis, don't assume there's nothing you can do to help. Try placing litter boxes throughout your home to make it easier for your cat to get to them; provide a ramp, purchase a box with lower sides, or provide steps or a cutout in the box for ease of entry and exit; and ask your veterinarian about feline-safe pain medication, treatments, or joint supplements to relieve creaky joints.

A trip to the veterinarian for a physical exam and some simple lab tests can rule out urinary disease, gastrointestinal problems, endocrine diseases such as diabetes, and musculoskeletal conditions such as osteoarthritis. A urinalysis by cystocentesis—painlessly drawing the urine out of the bladder using a very fine needle attached to a syringe—and medical imaging of the entire urethra to look for stones are some of the tests your veterinarian may recommend to get a complete picture of what's going on.

Your cat's age may also be a factor in the diagnosis. Cats who are less than one year old may be suffering from urinary stones or anatomical abnormalities. Cats who are one to seven years old are more prone to idiopathic (meaning the cause is unknown) cystitis and urinary stones. Older cats may have developed bacterial infections, renal failure, or certain metabolic diseases. This is really important because too often antibiotics are prescribed by a veterinarian or requested by an owner as a quick fix, but instead they only postpone the solving of the problem. When you know that fewer than 2 percent of cats who are one to seven years old are diagnosed with bacterial cystitis, then you can see that more than 98 percent of the time it's futile to send them home with antibiotics. Look deeper for the cause and try other fixes before resorting to a scattergun approach of antibiotics. The problem could be...stress! Some extremely intriguing research at Ohio State University suggests we underestimate how changes in a cat's routine or environment cause stress that leads to problems such as food refusal, frequent vomiting, and litter box avoidance. The study reinforces the recommendation that pet owners feed at the same time, keep litter boxes in consistent locations, and offer regular playtime. Relaxed cats are healthy cats!

BEHAVIOR-RELATED CAUSES OF HOUSE-SOILING

The ABCs of litter box management are Accessible, Big, and Clean. Let's see which of those, or other factors, may be pissing off your cat.

You've ruled out any medical problems as the cause of your cat's house-soiling. When infection, inflammation, pain, or other physical causes are not an issue, the two primary motivations for a cat's refusal to use the litter box are toileting, meaning the cat has decided he would prefer to use the bathroom elsewhere, thank you very much; or marking, the feline form of communication. Marking, also known as spraying, is most common in unneutered cats—an excellent reason to have your Tom or Kate Kitten altered at a young age—but it can also result from tension between two or more cats in the household, regardless of gender or alteration status.

How can you tell the difference between toileting and marking? The number one clue is the location of the urine. If the urine is on the floor or some other horizontal surface, especially if the cat is standing or squatting to urinate, he has a toileting issue. Most often, it's because he doesn't like the location or state of the litter box.

Urine sprayed onto a vertical surface such as a wall or door is a sign of scent marking, or territorial marking. Most cats who mark vertically don't have a medical problem. You can almost always chalk the behavior up to a cat's desire to communicate something, either to you or to other cats in the house. Cat pee is designed to stick on trees in all weather for as long as three weeks, so it's powerful stuff. When your cat uses it to send a message, you know he's serious about what he's saying. Don't ever tell yourself that he just missed the box.

Size Really Does Matter!

Your cat's litter box should be one and a half to two times as long as your cat. How big is that? Measure your cat from the tip of his nose to the base of his tail—heck, throw in the length of the tail for good measure. If your cat is 21 inches long, his litter box should be at least 32 inches long. That gives him enough space to turn around in the box and dig. If you can't find a commercial litter box that's an appropriate size, look for a litter box made for dogs weighing up to 35 pounds or purchase a plastic sweater box from a discount or home design store.

Sometimes a box is too big. You may have chosen a box that your kitten can grow into, but if he's too little to climb into it easily, he won't use it. Old cats or those who are on the tubby side can have a similar problem with high sided boxes.

So what can you do? You have one litter box per cat, plus one extra. You've placed the litter box in a private area with an escape route from other pets and no unexpected noises. You have at least one litter box on each level of your home. You're sure that the box is the right size. Even if you think you're doing everything right, cats will sometimes start going outside the litter box. That's when you have to dig a little deeper to discover the root of the problem.

Start with easy solutions, such as cleaning the litter box even more frequently, moving the box to an area the cat seems to prefer, or adding another box. You may even want to create a litter box cafeteria, giving your cat a choice of box styles and litter types. It's possible that his preferences have changed. For instance, if your cat has started peeing on the carpet, he may be trying to tell you that he'd like a litter that's more absorbent or one that has a softer feel beneath his paws. Offer him a fine, sandy, scoopable litter. You may have chosen a particular type or brand because of its cost or for environmental reasons, but cats like what they like. Be willing to defer to your cat's preferences, even if they aren't as green or as cost-effective as you'd like. He's not going to change his mind no matter how many times you tell him a particular type of litter is less expensive or more environmentally friendly.

Feline Fact

The domestic cat's relationship with people started in the Middle East some seven thousand to nine thousand years ago. Those early cats buried their waste in the sandy soil of their environment, and to this day most cats prefer litter with a fine, sandy texture.

Scented litter might appeal to you, but for most cats it's a turnoff. Try an unscented variety and see if that solves the problem.

Experiment with the depth of the litter. Most cats like it to be about one and a half inches deep, but your cat might like a little more or a little less. If your cat is urinating on a hard, smooth surface, try changing the distribution of the litter in the box. Put a thin layer of litter at one end and leave the other end empty. Placing the box on a floor with a hard surface may also help.

Clean up your act and scoop the box every time you see that your cat has used it, or at least twice a day. Cats can be a lot more finicky than your mother-in-law when it comes to having a clean bathroom. If your cat is peeing right next to the litter box, the message he's sending may be that it stinks so much he doesn't want to get into it. When you see a nasty stall in a public restroom, don't you move on to one that's cleaner? Cats are the same way. They need a small amount of odor to attract them back to the litter box, but too much is overwhelming and sends them off in search of a new spot. Here's a rule of paw: if you can smell the litter box, it's WAAAY too smelly for your cat.

Every week, dump the old litter and replace it with a fresh supply. Once or twice a month, wash the litter box itself with mild, unscented dishwashing detergent and fill the box with new litter. Plastic absorbs odors, so replace the entire litter box every six months to a year. It may be a little more expensive and time-consuming, but it's a lot less trouble than dealing with a cat who refuses to use the litter box.

Make sure the box is really in a place that your cat approves. If your cat is urinating and defecating in the same general area as the box, just not in it, or in an area where the box was previously located, she may be hinting around that she'd like you to move it. Try to meet her request if possible. There are any number of reasons your cat might not like the location, from privacy to protection to noise level.

Cats have a strong sense of privacy when it comes to elimination habits. Just as you wouldn't like having someone walk in on you in the bathroom, neither does your cat. When cats are urinating and defecating, they need to feel secure in the knowledge that nothing scary will interrupt them. (Would you want somebody opening the door of the bathroom at random while you're doing your business?) They're not fans of cavelike locations when they're using the box—too easy to be ambushed on the way out—so they may dislike covered litter boxes or a box that is placed in a cabinet or closet.

They can feel threatened if the litter box is placed in an area without any escape route, one that has a lot of foot traffic from other family members, including other dogs and cats, or one that is likely to have unexpected noises or activity.

You might think the laundry room is a great place for the litter box, but your cat may have an entirely different opinion on the matter. Laundry rooms tend to be noisy (spinning, bouncing machines), and they don't necessarily have an escape route if your dog sticks his head in to see if there are any "snacks" in the box or the twins run in to pull their soccer uniforms out of the dryer. And if the dryer buzzer goes off at a crucial moment and scares the heck out of the cat, that may be the last time he goes near that litter box.

What about the garage or basement? They're pretty good as far as privacy goes, although a garage door opening unexpectedly could put a scare into a cat. But because they're usually far from living areas, young cats may not always remember how to get to them at first or may not be able to make it all the way before they have to go. This is also an issue for aging cats with arthritic joints. And some cats like to leave their mark by making scratching motions in the area surrounding the litter box. Pawing on concrete might not be their cup of tea.

If possible, try placing the box in a little-used guest bathroom. A bathroom is ideal because you can scoop the waste right into the toilet and flush it away as long as you're using flushable litter, and it's likely to have a cabinet where you can store bags or boxes of litter. Just be sure the door is always open so your cat can enter and exit easily.

Whatever you do, don't place the litter box in the same area where your kitten or cat eats and drinks. Cats are fussy about cleanliness and would never dream of using the bathroom in the same place where they eat. You can't blame them, right?

I know it's hard to imagine, but you can try too hard to cover up the smell of a litter box. Go easy on air fresheners and potpourri. Sometimes they can mask odors a little too thoroughly, so much so that your cat can't find the litter box. Instead, to kill odors, use an enzyme breakdown product such as the Equalizer, Nature's Miracle, Arm & Hammer, or other enzymatics to clean areas where your cat has urinated or sprayed inappropriately. If you scoop the box often, change the litter, and clean the box regularly, odor shouldn't be an issue.

SPRAYING

If you ever come home to find that your cat has peed on your pillow or inside your suitcase, or sprayed your favorite cashmere sweater, you might think he was getting revenge because you went out to dinner after work instead of coming home and feeding him on time. It's an understandable belief, but it's not accurate. Cats are complex in many ways, but they live in the here and now. Plotting revenge just isn't up their alley. When your cat sprays your clothing or bedding, he's actually paying you a compliment, backhanded though it may be. Those items smell like you, and adding his scent to yours makes the cat feel comfortable, especially if he's feeling stressed for some reason. It might be because you went out to dinner and interrupted his feeding schedule, but it also might be a response to the presence of a stray cat in your yard, bullying by another cat in the household, or even some incident that you didn't notice but that made an impression on your cat.

What we have with cats who spray is not a failure to communicate but more of an undesirable attempt to communicate. While your cat may have a valid message to send to you or to one of his housemates or the stray cat who's been lurking outside his front door, his stinky method of getting it across is making you, well, cross. If your cat is urine marking, you need to reduce his need to communicate. That can mean spaying or neutering him or her, changing the environment, instituting a behavior modification plan, or administering pheromones

SOLVING LITTER BOX PROBLEMS

or medications that will help to decrease the anxiety that is often behind the territorial imperative to mark. Depending on the situation and the individual cat, a behaviorist may recommend one or a combination of these options.

Any cat, regardless of gender, can and will urine-mark if the message is important enough and once they are mature sexually. Spaying or neutering a kitten before such maturity is one of the best ways to prevent territorial marking. Females can reach that milestone as early as four months of age, and males are not far behind. Young kittens recover quickly from this surgery, so don't hesitate to have it done. Altering a cat after he or she starts spraying can help stop the behavior, but it doesn't work as well as early spay/neuter surgery. Spraying is less likely if you have female cats or a male and a female, but a few cats are just going to spray no matter what. For them, you may need to bring out the big guns of medication and behavior modification.

Environmental changes start with establishing an atmosphere of plenty. Give your cat multiple perches, toys, scratching posts, and places to eat and drink. If he doesn't feel as if he has to hoard his resources, he'll be more relaxed. Think of kids in day care. Kids are the happiest when they've got their own area and own toys. Some like to share, but most don't.

An environmental factor that may inspire a cat to continue to spray is the type of furniture you have. Items made of particleboard absorb odor much more intensely than furniture made of solid wood. (That's right; your cat is an interior design critic.) For a cat, spraying an object that will hold odor longer and better is a major plus. It's like buying airtime for an advertisement during the Super Bowl.

Keeping a Log Can Help Spot Patterns

The techniques behaviorists recommend to modify a cat's behavior will vary depending on the situation and the individual cat, but

(Continued)

some methods are universal, especially when it comes to problems caused by anxiety. Work directly with a behaviorist if possible, but if there isn't one in your area, the following advice may help.

Keep a record of when and where your cat sprays. Include details such as time of day, whether it seems to be in response to a particular stimulus, and even seemingly unremarkable changes in the household, such as getting your hair colored or your spouse shaving his mustache.

Give your cat a predictable daily routine. He should know that meals or playtime will always occur at the same time every day, as much as possible.

Ignore behavior you don't like and reward behavior you do like.

Use pheromones to chemically enhance your cat's environment. Pheromones are biological or chemical substances that influence sexual and other behaviors in animals. They are often used in conjunction with behavior modification or counterconditioning programs, so it's not always easy to tell whether it's the pheromone or the behavior modification plan that's really making the difference. Nonetheless, they are harmless and have a good track record of reducing spraying behavior. Feliway is a widely used pheromone that is dispensed via a plug-in diffuser. The diffuser covers five hundred to seven hundred square feet and lasts for thirty days. If the spraying behavior occurs throughout the house, you will probably need to use more than one diffuser. It's common to see results in three to ten days, and sometimes sooner.

If all else fails, bring out the big guns: medication (for the cat, not for you). Drugs such as fluoxetine (Prozac) and clomipramine are often effective in dealing with territorial marking, but they won't help with garden-variety house-soiling. Fluoxetine, formulated for people, is available inexpensively in generic form, but the beef-flavored version made for dogs is often more popular with cats and the people who have to pill them, as every molecule of the drug is coated with something tasty (fluoxetine is very bitter).

The downside is that drugs are not a quick fix and they work best in concert with a behavior modification program. You can't just give a pill and expect an instant result.

> **Feline Fact**
>
> **N**ever use ammonia-based products to clean up areas where a cat has urinated or defecated. To the cat, it just makes the area smell as if a tiger has let loose in the room. That's not going to do anything to help with his anxiety! Instead, use an enzyme-based cleanser that will eat the odor—actually devours the molecules or urine like Pacman—and make it disappear.

Until your cat's marking behavior is under control, here's a tip that may help prevent stains and odor and make cleanup easier. It's most effective if the cat sprays in one specific area. Lean an empty litter box against the wall or other surface where the cat sprays. It will prevent the urine from hitting the wall or sofa and contain it until it can be cleaned up.

SOCIAL DISCORD

Conflicts with other pets or changes in the household such as a new spouse or baby can also cause cats to stop using the litter box or to urine-mark. Some aggressive cats will guard the litter box so that other cats can't use it. Would you want to go to the bathroom knowing that there might be a bully lurking along the way ready to pounce on you? No! That's why it's so important to have boxes in separate areas. A treatment plan devised by a behaviorist can help you solve the problem.

While many cat lovers don't mind—or at least grudgingly accept—cats on the furniture, if you're not one of them there are a few strategies you can use to keep your pet off.

Chapter 14

CORRECTING BAD BEHAVIOR

Cats have a reputation for being easy-care companions, but when they ain't happy, ain't nobody happy. Cats with issues usually express their displeasure in the least pleasant way possible. They urinate or defecate outside the litter box, spray furniture or other objects with urine, or fight with one another. Sometimes they chew or suck on wool or other fabrics or even plastic bags, or groom themselves to the point of fur loss. The latter is an example of a normal behavior that becomes repetitive or sustained, makes no sense, and interferes with the cat's ability to function normally: compulsive, in other words. Compulsive behaviors can become so extreme that they affect the cat's well-being, not to mention that of the people who have to live with him.

Behaviors such as wool sucking may have a genetic basis—it's most often seen in Siamese and other Oriental breeds—but most often a cat who sprays, becomes destructive or aggressive, or develops some type of compulsive behavior is suffering from anxiety. Like the rest of us, cats become anxious when they feel as if they don't have any control over their environment. Unfortunately, while a cat's response to anxiety suits him just fine, for us it's usually unpleasant or destructive.

If your cat's behavior has gone from mild to wild, delight to bite, it might be due to stress, dislike of his surroundings, conflicts with other animal or human members of the household, a case of separation anxiety, or often undiagnosed pain or illness. For example, cats who don't get enough physical or mental stimulation can develop behavior problems. In conflict situations, the cat may have trouble choosing between two different types of behaviors, or he might not feel as if he has any course of action that he likes or that is safe. Cats with separation anxiety are often those who were orphaned or were weaned at too early an age. Older cats may develop separation anxiety after the death of an owner or loss of a favorite person because of a divorce. These cats express their fears by sulking, crying, refusing to eat, becoming depressed, not using the litter box, spraying bedding or clothing, vomiting, compulsively grooming, or becoming destructive.

Sometimes, though, the cause of a cat's anxiety or compulsive behavior is unknown, triggered by a situation that went unnoticed at the time. And the longer a behavior continues without intervention, the more disassociated it becomes with an actual trigger. The cat starts doing it "just because." It's also possible that engaging in repetitive behaviors releases endorphins, substances produced by the pituitary gland and the hypothalamus that give a feeling of pleasure or relaxation, making it rewarding for the cat to continue.

It's easy to become frustrated with those behaviors—believe me, I understand—but don't punish your cat (that can make things worse!), banish him to the outdoors, or take him on a one-way trip to the animal shelter. Help is available in the form of veterinary behaviorists or certified applied animal behaviorists.

There's a lot to know about cat behavior, and when you think you've tried it all, a behaviorist can show you some new tricks to try. A qualified behaviorist is trained to evaluate your cat's environment, activity level, eating habits, and interactions with other animals and people in the home; interpret his behavior and figure out the underlying cause, including diagnosing any type of anxiety disorder that may be contributing to the problem; and plan a strategy—including chemical crutches, if necessary—to bring your cat's behavior back to normal.

Don't be shy about consulting a behaviorist. Behavior problems don't just go away. The longer you go without addressing a cat's behavior problem, the more difficult it will be to solve. Working with a behaviorist can be successful, though, only if you're willing to make changes in your cat's environment and carry out behavior modification exercises to help him deal with the circumstances that trigger behaviors and learn new ways to cope with them. The reality is that no cat is ever going to change his behavior on his own. For the cat, spraying or sucking on wool or chasing his tail is working for him to relieve his anxiety. As far as the cat is concerned, you are the one with the problem. The solution is to change the environment so the cat's behavior is compatible with your life. If the environment can be changed so that the reason for the cat's behavior disappears, or at least is reduced to a level that doesn't elicit what may be a perfectly normal but undesirable behavior, then the problem is solved. A behaviorist can help you do that effectively.

BEHAVIORISTS, VETERINARY AND OTHERWISE: WHO THEY ARE, WHAT THEY DO

Lots of people claim to be cat behaviorists, but you want one who's the real deal. Credentials count. Look for a veterinarian who has advanced training in behavior or a professional whose title includes the initials CAAB: certified applied animal behaviorist.

Board-certified veterinary behaviorists have completed an internship and residency at an approved behavior training program. Their prep work includes publishing peer-reviewed scientific papers and case reports and passing a tough two-day exam. When you see the initials DACVB behind a veterinarian's name, that means she's a diplomate of the American College of Veterinary Behaviorists and has met all those requirements.

A behaviorist who's a veterinarian can give your cat the physical exam and run the lab tests to see if a health problem is behind the behavior issue. If that's the case, she can prescribe any necessary medication. The bad news is that a veterinary behaviorist is not your everyday specialist. Unless you live in a major metropolitan area, you may have to drive a ways to find one, or you may be able to solve the problem through phone or fax consultations. Ask your general practice veterinarian for a recommendation, or contact your state's veterinary college (which sometimes is located in the state next door).

Someone who sports the initials CAAB after his name has an advanced degree in behavioral science, biology, zoology, or some similar discipline and may or may not be a veterinarian. Before he can use the initials CAAB, he must pass difficult oral and written examinations, published articles in scientific journals, and managed behavior cases under the supervision of a qualified behaviorist.

Like their veterinary counterparts, behaviorists with this certification can help you understand why your cat behaves the way he does. Sometimes they team up with a veterinarian to confirm whether your cat has a health problem that's causing him to act out. You can find a certified behaviorist through a referral from your veterinarian or through the Animal Behavior Society.

Whichever type of behaviorist you choose, the first step in a diagnosis will be ruling out a medical cause for the behavior. Some medical conditions can trigger repetitive behaviors or behaviors that appear to be compulsive. Cats who groom themselves excessively may have a skin or other health problem that's causing the behavior. Tail chasers may be reacting to spinal disease, neurological disease, or some sort of change of sensation in their limbs. Cats who are yowling excessively may be in pain, reacting to an overactive thyroid, or experiencing the onset of kitty dementia. All of those are health problems that can be treated with medication.

If your cat has a clean bill of health, be prepared to feel as if you're the one in therapy. No detail is insignificant, so get ready to spill your guts about your cat's life. The information you provide will help the behaviorist understand what's going on so she can plan the best way to modify your cat's behavior. Here are some examples of what you might be asked:

☙ How old is your cat?
☙ How old was your cat when you acquired him?
☙ Where did you acquire your cat?
☙ What is the cat doing that's a problem?
☙ When did the behavior begin?
☙ Do you know of a particular incident that precipitated the behavior?
☙ How often does the behavior occur?
☙ Does the behavior occur at certain times of the day?
☙ Do any specific conditions trigger the behavior?
☙ Can the behavior be interrupted?

- What methods have you tried to stop the behavior?
- How would you describe your cat's temperament?
- How many people live in the house?
- What other animals live in the house?
- Does the cat share food or water dishes with other pets?
- Have you moved recently?
- Have there been any changes in the household?
- Does the cat's daily routine change frequently?
- Does the cat get played with during the day?
- Does the cat have places to climb in the home?
- How many litter boxes do you have?
- Where are the litter boxes located?
- What type of litter do you use?
- How often are the litter boxes scooped/cleaned?
- Describe how the cat gets along with other people and animals in the home.

Once she has the dirt on your cat—and the results of a veterinary exam and lab tests, if necessary—a behaviorist can start to figure out what the problem is and how to fix it. That might include making changes in the home, such as moving the litter box or adding more litter boxes; changing the way you act toward the cat; changing the ways or places the cats interact with each other; providing more exercise or play for mental and physical stimulation; or using medication to help relax the cat and assist in behavior modification.

How to Separate Fighting Cats

When you hear that low-pitched *mrrrooooowrrr* sound coming from one or more of your cats, you know trouble is brewing. To stop it before it gets to the fur-flying stage, make a loud noise by clapping your hands, banging a book down, or clanging a pot lid—

(Continued)

whatever's handy. If the combatants are already having at each other, do the same thing, only louder, if possible, or squirt them with water. Whatever you do, don't try to grab one or both of them. You will get hurt!

Working with a behaviorist may involve a phone or fax consultation, a meeting at the behaviorist's office—cat in tow—or a meeting at your home. Because your cat is probably most comfortable on his own turf, an in-home visit may give a behaviorist the most detailed picture of what's going on, but it's not always necessary. Sometimes all it takes is the behaviorist's knowledge combined with a fresh eye on the problem. You might not recognize or even notice certain postures or vocalizations that lead to cat fights or territorial marking. For instance, cats who spray urine at windows or doorways inside the house may be agitated by the presence or scent of another cat outdoors.

A behaviorist can help you recognize and understand your cat's body language and vocalizations. When you know those subtle behavioral signals, you can learn to interrupt or redirect the behavior before it happens.

Keep a diary or calendar noting what your cat does and when. Writing down dates, times, and other observations can help you and the behaviorist see patterns that might otherwise not be obvious.

Depending on how long the problem has existed, the cat's temperament, and whether you can make the recommended changes, success can come quickly or it may take as long as a year. For instance, separating fighting cats in a home with an open floor plan may call for a little creative thinking and a lot of persistence. Other times you get lucky. In the best-case scenario, separating two aggressive cats and then gradually reintroducing them does the trick. Another way to deal with conflicts between cats or anxiety caused by the presence of a new baby, dog, or spouse is to make more positive associations with the other animals or people. Separation anxiety is often managed with attention, diversions such as new toys and food puzzles, and sometimes medication.

Keep in touch with the behaviorist. She can't help if she doesn't know what's working and what's not. Follow-up visits or phone calls can allow her to fine-tune the plan for changing the cat's behavior. It's the only way to get the best results.

MEDICATIONS CAN HELP WITH BEHAVIOR

Sometimes changing a cat's environment and instituting behavior modification techniques aren't enough to solve the problem, especially if a behavior has gone on for a long time. In these cases, medications such as Reconcile and clomipramine can be effective in reducing the cat's anxiety to a level where behavior modification will work. When the cat is less stressed, he can learn new rules or ways of living and come to accept that not all change is bad.

Why can't you just give the cat a pill and skip all the effort involved in changing how he lives and trying to modify his behavior? Much as we might like them to be, anti-anxiety medications aren't a quick fix, and they can't solve the problem on their own. Drugs simply raise the cat's tolerance level for whatever is making him anxious. Behaviorists view medication not as a cure but as a useful tool for getting cats to a mental or an emotional state where they can be helped. Without changing the cat's underlying reaction to his environment or his motivation to scent-mark or to lick off all his fur, the problem can never be solved.

How long it will take medication and behavior modification to work depends on how long the problem has existed. In the case of a cat who has been peeing under the window for a year, then moves on to peeing on the owner's head for three months (true story!), treatment could require a year for the medication and behavior modification to take effect, a year to stabilize the result, and another year in which to wean the cat off the medication. On the other hand, when a cat receives treatment as soon as the problem begins—within a month—the problem can often be resolved very quickly, often without medication.

Hardwired Behaviors Won't Go Away

Not all behavior problems respond to medication. For instance, hunting behavior can't be modified. That's hardwired into the cat. No drug stops it, and diazepam (Valium) or its derivatives have been known to increase it. For some cats, more play activity helps, but the behavior of true hunters can't be softened or redirected. Think of them as avatars of the cat as he was before domestication, when he lived among but not with people, appreciate them for those qualities, and try to meet their needs with a large outdoor enclosure or cat-fenced yard where they can exercise their hunting prowess.

Figuring out which drug will work best for a particular cat or a particular behavior problem is a matter of trial and error. It will remain that way until we know more about the molecular biology of the feline mind. The good news is that most cats respond well to behavior modification and, if necessary, medication, to a point where they and their people can live happily ever after.

Carriers need to be part of the furniture, not something that gets pulled out whenever something bad is going to happen. Treats can help a cat learn to accept that a carrier is nothing to fear.

Chapter 15
TRAINING FOR FUN AND SAFETY

TRICK TRAINING FOR FUN AND EXERCISE

You can train a cat to do anything he wants to do. You just have to persuade him that he wants to do it and be more persistent than he is. But seriously, there's a lot more to teaching cats tricks than simply getting them to do what you want. Trick training is absolutely a great way to prevent unwanted behaviors—I won't call them bad behaviors because they're perfectly natural for cats—but it's also the best way to develop a relationship with your cat, have fun with your cat, and give your cat the stimulation he needs to remain mentally and physically alert. Cats like to solve puzzles and do things that are interesting, so give them the chance to exercise that intelligent feline brain.

CLICKER TRAINING FOR CATS

You don't need a whip and a chair to train cats, just a clicker—a children's toy that makes a *click* sound when you press and release it—and some really tasty nom-noms (think stinky cheese, Vegemite, Kong stuffing, or liver bits). Keep the treats tiny; you don't want your cat to get fat from his training sessions. I've found cats like freeze-dried chicken or pieces of shrimp the best. (You can find clickers in any decent pet supply store these days.)

Clicker training is based on a principle called operant conditioning, which you may remember from your Psych 101 class. The basic idea is that if animals (or people, for that matter) are rewarded for doing something, they're likely to repeat the behavior in the hope of getting another reward. Sort of the same way that slot machines in Vegas work: you get one payout and you keep feeding in more quarters in the hope of getting another, bigger jackpot. Cats are no more immune to the lure of getting prizes than the rest of us.

A clicker allows you to reward your cat for performing actions that he would do naturally and then shape those into useful behaviors. To clicker-train your cat, all you need to do is let him know when he does something you like, using his scratching post, for instance. When you see him scratching away, click, then give a treat. The click lets the cat know that you like what he did, and the treat is his payment for it. Cats don't work for free, you know! Good behavior, click, treat. Easy as pie! This simple sequence works for touching his nose or paw to an object, playing with a toy, even something as simple as sitting. What's happening is that your cat is learning how to learn and you're learning how to communicate with him in a new and meaningful way.

FIVE TRICKS AND HOW TO TRAIN THEM

Teaching your cat tricks is a fun and easy way to learn how to communicate with him and build an unbreakable bond in the process. And a trick is not always just a trick; sometimes it has an underlying purpose, like being able to find your cat during an emergency or getting him to move away from someone who's allergic.

Think cats can't learn tricks? Prepare to be surprised at just how smart—and maybe just how much of a ham—your cat really is.

Sit

This is probably the easiest, fastest trick you can teach a cat. Some learn it within minutes. Here's how.

Take a treat your cat likes, preferably something with a strong aroma, and hold it next to his nose. As the cat sniffs, slowly move the treat upward until it is above his head. Your cat will naturally look up to follow the progress of the treat, and just as naturally his rear end will go down. Now, calmly say "Sit" and give him the treat. Practice this a few times a week, and pretty soon your cat will sit whenever he hears you say the word. Once your cat knows how to sit, you can build on that trick to teach him to stay, sit up on his hind legs, and wave a paw.

Train with a Calm, Direct Voice

Always ask your cat to do something in a calm tone of voice, and don't say it repeatedly. "Sit, sit, sit, SIT" just teaches your cat that he doesn't need to respond the first time you say it. If he doesn't want to play the game, walk away and try again later.

Come

Cats need to learn to come when called just as much as dogs do. It's essential for when you need to find your cat in a hurry. As with other behaviors, the secret to teaching this trick is in associating the word *Come* (or whatever word you choose) with a cue and a reward.

Figure out what your cat loves best, whether that's a bit of deli turkey or freeze-dried chicken, being fed a meal, or a few minutes batting at a peacock feather. Choose a prompt to elicit the behavior. It can be a word, a whistle, or a bell. Trainers like using a bell or a whistle because they can be operated by anyone and the cat can hear the sound from a distance. If you're away from home, for instance, you want your spouse or the cat sitter to be able to get the cat to come for his meals. Don't use a clicker; you'll want to save that for teaching other behaviors.

Make the sound that you've chosen and then give the reward. Do this several times—noise, reward, noise, reward, noise, reward—so the cat quickly learns that something good happens when he hears that sound. Pretty soon, your cat will come running when he hears that sound. Reward him big-time when he does.

Then practice making the sound in different parts of the house. Start by going across the room where you started or around the corner. Move to different rooms so your cat learns to seek you out when he hears the cue. Once your cat knows this command, practice it every once in a while just to keep him sharp. Practice time can be daily, weekly, or monthly; whenever you can fit it in. If you have kids, turn kitty training practice into a short but fun game. Station each child in a different room. One at a time, have them call the cat. When the cat goes to the correct child, he gets rewarded. Then the next child calls him and rewards him for responding. Repeat until the cat gets bored, which will probably be in about two minutes. Until then, it's good exercise and good reinforcement of his training.

Words Don't Matter—Consistency Does

There are no magic words when it comes to teaching cats tricks. You can choose any word you please and give it a particular meaning to your cat. Try it! You can teach him to come or sit using the word *pumpkin* if you'd like (unless that's his name, of course). You are simply creating an association between a certain word and the corresponding action.

Go to Your Place

This is a great phrase to have at your disposal. Use it when you want your cat off the kitchen counter or out from under your feet when you're preparing a meal.

Using a favorite treat, lure the cat to the spot you want him to go. It can be a cat bed, a window perch, his cat tree, whatever works best for you. When he gets on it, click and give him the treat. After you've done this a few times, add a verbal prompt: "On spot" or "Place" or any other word or phrase you want to use. It doesn't matter what you say;

you are simply creating an association between the word or phrase and the action of going to a particular place.

The companion phrase to "Place" is "Off." When you want your cat off the dining room table or the bed or wherever he's not supposed to be, calmly pat the object and say, "Off." Then set the cat down so he understands what you want. Repeat this until he relates the patting of the hand to the understanding that you want him off that particular piece of furniture. When he starts to respond to the word or the gesture, click and treat to reinforce that he's done something you like. With practice, you'll soon be able to just touch the edge of the table and your cat will jump off. Between cats and people who have a strong, close relationship, a glance is enough to get the message across.

Teach Your Cat to Love the Carrier

I think one of the reasons cats don't get as much veterinary care as dogs is that people sometimes find it difficult to get the cat to the clinic without a lot of stress for all involved. Some cats just plain disappear when they think a trip to the veterinarian is in the air, causing the appointment to be canceled. Teaching a cat to "load up" (get in his carrier) makes a car trip to any location more of a pleasure than a pain. It requires a little more patience than some of the other tricks, but it's well worth the time.

Start by leaving your cat's carrier out. Most cats are curious—they wouldn't be cats if they weren't—and will walk in and explore the carrier on their own. If your cat is on the cautious side, lure him into the carrier with a toy or treat, or scratch at it so that he becomes intrigued by the sound. If all else fails, try catnip. Whenever your cat gets into the carrier on his own, give him a treat. For the not-so-curious kitty, reward even small movements into the carrier, using a clicker and treats. If he puts his head or paw in, click and treat. Gradually require him to step in farther before he gets the click-treat: two paws, three paws, all four paws. It's easy to become impatient, waiting for the cat to offer the behavior you want, but keep at it. Reward him anytime you see him inside it. You want the cat to learn that something good happens every time he goes in the carrier. Other ways to encourage the cat to go into his carrier are to spray it with Feliway, put his meals in it, or to toss treats in it once a day so he has to go in and get them. Right before bed is a good time to do that.

Once your cat willingly goes into the carrier, add a verbal cue: "Load up," or even just "In." It's great if your cats enjoy going into the carrier, but you want to associate a word or phrase with it so they'll do it in a hurry if necessary.

Don't worry that getting your cat to go in the carrier and then taking him to the veterinarian will sour him on this trick. If you play your cards right, your cat will get treats for going into the carrier a lot more often than he will have a bad experience at the veterinarian. There are 365 days in a year. If your cat gets in the carrier and something good happens on most of the days, he's not going to worry too much about the two days that he got in the carrier and something happened that he didn't like. In other words, cats know when the odds are to their advantage.

Walk on a Leash

Teaching a cat to walk on leash requires more time and patience than most tricks, and not every cat will take to it, but it's well worth the effort if you plan to travel with your cat or would like your cat to be able to enjoy the outdoors safely. Among the cat breeds that are best known for enjoying walks on leash are Siamese, Abyssinians, Ocicats, and Ragdolls, but any cat with an outgoing nature who likes to explore can learn. It's best to start leash-training a cat when he is four to six months old, but with the right equipment and incentives, even senior cats can take to walking on leash.

Start by choosing the right harness. Cats are most comfortable wearing a harness that is stretchy and lightweight. A harness with these qualities will move and stretch with the cat so he doesn't feel restricted. It should fit snugly so he can't squirm out of it. For small, slim cats, look for a harness made for ferrets or rabbits. An alternative, especially for larger cats, is a jacket-style harness that wraps around the belly and fastens on the side.

Before you put the harness on your cat, give him plenty of time to get used to it. Leave it out for several days in a place where he can sniff it and play with it. Sprinkle a little catnip around it if you want, but otherwise just ignore it and let him get familiar with the harness at his own pace.

Once your cat has adjusted to the presence of the halter, put it on him and adjust it for comfort. Stop! Don't do anything else. Your cat will now either run around like a maniac or fall over as if he's paralyzed. Both are normal reactions. Leave the harness on for a few minutes and ignore his antics. Then calmly take it off and give him an extra-special treat or feed him if it happens to be breakfast or dinner time. Repeat this two or three times a day for a week or two. Remember that cats learn through repetition. At first, they think wearing the harness is going to kill them. After seven to ten days, wearing it starts to become a routine part of the day.

I said this would take a while, didn't I? If you are patient, though, you should be successful. Now it's time to attach the leash. Again, leave it on for a few minutes at a time, two or three times a day, letting the cat drag it around if he chooses. He might just lie there. Do this for up to a week. Because he is already used to the harness, adding the leash shouldn't be as much of a shock to his sensitive feline nervous system. By the way, you might want to make sure your other pets don't drag your leashed cat around on the floor. Don't laugh! I've seen this on YouTube, one cat pulling another by the leash. That particular cat didn't seem to mind, but not all cats will be that laid-back.

When the leash and harness are an accepted part of your cat's life, it's time to practice walking around. Do this indoors at first. Hold the leash and encourage your cat to walk toward you. Offer a treat to sweeten the deal. If he walks toward you, say "Come" and praise him. Continue to be patient as he gets the hang of this new way of moving around.

As your cat gets comfortable with walking on a leash, move the lessons outdoors, to a fenced yard if possible. This is where he discovers how fun leash-walking can be, offering the opportunity to sniff, nibble some grass, roll around on his back, and lie in the sun. Keep encouraging him to walk alongside you or in front of you. Use a wand or fishing-pole toy to get his attention and keep him moving in the direction you want him to go. Just be aware that walking a cat is never going to be the same purposeful activity as walking a dog. Expect to stop and start a lot and go off in odd directions, depending on your cat's whim.

That doesn't mean you should let him pull you around. If he starts to head in a direction you don't want to go, stand still. If he turns to look at you, click and reward him with a treat. Repeat if he moves toward you. Encourage him to move in the direction you want to go and click and reward him if he does so.

Cats who are well socialized can come to enjoy leash-walking for its social aspect, not to mention the opportunities for bird-watching and bug stalking. If you train him patiently, he will look forward to his walks, not only for the activity but also for the attention from you. The only drawback is that he might start demanding walks all the time!

Now that you've taught him these tricks, your cat is ready to be a star. Videotape him demonstrating his talents and post the film on YouTube so the whole world can see just how smart your cat is. Amaze your friends when your people-loving cat provides the entertainment at your next party.

PART FOUR
IN SICKNESS AND IN HEALTH

Veterinarians have long recognized something very sad and very wrong about how cats are treated: compared to dogs, cats aren't given much medical care at all. Even as much as we love our cats, and as popular as cats have become, there's something about the idea that our feline companions are just fine on their own that has cat lovers adopting a wait-and-see approach when it comes to cats and veterinary care.

And that's just not right.

We know more about the care and treatment of cats than ever, and as veterinarians we want to share what we know and what we can do for the good of cats everywhere. Think preventive and proactive rather than reactive when it comes to veterinary care—heading off problems before they become major, or preventing them entirely. And when cats do get sick, we veterinarians not only want to address little health problems before they become big health problems—and sometimes become untreatable—but we also want to help treat those problems in ways that are less painful to our patients.

The word is getting out, but too slowly for my taste. That's why in this section I've stressed getting your cat the best veterinarian before your cat gets sick, and working with that veterinarian to prevent illness, and to address illness early when it happens. And I also want you to know what illness looks like, so you can get your cat in soon to get help fast.

You owe that to your cat, don't you? I think so, and I hope you do, too. So read on!

"Never take a live pet to a veterinarian with dead plants" is a good rule of thumb, but there are others. A good veterinary practice has an eye to detail and a nose for odors. Look for diplomas and pictures that hang straight (not crooked) on the wall and an odor-neutral smell that comes from a facility where clean is important.

Chapter 16

FINDING A GOOD VETERINARIAN

Time passes at such a crazy pace—and if age creeps up swiftly on us humans, then it practically gallops as it makes its mark on our pets. By the time your cat turns two or three, he has passed through the canine equivalent of infancy, childhood, and adolescence. After age seven or so, your cat has hit middle age. And at just twelve years old or so, most cats are seniors—not the kind found on a wild spring break, but the kind that gets the early-bird discount at restaurants.

Because cats age more quickly than people, they may get illnesses earlier than you'd think. Cats who live indoors can live well into their teens, more than a decade or so on average than a cat who roams freely among the many hazards of the outdoors. But the relatively sedentary lifestyle of indoor cats has its hazards, too, most of which can be avoided by careful attentiveness to your cat's physical and mental needs, and regular pet check-ins with a veterinarian.

Making sure your cat has regular checkups with the veterinarian is the best way to catch and treat developing health issues before they become serious problems. I recommend twice-yearly wellness visits. Just as in human medicine, veterinary care has come a long way in the ability to detect health problems before they become symptomatic—and to treat many of those problems simply and effectively. Veterinarians have the experience and training to look past obvious problems to potential ones. Preventive, proactive veterinary care can add years to your cat's life and good health.

The place to start a good preventive-care regimen? With a good veterinarian, of course.

YOUR PARTNER IN YOUR PET'S HEALTH: CHOOSE THE RIGHT VETERINARIAN

Into every cat's life must come a relationship with a special person with some special letters after her or his name—DVM, VMD, or even MRCVS (for veterinarians trained in the United Kingdom). For some cats, the veterinarian is just a vaguely familiar person who gives them treats and rudely palpates their privates once a year. For others, though, this is someone associated with all kinds of discomfort—strange and disturbing odors, barks and howls of unfamiliar pets, and memories of pain from visits during an illness or following an accident. The veterinarian's office can be a scary place, indeed.

But it doesn't have to be that way, and it shouldn't be.

Making sure you and your pet have found the right veterinary practice can cut way down on the stress and strain of your cat's visits. Having a practitioner—and a veterinary practice, from front desk to veterinary technicians and more—you can trust and count on when it comes to your cat's health care is essential to your cat having as long, healthy, and happy a life as possible. Because without a well-run practice, an expert team, and great veterinarians, neither you nor your pet will be likely to go as often as you need to, and that means less than optimal health for your cat. And while this is true for dogs as well, it is especially true for cats, for studies show cats don't get the care dogs do, for reasons ranging from the idea that cats don't need care (wrong) to the concern that cats are too difficult to take to the veterinarian (often true, but fixable—and I'll get to that later).

Does your cat's veterinarian put you at ease?

Do you feel comfortable calling or coming in with any question or concern? Are you taken seriously when you bring your cat in for something nonspecific, like "He just ain't doing right," or a slight change in bathroom habits?

Does the veterinarian acknowledge your role as a pet "parent"?

A good practitioner respects the fact that you are her eyes and ears at home. You're the one who knows your cat's normal habits and attitudes, and you can be trusted to raise an alarm when something is wrong or your cat is just a little off.

Do you like the way pets are treated at the practice?

It's fair to expect to feel confidence in everyone from the receptionist to the surgeon in your cat's practice. Ask for a tour of the entire clinic before becoming a client. Beyond reception areas and exam rooms are the areas where the nitty-gritty work of the office takes place, and most veterinarians will be happy to show you around. Employee- and pet-only rooms should reflect the same level of care, compassion, and cleanliness as the ones out front. In fact, they must. I have a mantra that you should demand from your veterinarian: that they treat your pet exactly as if you were standing there looking over their shoulder.

Leveling with You: Details Count

As you might imagine, I've seen a lot of veterinary hospitals and clinics, front to back and in every nook and cranny. What always catches my attention when I walk in for the first time is odor—or better yet, the lack of it.

A veterinary hospital should be what I think of as "odor neutral," which is to say that if I walk in and can smell anything, it doesn't make me happy. I don't want to smell foul odors, nor do I want a strong fragrance. Frankly, if I smell something, it makes me wonder about how much the hospital cares about its sanitary practices. When I owned veterinary hospitals, I never tolerated bad odors. And even now, when I'm just too busy to own my own hospital, the

(Continued)

practices where I work when I'm not on the road are clean as clean can be—and I don't think I could work in them if they weren't.

Now, I want to confess. Laugh if you want to, but I also can't stand it when diplomas and pictures are crooked in a veterinary practice or lightbulbs are burned out. No, it's not as big an issue as a problem with odors, which may signify a bigger problem with sanitary procedures. But I'm a firm believer that when a hospital's staff pays attention to the smallest of details, they're not as likely to miss things—big or small—when it comes to your pet's care.

Does the practice take your pet's discomfort seriously, whether the pain is physical or mental?

Cats have huge ranges of pain tolerance and some are more nervous than others, but you want a veterinary practice that works to keep your pet comfortable and pain free—even if your cat isn't showing the pain she's in. If it's consistent, your veterinarian's work to keep your pet physically and mentally comfortable will help your cat see a trip to the vet as something more like a field trip rather than a forced march. When discussing any procedure, surgery, or chronic health condition, pain management should emerge as a priority issue. Ideally, your veterinarian will address both pharmaceutical options and "creature comfort" matters like bed padding or hot water bottles.

Is the cavalry on call?

Your veterinary office doesn't have to house a host of specialists to provide top-notch care, but it does need to have good relationships with specialists and a willingness to ask for help if your pet's case gets complicated.

Is there a crisis plan in place?

Even if the office is open only bankers' hours, your practitioner should help you plan for emergencies. Where would you go and who would you call if your cat had an accident at midnight on a Friday, over a holiday, or during a natural disaster? You and your veterinarian should be in agreement on how to handle an emergency right from your first appointment.

Is the approach to care thorough, and does it go beyond the initial concern?

Whether your cat is limping a little or sporting a sore on his nose, a good doctor will take advantage of the up-close-and-personal time to perform a full exam, make a general health assessment, and update your cat's medical information. A good veterinarian will look past obvious problems—the entering complaint or something as obvious as a bleeding wound and flip the lip, look in the ears, check the eyes with an ophthalmoscope, feel the lymph nodes, listen to the heart and lungs with a stethoscope, palpate the internal organs such as the liver, spleen, and bladder, move limbs through their range of motion, and rub his hands on the curvatures of the body. A good vet will treat the problem you brought the cat in for. A great veterinarian will prevent problems when possible, detect other problems at their earliest phase, and always recommend everything you need but only what you need to keep your pet happy and healthy. Put another way, a good vet is an advocate for your pet.

Does the veterinarian know your cat?

A health professional who knows and remembers your cat (name, sex) and his health and lifestyle is, as they say in the credit card commercials, priceless. Even if you choose a big veterinary practice, try to build a relationship with one person who can serve as a touchstone for your cat's health all his life. If you see your veterinarian away from the practice—at a grocery store, church, or sporting event—and they remember your pet's name and ask about them, you've got a keeper.

Do you feel that your concerns are addressed, no matter what they're about—costs, billing, care, what food to buy at a place that's convenient for you, options for prescriptions, even waiting time?

While misunderstandings and disagreements are often unavoidable in life-or-death situations, you want to know that your veterinarian and the entire staff are interested in helping your pet—and keeping your business. In the practices I work at we have a philosophy that every client gets treated like number one.

If you're satisfied with all these factors, then congratulations! You've found a strong, capable advocate for your cat's well-being—in sickness and in health.

Feline Fact

Cats are more sensitive to light than humans and are able to see better in the dark than we can, which is what you'd expect from a nocturnal animal. But even cats can't see in total darkness.

They can get pretty close, though. They have adapted to low-light conditions, which causes the eyes-that-glow-in-the-dark phenomenon anyone who drives at night has observed.

The "glow" is actually light reflected back from a layer of cells behind the retina called the *tapetum lucidum*, which is Latin for "luminescent tapestry." (We love showing off our Latin, even if we had to look it up first!)

Add to that the fact that a cat's pupils can dilate three times the size of ours, and they also have larger corneas, and you can see why a cat has no need for night-vision goggles. The bottom line: a cat can see in conditions that are over five times less bright than what we require.

Long before any cat ever was caught in the headlights, the ancient Egyptians had another theory for the glow of a cat's eye at night—they believed the eyes of a cat reflected the sun, even at night when it was hidden from humans.

THE PLACE TO START: THE WELLNESS CHECK

As great as you may be in your role of pet "parent" at home, there's no substitute for your cat's regular wellness checks with the vet. When you consider these visits, think of your cat for a second as a trusty, well-loved car. You see that car every day—and you know how it looks and how it sounds. But do you really understand what goes on under the hood? Your cat's veterinarian is responsible for checking your cat's internal systems and making sure he's running right. Long years studying every aspect of animal health and learning the ropes of feline medicine make your cat's veterinarian the pro at not only diagnosing but also anticipating health issues and troubles. Veterinarians know what problems can be triggered at what age.

For most young, healthy cats, an annual checkup after kittenhood should be enough. Your cat's veterinarian may order basic lab tests to provide baseline information on what's normal for your pet at the time your pet is spayed or neutered and then again in middle age for an early comparison. Some people think of a spay/neuter as routine as a lube/oil/filter change in a car. It's not! This is perhaps the only major surgery your pet will ever have, and it's important to test the function of the organs that will eliminate the anesthetic and catch worrisome problems early on. Every visit, your cat should get a nose-to-toes examination and an objective assessment of his general health and body condition.

As your cat enters middle age, your veterinarian may recommend bringing him twice a year for routine exams—I certainly do. These semiannual exams can actually save you money and your pet pain, spotting problems early and slowing or even stopping some problems of aging for a good long while. When you factor in any increased risk of health problems, frequent wellness checks become the number one tool available to you in keeping your feline companion in good health and saving you money in the long run.

Help Your Pet Stay Calm

If your cat gets apprehensive about visiting the veterinarian—and many do—there are a few tricks you can use to help him relax and even enjoy the experience. For starters, ask your veterinarian or take a trip to your local pet supply store and pick up some Feliway. This product is kumbaya in a bottle for cats. These pheromones

(Continued)

don't have any effect on humans, but spritzing your cat's carrier will make him feel better. Many veterinarians also use it in exam rooms and even on themselves. My daughter Mikkel and I practically bathed in Feliway before taking the pictures for this book, to ease the stress on our feline models.

In addition to using pheromones to help your cat relax, remember that he takes many of his emotional cues from you. Use your happy voice in the car and in the clinic. Encourage veterinary staff to get in on the act, too. When a cat gets anxious, don't push it: back off before the situation escalates. You may be on a tight schedule, but if your cat really blows up, you aren't going anywhere. So chill. To make your cat feel at home at the veterinarian's office, bring the cat's favorite treats and toys with you. When at home, practice regular care routines like grooming, nail trimming, and teeth brushing. Pretend to do routine veterinary procedures with your cat. You can do this by touching the cat's face, ears, feet, and tail. This should help your cat adjust to the veterinary hospital and any needed home care. Make trips to the veterinary hospital for visits involving no examinations or procedures, such as checking the cat's weight. It gives the staff a chance to interact with your cat in nonthreatening way.

If a pheromone spritz and encouraging words fail to calm an anxious cat, don't be afraid to ask the staff to dim the lights or even switch personnel. In the north Idaho practices where I work, if one of us can't win over a pet even with an effort worthy of *The Bachelor* or *The Bachelorette*, we tell the pet owners that we're going to switch with a veterinarian of another gender and we dim the lights before the entrance. More than half the time the pet ends up being a happy camper.

WHAT IS YOUR VETERINARIAN LOOKING FOR?

Depending on the practice, your veterinarian's technician may get some basic information first, such as if you've noticed anything odd or that concerns you. The tech will also get the basics including a weight before you head into the exam room, then temperature and heart rate, body condition scoring, and dental health, and will check the status of vaccinations and parasite control. All will be noted in the chart for your veterinarian to discuss with you further if there are problems.

Shiny on the outside. The first, simplest indication of feline good health is a shiny, healthy coat. Some cats have a luster to their fur that's like a neon sign advertising their vitality. This Healthy Cat Here sign is any veterinarian's first indication that a cat is being fed a high-quality diet and gets good care at home. It's a low-tech health barometer, the feline equivalent of a glowing complexion.

Signs of trouble in your cat's coat can sometimes be masked by stress-related shedding in the veterinary office, which is perfectly normal for many cats. Your veterinarian looks beyond the shedding for lumps or bumps, bare patches, thinning areas, a lack of shine, and any visibly irritated skin.

Walk this way. Your cat's veterinarian is looking for surefooted steps and balance. Symmetry is a clue that things are working properly. If your cat favors a leg, doesn't want to stand with equal weight on all four, walks as if on eggshells, or adopts a bunny-hop gait, your veterinarian may want radiographs to help pinpoint the root of the problem.

An uneven gait doesn't always point to an orthopedic issue—it can also be the first sign of a neurological problem or a symptom of a severe ear infection. If you notice your cat having more difficulty rising to his feet, not wanting to exercise or play as much, not jumping up on the couch or going up stairs, leaning to one side, or suddenly seeming clumsy in his walk, be sure to mention this.

Flip the lip. A healthy mouth is critical for a cat's overall health and happiness, but it's the most overlooked part of feline care. Not only will a cat with dental disease be in constant pain, but those infected gums become breeding grounds for bacteria that are sent through your cat with every swallow, putting strain on all internal systems. When your veterinarian looks at your cat's mouth, she'll look first for signs of periodontal disease including plaque, tartar (brown mineralized matrix adhered to the outside surface of the tooth), and red, bleeding gums. Then she'll rub her finger along the teeth and gums to feel for lumps and for the roughness that indicates periodontal disease. She'll check for healthy gums that are firm and not pale. Gums should feel equally firm on both sides of the mouth—bleeding or swelling in any area indicates a potential problem.

Tuna breath, believe it or not, is not normal. If your cat's breath makes you gag, you're already looking at dental disease that likely needs your veterinarian's attention, with full cleaning under anesthesia that will include dental radiographs for broken teeth and rotting roots, and may require extractions of teeth too far gone to be saved. Veterinarians not only use special machines to vibrate the tartar off of the visible tooth surfaces; they also go deep under the gum flaps to root out infection you can't even see with the naked eye and no cat would tolerate if not anesthetized. Because cleaning leaves the surface of the teeth rough, the next step in a veterinary dental is to polish the teeth so that plaque has a much harder time adhering. The final step is to put a dental sealant on the entire dental arcade. If you've noticed your cat favoring one side of his mouth when eating, or drooling, or of course has bad breath, you'll want to mention all these issues to your veterinarian.

The ears have it. Healthy ears are light pink and clean on the inside. A little yellowish or brown wax is normal, but any kind of crust, brown speckles, or the dreaded dark brown muck of an infection is a concern. When your cat's veterinarian checks the ears, he's feeling for abnormal warmth in the area, looking for discharge, and sniffing for abnormal odor. You'll want to mention any head shaking you've noticed, even if it has stopped.

Eye for good health. Healthy eyes don't have excessive tearing and are bright and shiny, and the whites are white—not yellow. A yellow tinge to the whites of a cat's eyes can mean he has jaundice, which can be a symptom of a number of serious illnesses. The lining around your cat's eyes should be pink, not red or yellowed.

Any kind of irritation on or around your cat's eye is reason enough for a visit to the veterinarian, as untreated eye injuries or infections rarely clear themselves up. Any injury to your cat's eye, by the way, is an emergency situation that needs prompt veterinary attention.

Nose news. The moist soft nose attracts more molecules of scent, something very important back when cats had to sniff out supper. Dry conditions won't concern your veterinarian as much as when a nose is draining—sure sign of something going wrong further up. If the sound of the breathing through the nose is a wheeze, the concern is an obstructed airway. Your veterinarian will also look for cracks, lumps, bumps, and irritations, which can be symptoms of many different problems, including chronic disease having nothing actually to do with the nose.

Checking the lymph nodes and internal organs. As your veterinarian continues the nose-to-toes-to-tail examination, she'll be feeling for abnormalities in areas you may not even know your cat has. Your veterinarian will also press into your cat's abdomen to palpate the internal organs, feeling to make sure everything is as it should be.

Give a listen. The heart is the most important muscle in the body, which is why your veterinarian will put on that stethoscope—no, it's not just for looking cool—and listen to your cat's heart and lungs, and for the sounds of normal digestion. When it comes to the heart in particular, she'll be listening for problems such as murmurs that may be the sign of a chronic cardiac problem that will need lifelong management.

Lean and fit is best. The best gauge of a healthy weight is your veterinarian's assessment, and the history of your cat's gains and losses over a lifetime. For this reason alone, your cat should get on that scale in the vet's office at least twice a year.

Veterinarians see fat cats every day—it's estimated that more than half of all pets are over their ideal weight—but they're sometimes loath to say much, especially if the owner is likewise overweight (or if the veterinarian is!). But this is a discussion you must have. Here's how veterinarians determine ideal body weight:

❧ **A look from above.** When seen from above, a cat should have a waist—an indentation between the ribs and hips, the shape of a modestly proportioned hourglass. A bulge between ribs and hips, however, is bad news on any cat—the equivalent of a potbelly on a person. Ideal weight: well-proportioned; observe waist behind ribs; ribs palpable with slight fat covering; abdominal fat pad minimal. Too thin: ribs visible, no palpable fat; lumbar vertebrae obvious; pronounced abdominal tuck. Too heavy: ribs not palpable under heavy fat cover; fat deposits over lumbar area, face, and limbs; distention of abdomen with no waist; extensive abdominal fat deposits.

❧ **A peek at the side.** A cat's abdomen should never hang down, making even male cats look pregnant, and ribs should have a little bit of fat, but not much.

No Bikini Season for Cats

The simple truth is that keeping your cat at a healthy weight is like leading him to the fountain of youth and pouring him a long drink. Pets kept at a healthy weight live an average of 20 percent longer than those who are overweight or obese—an average of two years.

If your cat is overweight, your veterinarian will have strategies to help you get him back where he should be, from an exercise plan to special diet foods to medication that may take the edge off the hunger. Remember: Your pet's weight is yours to manage, since your cat won't be snacking or overeating if you don't let him. Food is not love: good health is.

How to Become a Veterinary Favorite

Let me tell you an insider secret. There are certain people we veterinarians can't wait to see come in with their pets. What makes these clients VIPs, how do you become one, and what will you receive in return for your efforts? The more items you tick off this list, the higher your ranking as a veterinary VIP:

🐾 You're a tiny bit early for your appointment.

🐾 You treat the entire staff with respect, warmth, and good humor.

🐾 You come armed with a full history of your pet's medical problem, the more detailed the better (e.g., vomited three times yesterday; it was slimy, yellow, and contained bits of cardboard packaging).

🐾 You've trained your cat to welcome, not fear, a veterinary visit, and you went through gentling techniques with your pet, so we can easily examine everything.

🐾 You accept our recommendations.

🐾 You pay your bills.

🐾 If we exceed your expectations, you recommend us to others with enthusiasm and frequency.

🐾 On occasion, for any or no reason, you bring us a plate of brownies or cookies to feed a tired crew.

In return you get:

🐾 People who fight to take your call and veterinarians who fight to win you as their vet.

🐾 A veterinary team who lights up even brighter when you walk through the door.

🐾 Somehow we find a spot on an overbooked schedule for you or find a place to board your pet over a holiday, even though we've been booked full for months.

🐾 We don't watch the clock as closely when it's your turn in the exam room.

🐾 Perhaps most important, you can call us 24/7/365 for help when you most need it, and we'll either pick up the phone to talk you through it, race to the practice to meet you, or refer you to someone else and tell them to take extra-special care of you.

Once your cat has gotten a thorough physical—and a clean bill of health from your veterinarian, the discussion of how to keep him that way begins.

"Shots" are no longer one size fits all, and they're no longer a yearly event. Your veterinarian will tailor your cat's vaccines to be given based on risk, and less frequently as well—once every three years is common.

Chapter 17

FOCUS ON PREVENTIVE CARE

When you first get a kitten or adopt an adult cat, chances are that one of the first things you do is visit your veterinarian for that all-important checkup. That's why the last chapter was about what your veterinarian does when going over your cat—what he's looking for and why—and how regular wellness checkups with a good veterinarian are the cornerstone on which to build a healthy, long life for your cat.

But once that physical exam is over, the next phase of the veterinarian's work begins—helping you to make choices to keep the good health coming, with decisions that will focus on preventing illness in your cat. The preventive-care options your veterinarian will discuss with you include vaccinations, parasite control, and spay/neuter surgery.

THE SIMPLE "YEARLY SHOT" ISN'T EITHER ANYMORE

Safe to say that everyone knows cats need shots, but that's about all they can say on the topic. Most people don't even know what they're vaccinating their pets against, much less how often those vaccinations are needed.

Vaccines are weakened doses of the very diseases they protect against, and they're administered, usually by injection, to teach the immune system to recognize and destroy a stronger attack of the disease. The system works because of antibodies, the body's warrior particles that surround and destroy viral and bacterial intruders.

In adult cats, one dose usually offers immunity for a long time— more on how long next—but that's not how it works in kittens. While a challenged immune system gives grown, healthy cats a fighting chance against disease, even strong, healthy kittens lack that ability, because their immune system isn't yet functioning fully.

Kittens are initially protected from disease by antibodies passed to them through their mother's milk. This protection declines as a kitten matures, but its presence interferes with the preventive-care benefits provided by vaccinations. Because it's not feasible to pinpoint the moment when a vaccination will be effective, kittens are given a series of shots over the first three to four months of their lives.

For all kittens and cats, vaccines can be divided into two major categories: core and noncore. Core vaccines are the ones designed to protect against major, potentially fatal diseases that could threaten any cat. Known as the FVRCP vaccinations, they are for feline viral rhinotracheitis, feline calicivirus, and feline panleukopenia virus. A feline leukemia virus shot for kittens and a rabies vaccination are also strongly advised.

Most veterinarians now recommend an initial FVRCP vaccination at the age of six to eight weeks, and then every three to four weeks until the kitten is older than twelve weeks. Kittens should also be vaccinated against feline leukemia virus, receiving two doses three to four weeks apart. Veterinary immunology experts recommend the use of modified-live vaccines that do not contain adjuvants, substances that have been implicated in the development of vaccine-associated sarcomas in cats.

A single, separate rabies vaccine can be given when the kitten is twelve to sixteen weeks old. Because rabies can be transmitted to people and can be fatal, it's wise for cats to be vaccinated against it. Even if your locale does not require cats to have a rabies vaccination, it offers important protection in case your cat ever encounters a rabid animal— which is not as unlikely as you might think. Even in suburban areas, bats can fly into homes (I've even had them in our bedroom at Almost Heaven Ranch!), and it's not uncommon for cats in their own yards to come in contact with skunks and raccoons, which often carry rabies.

Be sure your kitten completes the entire series of vaccinations. Stopping after just one shot leaves her at risk for disease.

Every cat should have the core vaccines as a kitten and then as the veterinarian advises in adulthood. In the past, most vaccines were given annually, at a cat's routine exam. (In fact, many folks mistakenly believed the vaccines were the only reason for that annual exam.) However, recent research has revealed two important issues with that schedule: First, many vaccines are effective for longer than a year. Second, unnecessary vaccinations can carry health risks of their own, and a small percentage of cats do have bad reactions to their shots, developing tumors at the site of the injection. Now, it's recommended that after booster vaccinations at one year of age, the core vaccines for feline rhinotracheitis, calicivirus, and panleukopenia be given no more often than once every three years.

The risk of contracting feline leukemia virus decreases with age. Talk to your veterinarian about whether your cat's lifestyle requires further vaccinations for the disease. Cats who go outdoors or who are exposed to other cats who go outdoors probably should be vaccinated and tested annually for the disease because their exposure to it can't be controlled.

When it comes to revaccination timing, the recommendations for rabies are a little different. The best choice of rabies vaccine for cats is one that is given annually rather than triennially (every three years). It is what is known as a recombinant vaccine, and it does not contain an adjuvant. Veterinary immunology experts recommend giving cats this rabies vaccine annually rather than a triennial vaccine that does contain an adjuvant.

Noncore vaccines are available for giardia, feline infectious peritonitis, feline immunodeficiency virus, and virulent calicivirus. These noncore vaccines for cats have little to no efficacy, and immunology experts do not recommend their use for household pets.

Vaccination recommendations continue to change and are always being debated. The key takeaway is that your cat should get what he needs and no more, and no more often than is necessary. Your veterinarian will discuss what she believes is necessary and why, but the final decision is yours.

Don't Listen to the Antivaccination Crowd

Just as in human medicine, there's a sizable camp of people who believe vaccines cause more disease than they prevent. Some of them refuse to vaccinate their pets at all, counting on the health and vaccination status of other pets—so-called herd immunity—to protect their animals from the small risk of vaccines.

Don't believe what you read on the Internet: a good, sensible vaccination program is key to your cat's health.

Just as in human medicine, contagious disease used to sweep through regularly, causing misery and death by the millions. Vaccines are one of the true success stories of modern medicine, a life-saving measure of near-miraculous importance. Manage this risk with your veterinarian's help, vaccinate no more than you need to and no more often than you need to, and you'll be doing what's best for your cat. My cats come in contact with no other cats. But I still follow the vaccination program that I'm outlining for you.

DON'T LET PARASITES BUG YOUR CAT

There are two kinds of parasites to worry about, and worry you should. These voracious freeloaders cause your cat discomfort and disease, and they aren't so great for you and your family, either. That's why you need to keep on top of parasite control, both inside and outside your cat.

Let's start on the outside. Did you know that a single flea lays forty to fifty eggs per day? If there are ten female fleas in your home, that means you're talking four hundred or more flea eggs a day. Under the right conditions, that can multiply in less than a month to a thousand or more fleas in your home to torment your cat. And a single flea can bite your cat up to four hundred times a day. One flea can make your cat's life miserable—and if you don't get a burgeoning bug problem under control, it can make you pretty unhappy, too.

Feline Fact

In 1834 a Frenchman by the name of Bouché took a flea off of a cat, described it in some literature, and gave it the name *Pulex felis* (*felis* for "cat"). He actually got the genus name wrong, which was later named *Ctenocephalides*. He was, however, the first to use *felis* as a species name for a flea. The Entomological Society gives all insects a common name, so *Ctenocephalides felis* was named the cat flea.

This Frenchman could have taken the same flea species from a dog, fox, or lynx in France, and today we might be calling it the dog, fox, or lynx flea. There is a dog flea (*Ctenocephalides canis*), which, as you might suspect, was first described after removal from a dog, hence the species name *canis*. However, this is a rare species and has been rarely recovered from dogs in North America over the past twenty years. In most countries in the world the cat flea is the most common flea found on dogs and cats.

It's important to control fleas not only because of the itch-scratch syndrome and the "ick" factor—they leave their eggs and feces on cats and in the environment—but also because they transmit diseases that can affect cats and people. Those diseases include mycoplasma (bacterialike organisms that cause anemia in cats) and bartonella, the cause of "cat scratch disease" and other infections in people, as well as various infections in cats. Regardless of whether your cat goes outside, it's important to have her on a safe and effective flea preventive.

If you are using a spot-on topical product to ward off fleas, apply it high enough on the neck that your cat can't lick it off. The best spot is in the middle of the neck, right behind the ears at the base of the skull. Don't apply these products to your cat's shoulders or down his back because when he licks them he will foam at the mouth, become excitable, and may throw up.

The best way to control fleas is to work with a veterinarian to make sure your cat never gets them at all. Ask your pet's veterinarian what management program would work best for your cat, and then stick to it. Modern medicine has come up with some pretty sophisticated flea and tick preventives. A product given monthly can control fleas, internal parasites, and heartworms. Getting that started in kittenhood and using it consistently and appropriately can practically eliminate the potential for parasite infestations in cats.

A great low-tech, low-cost complement to prescription flea control is to use your vacuum and washing machine to remove fleas from your home before they can reproduce. Vacuum all carpeted areas and any upholstery your cat comes in contact with at least once a week until all signs of fleas are gone. Be sure to pick up cushions, lift furniture, and get in the corners. Fleas are most comfortable burrowed down in dark, sheltered spots—so you've got to really clean aggressively to get them out. And wash pet bedding—and your bedding, if your cat sleeps on the bed, as many do—weekly in hot water. Getting fleas out of the environment is as important as killing fleas in the environment.

Flee, Fleas!

Often people complain that flea-control products don't work, when the real problem is that they aren't doing everything that's necessary to make fleas feel so unwelcome that they pack their bags and move along. To get a handle on a flea problem in your home and yard, start with a little detective work—flea CSI, if you will. Do possums, raccoons, feral cats, or stray dogs pass through your yard? They all carry fleas and shed flea eggs into your environment. Don't leave pet food outdoors, don't give them access to your home through pet doors—for real, they will come inside!— and put up latticework or some other barrier to prevent them from having access to your crawl space, deck, or porch. Apply a flea-killing product to your yard. Most important, treat every cat and dog in your home with a flea-control product every thirty days. If you can't afford to do that, talk to your veterinarian about alternative methods of environmental control, such as twice-yearly use of an insect growth regulator (IGR) product for the home to prevent development of flea eggs and larvae, or environmental use of a borate flea powder such as Fleabusters to kill fleas.

Like fleas, ticks carry diseases, so if you live in an area where ticks are common, your cat should be on a tick preventive that contains fipronil, such as Frontline Plus for Cats. Ticks aren't as much of a problem for cats as they are for dogs, but in parts of the southern and midwestern United States ticks can transmit a serious and frequently fatal disease called *Cytauxzoon felis*. Cats with this infection rapidly develop a high fever, anemia, and circulatory collapse and can be dead within a couple of days. In many places the mortality rate is 90 percent, even with treatment.

Ticks can and do transmit other diseases to both pets and people, so it's essential to be proactive when dealing with these pests. If you're in a tick-infested area, be sure to go over your cat carefully anytime she goes outdoors. Run your hands over her, checking for small, telltale lumps. If you find one, part the fur to get a look at the skin and see if your cat has an eight-legged hitchhiker.

Removing a tick is a simple procedure you can do at home. Using a pair of fine tweezers (a curved jeweler's tweezer is ideal) or a tick removal tool (Tick Key and Ticked Off removers are two brand names), firmly grasp the tick as close to the skin as possible and steadily pull. Don't twist the tick, or you may end up leaving part of it attached to your cat's skin. The tick will release its hold if you apply steady pressure. Never touch a tick with your own bare hands, and always dispose of them after removal. The best way to get rid of a tick is to submerge it in a small container of rubbing alcohol, then toss it out. Don't panic if you see a part of the tick left behind. Just check in a day or two for swelling and infection, and talk to your veterinarian if you see a lingering problem.

Always Follow Directions

I've been a practicing veterinarian for more than thirty years, and in that time I have seen a huge change in our ability to prevent parasites that once made our pets' lives miserable and our own lives more dangerous. I remember all sorts of noxious dips, and soaps that you practically needed a respiratory mask (and definitely gloves) to handle, and I remember all kinds of snake-oil suggestions that were sold (and, let's face it, are still being sold), to people who wanted fewer fleas with less side effects. Magic crystals, anyone?

It was common to see patient after patient come in—usually for other reasons—crawling with fleas. And while I'd be talking to the client, I'd notice flea bites on them as well.

Words cannot express how much better we have it today. While no medication is or can ever be completely safe, today's flea-control products are more effective and safe than we could have ever hoped for or dreamed of when I was just starting out as a veterinarian. The biggest problem we have with them: people who don't follow directions, such as applying as indicated, in dosages appropriate for their pet, and using a medication meant for one species on another.

Ear mites rank right up there with fleas as some of the most maddening parasites to take up residence in or on cats. They are most common in kittens and cats who have come from community situations such as feral colonies or, in some cases, rescue or shelter housing, but any cat can get them.

The tiny invaders love the warm, moist darkness of the ear canal and settle in, piercing the skin to feed and reproducing rapidly. Their presence causes intense itching. Cats with ear mites constantly shake their heads and scratch at their itchy ears. In severe cases, they end up with raw skin or hair loss around the ears, often complicated by a bacterial infection.

If your kitten or cat's ears have a dry, crumbly, dark-brown waxy discharge that looks like coffee grounds, chances are good he has ear mites. If you have sharp eyes and examine a sample of the discharge through a magnifying glass, you may see the tiny white mites, about the size of a pinhead, moving around inside the ear wax. (Or, it could be an environmental allergy, so let your veterinarian—the expert!—decide.)

Ear mites don't affect people, but they are highly contagious between cats and can be spread to dogs as well. That means that even if only one cat is diagnosed with the itchy critters, you'll need to treat not only him but also any other pets in the household.

The good news is that it's much easier these days to treat ear mites. Your veterinarian or her technician will thoroughly clean out the ears and apply a topical medication inside the ears. Back in the bad old days, a cat's ears had to be medicated frequently for as long as a month. Now, medicated ear drops in combination with a whole-body or systemic parasite treatment will get rid of mites much more quickly and easily. Other skin mites may inhabit cats, too, although they are less common than ear mites. A good flea preventive will keep them under control.

And what about worms—the parasites on the inside? Cats are hosts to a variety of worms, from the roundworms that virtually all kittens get, to heartworms that are so dangerous that the best "cure" is prevention, to tapeworms that go along with flea infestations. Other intestinal parasites that can invade cats are hookworms, coccidia, and giardia. Intestinal parasites are usually transmitted by the mother to kittens or from one cat to another, and it's possible for cats to carry the parasites for a long time.

Roundworms look like miniature earthworms and may occasionally be seen when a cat passes them in feces or vomits them up. Coccidia, giardia, and hookworms are not visible, but most intestinal parasites make their presence known when kittens fail to thrive or develop intestinal problems such as diarrhea.

A protozoal parasite called toxoplasma is a problem for cats not so much for the disease it causes in them but because people, in particular women who are pregnant, are concerned that the infection can be spread to them.

Cats usually get infected with toxoplasma after eating infected mice. They can then pass toxoplasma organisms into the soil, where they can be ingested by other animals, including people. The important thing to know is that even if your cat is infected, you cannot get toxoplasmosis directly from her. If you are pregnant or immunocompromised, avoiding infection is as simple as delegating the job of scooping the litter box to someone else in your household. There is no need at all to get rid of your cat or to make her live outdoors.

Have your veterinarian perform fecal analyses once or twice a year if your cat lives indoors; more frequently if she goes outdoors or interacts with other animals who do.

Mosquitoes transmit heartworms to cats, just as they do to dogs. But in cats, the worms are less likely to invade the heart, instead settling in the lungs. Once a cat has been infected with heartworms, the damage they cause can lead to coughing and vomiting. Think "hairball cough"—that awful gagging sound might actually be the result of heartworm disease. At that point, the disease can be difficult to manage because there is no treatment once the immature heartworms have entered the cat's bloodstream. If you live in an area where dogs need heartworm preventive, your cat should be taking a monthly preventive, too, even if he lives indoors.

What about tapeworms? They are about the size and shape of rice grains or cucumber seeds and can be seen wriggling on the feces.

Your veterinarian can recommend an appropriate preventive program based on your cat's lifestyle—indoors or outdoors—as well as your climate and the prevalence of parasites in your area. For instance, in areas with harsh winters or hot, dry climates, neither of which is favorable to the fleas or mosquitoes that give cats grief, you may not need to give preventive year-round. And several products can prevent multiple parasites. Selamectin (the active ingredient in Revolution) treats many internal and external parasites, including heartworms, as does the combination of the compounds imidacloprid and moxidectin contained in Advantage Multi. For tick control, products containing fipronil (Frontline) are effective, but they don't treat or prevent internal parasites.

Most important—ask your veterinarian what's safe and effective. Not everything "natural" is safe, especially when it comes to cats. Products derived from citrus agents and chrysanthemum-based pyrethrins are toxic to cats. And never use a product made for puppies and dogs on a cat.

THE KINDEST CUT OF ALL: SPAYING AND NEUTERING

The vast majority of pet cats these days are spayed or neutered, and this has had many benefits. The near-total acceptance of spaying and neutering has helped to steadily drop shelter populations. And spay/neuter surgery makes cats much easier to live with. Altered males are less likely to mark their territory with stinky urine to ward off other males and attract females, and they're less inclined to roam because they don't have that urge to find a mate. With spayed females, there's none of that noisy, insistent yowling emitted by intact females eager to find a male to satisfy their reproductive desires.

Because cats reach sexual maturity at a very early age, usually before they are six or seven months old, the sooner you alter them, the better. Kittens having kittens is never a good thing. Talk to your veterinarian about the best age for scheduling your kitten's surgery.

Neutering a male cat is a very easy procedure, but spaying is major surgery: the removal of the uterus, fallopian tubes, and ovaries through an incision in the abdomen. Your veterinarian may require you to return to have the stitches removed in about ten days, or he may use stitches that are absorbed into the body. Unlike women who have hysterectomies, though, cats feel better quickly. To help speed recovery, limit your cat's activities for the first few days afterward: no jumping or boisterous play. Recently, this surgery has been made even easier on the animal with the introduction of laparoscopic surgery, which requires not an incision but small holes through which surgical instruments are inserted. Recovery time is faster and pain is even less.

"Cheap" Surgery: You Get What You Pay For

Because spaying and neutering are common procedures, people tend to think they're easy ones, too. And while that's not too far from the truth with male cats—who have thoughtfully arranged to leave their removable pieces hanging out like ripe fruit for the picking—that's not the case with females.

I understand the desire and the need to save money, but price-shopping for surgery really isn't the best place to do that. When you get rock-bottom prices, you're often getting only the most basic of care. And while that's probably necessary for the clinics working to keep feral cat populations down, opting out of top-quality care may not be the choice you want to make for your own pet.

Don't make price the bottom line. If you're going to price-shop for surgery—and I don't recommend it, honestly—be sure you're comparing apples to apples. What sort of anesthesia protocol will be used? Will the anesthesia be monitored? Pre-op screening? Pain medications? Warm pads for recovery? All of those things make surgery safer and recovery easier.

An informed decision is the only kind to make, and that requires knowing what's involved and considering all the options, not just knowing what your final bill will be.

DENTAL CARE: HEALTHY TEETH AND GUMS ARE KEY TO A HEALTHY CAT

Dental health is another of those areas where veterinarians' recommendations have changed a good deal—and for good reasons. We now know that the health of teeth and gums are important not only for quality of life but also for longevity. A mouthful of rotting teeth and gums is home to bacteria that put stress on a cat's internal systems, and that stress leads to a shortened life span.

Yes, I'm aware that a lot of people my age—and I've been a veterinarian for more than thirty years, so you can guess I'm in the AARP range, and happily so—consider dental care for cats to be at best a joke and at worst a rip-off. Let me just say that those people haven't seen what veterinarians see every day and aren't aware of the suffering a mouthful of disease can cause. But let me bring this home: Have you ever had a tooth break? Had periodontal work? Needed a root canal? Did you enjoy waiting for those procedures, or were you begging for pain medications?

Now, consider that every day veterinarians see cats who have not one of those problems but all of them—advanced dental disease. You can smell them coming by their bad breath and you can feel their pain and admire their stoicism. But mostly, as a veterinarian, what I really want is to not see cats in that condition.

And that means preventive dental care.

Dental care starts with a veterinary exam to go over the teeth and gums to spot problems. There's more to feline dental health than gum disease. For instance, cats don't get cavities, but they can suffer an extremely painful condition known as a cervical line lesion. If your cat flinches when you take a cotton swab and press it on his gum line, he probably has one of these lesions. Veterinary treatment typically requires extracting the diseased tooth.

Breed-Specific Dental Problems

Abyssinians, Siamese, and Persian cats can develop juvenile onset periodontitis, sometimes called red gum disease. It begins when they are as young as six or eight months old and can be irreversible by the time they are one or two years old. Without daily care, the cats who get it end up losing a lot of their teeth by the time they are two or three years old.

If you're starting out with a kitten, or a cat with no plaque buildup or gum disease, prevention is easy and inexpensive. Your veterinarian or one of the technicians will go over home preventive care—brushing your pet's teeth daily and using pet-friendly toothpaste (unlike humans, pets swallow the toothpaste), dental wipes, and rinses. Depending on your cat's dental health, your veterinarian may suggest a diet that will help by abrading the teeth with every bite or the use of dental treats or toys that will help to clean your cat's teeth.

If there are already dental problems, however, your veterinarian will likely recommend X-rays and a more complete examination under anesthesia, along with treatment as needed, removal of any broken or diseased teeth, and scaling and polishing to get the teeth back to a healthier state. Because of bacteria issues, it's likely your cat will be started on antibiotics before the procedure and continue on the medication after, possibly along with pain-control medications.

After your pet's mouth is restored to good health, you can stretch the period between cleaning with home care, but do be aware that some cats are prone to plaque buildup and will likely need regular veterinary care under anesthesia once or twice a year for life.

I know what you're thinking: *Do I really have to brush my cat's teeth?* Well, I'm not going to call the cat police on you if you don't, but I can guarantee that you and your cat will be happier if you do. You will because your cat's breath will smell nice, not nasty, and your cat will because she'll need fewer visits to the veterinarian for painful gum disease. Your wallet will be especially happy because you won't have to spend as much money on professional veterinary cleanings to keep your cat's mouth healthy.

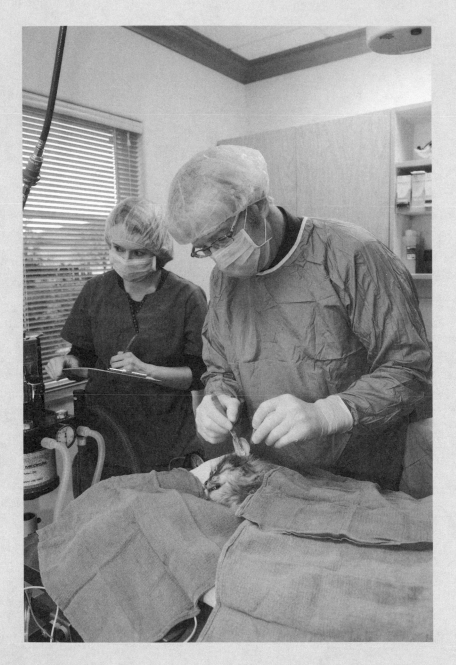

Get off the 'Net and call your vet for feline health information. Trying to figure out what's wrong with a gravely sick pet may mean a delay in getting care, which may cost your cat his life.

Chapter 18

HOW TO HANDLE
AN EMERGENCY

No matter how careful you are about providing preventive care, how much you've worked to control such things as your cat's access to the outdoors or to dangerous plants or chemicals, accidents happen. That, as they say, is why they're called accidents.

Your cat could misjudge a leap onto or off of a high place and injure himself, or he could escape through the door when no one is looking and get injured in a fight or hit by a car.

So what do you do?

Unless you're living with a veterinarian, chances are you're still going to be the first person to deal with a feline health emergency. You need to know what's an emergency and what's not, who to call and where to go, and what to do before you can get help.

While I believe every word in this book can help to make your cat healthier and happier, this chapter can save your pet's life. Read it now, and know what you need to do before you need the information. Because the time to be looking in the index of a book (or checking the Web) is not when a life is on the line and minutes count.

SYMPTOMS THAT SAY "GET HELP NOW"

Those of us who've worked at veterinary hospitals have our own stories of the emergencies that weren't—the pet owner who was sure the animal's intestines were coming out the back end when even the greenest kennel attendant could tell you they were worms, not guts. The cat who's "high" from catnip for the first time. The cat whose screeching isn't from an injury—she's in heat, so please schedule that spay, okay?

Knowing what's not an emergency can save you money, since after-hours care is almost always more expensive. But knowing what really is an emergency is going to save you something more important than money—it's going to save your pet's life.

Animals, especially cats, instinctively try to hide signs that they are sick or injured. For this reason, always treat any serious incident (like being hit by a car, a fall, or a possible overheating) as something that requires veterinary care—even if your cat seems to be bouncing back. Internal injuries could be killing him.

Here are some signs that should have you heading for a veterinarian, day or night:

- 🐾 Straining to urinate or defecate
- 🐾 Seizure, fainting, or collapse
- 🐾 Eye injury, no matter how mild
- 🐾 Vomiting or diarrhea—anything more than two or three times within an hour or anytime there's blood
- 🐾 Allergic reactions, such as swelling around the face, or hives, most easily seen on the belly
- 🐾 Any suspected poisoning, including antifreeze, rodent or snail bait, or human medication
- 🐾 Snake or venomous spider bites
- 🐾 Thermal stress—from being either too cold or too hot—even if the pet seems to have recovered (the internal story could be quite different)
- 🐾 Any wound or laceration that's open and bleeding, or any animal bite
- 🐾 Trauma, such as being hit by a car, even if the pet seems fine (again, the situation could be quite different on the inside)
- 🐾 Any respiratory problem: chronic coughing, trouble breathing, or near drowning

What kind of trouble is your kitten or cat most likely to get into that could become an emergency? The good news is that cats are a lot smarter than dogs and are less likely to eat toxic things. The big exception here is lilies. Never, never, never let your cat have access to them. Cats like to chew on plants, and all parts of the lily, even the pollen and the water in the vase, are highly toxic to them. Exposure to lilies is often fatal because by the time cats begin to show signs of toxicity, it has been several hours to several days since they came in contact with them. If you have cats, don't bring lilies into your home or yard.

Know Your Plants

It's possible to have cats and keep plants successfully, if you choose the right ones—plants, that is. There are plenty of plants out there that won't cause any ill effects, but you should still know what they are. Nibbling on any plant can make a cat vomit, and you can save a lot of money and worry if you are able to tell the veterinarian the name of the plant when you call for advice. Then she can give you instant advice: "Not a problem" or "Bring him right in." Write down the names of the plants in your home (and yard if your cat goes outside), and keep the list with your veterinary information so it's easily available.

Cats aren't exempt from emergencies, though. One of them is swallowing human or veterinary drugs that aren't meant for them. Cats do not metabolize drugs in the same way as people or dogs, so if they swallow the wrong kind of pills, the result can be deadly. Common drugs such as nonsteroidal anti-inflammatories (NSAIDs) are especially toxic to cats and can result in severe kidney failure and stomach ulcers. A single acetaminophen tablet can be fatal. Other pills, such as certain antidepressants, seem to attract cats because of their scent or flavor. Anytime you discover your cat has ingested a drug not meant for him, take him to the veterinarian immediately.

Exposure to household chemicals or insecticides or treatment with topical flea and tick medications made for dogs can also cause cats to develop signs of poisoning. Never apply anything to a cat without first reading the directions carefully, and don't let your cat walk through a yard or across a floor or other area that has been treated with chemicals or cleaners until it has dried. Cats can become poisoned by licking their paws, licking other animals, having too much of a product applied to them, or having the wrong type of product applied to them. The result can be severe drooling, vomiting, tremors, difficulty breathing, and life-threatening seizures.

Among the weird things your cat might try to taste-test are glow sticks. These items contain toxins that can cause heavy drooling. They aren't necessarily deadly, but they taste nasty—one reason why your cat probably won't get poisoned by them. Offer him some nice chicken broth or canned tuna in water to help him get the bitter taste out of his mouth. If he has any "glow juice" on his fur, wash the area thoroughly so he doesn't lick it off and start drooling again. Take him to the veterinarian if the drooling doesn't stop, if he's squinting or his eyes appear red, or if he's not eating.

Potpourri and mothballs are other seemingly innocuous household items that can be toxic to your cat. Potpourri contains essential oils that can cause cats to vomit or even threaten his life by damaging the ability of red blood cells to carry oxygen. If your cat collapses or has seizures after getting into potpourri, take him to the veterinarian immediately. Fortunately, most cats are put off by potpourri's strong scent, but it's still a good idea to keep it out of kitty reach.

The scent of mothballs tends to deter cats as well, but if you catch your feline delinquent sniffing their fumes or even eating them, you should take him right to the veterinarian. Ingesting mothballs or inhaling their fumes can lead to liver damage or neurological damage.

WHAT TO DO BEFORE YOU CAN GET HELP

Being ready for an emergency is the next best thing to handling one. It's amazing how much better prepared a pet owner can become by spending just one afternoon organizing a few documents and tools.

When you do your emergency prep, keep in mind that another member of your family or a pet sitter might just be the one nearby if your cat has a crisis. Posting a single page with clearly written instructions for how to find help and where to find your pet first-aid kit could one day save your cat's life. These are the main issues to address:

Emergency Contact Information

At the very least, every household with a cat should have an easy-to-find, clearly worded list of emergency contacts with phone numbers. Don't call 911 when your pet is sick: these emergency services are for people, and the operators are neither trained nor allowed to give you veterinary advice.

Your emergency-care sheet should include:

❧ YOUR CAT'S VETERINARIAN: name, office hours, address, phone number
❧ URGENT CARE OR VETERINARY EMERGENCY ROOM: name, address (detailed directions if you've never been there), phone number
❧ ASPCA POISON CONTROL HOTLINE: 888-426-4435 (there is a charge for this service, but in an emergency when your veterinarian is not available, it is well worth the fee)
❧ A TRUSTED FRIEND, NEIGHBOR, OR PET SITTER: name, phone number
❧ Program all this information into your smartphone as well, under the contact name "ICE"—in case of emergency.

Cat Identification

You can't help a cat you can't find. Your cat should always wear a collar with multiple phone numbers on it—your cell, your home, your veterinarian, and at least one number out of the area in case of a major disaster. Because collars can get hung up and strangle your cat, protect him with a breakaway collar. These collars give when they need to, and can save your pet's life. Also, make sure your cat has microchip ID, that you know the number, and that the number is registered to you with the information kept current.

You should also keep good pictures of your cat from all angles with a clutter-free background, in case you ever need to make a "lost cat" poster.

First-Aid Kit

If your cat has a health crisis, the last thing you need to be doing is digging around in the cupboards for a carrier, a pair of scissors, or bandages and tape. Spending an hour now to prepare for an emergency later is the best way to ensure this doesn't happen to you. Besides, if you believe in Murphy's Law, you can rest easier knowing that once you've gone to the trouble to make the ideal emergency kit, you'll probably never need it!

If you have the space for it and if your cat goes to your vacation home with you, a second kit to keep in the car will give you double the peace of mind. Here's what to include:

- A clearly printed label with your cat's name, your name and phone number, your veterinarian's contact info, and a note listing your cat's medical conditions and any allergies
- Leash and collar
- Disposable medical gloves
- Antiseptic
- A tube of K-Y jelly
- Styptic powder (from pet supply retailers in the grooming section, to stop bleeding)
- Bandaging supplies: sterile gauze, cotton pads, first-aid tape, bandages, scissors
- Tweezers
- Flashlight
- A bottle of 3 percent hydrogen peroxide solution
- Over-the-counter antihistamine
- 10cc syringe for giving medicine orally (no needle!)
- Clean washcloth, towel, and blanket
- Resealable plastic bags in different sizes

THE SHARED MEDICINE CHEST

Some "people meds" can be helpful in a feline health crisis, but others are quite dangerous. When in doubt, call your veterinarian to ask about the use of any product from your own medicine cabinet. *Never* give your cat anything that contains acetaminophen or ibuprofen—both of these pain medications are toxic, and potentially deadly, for cats.

The products listed here are all safe for occasional feline use. Always call your cat's veterinarian to let her know you are giving medication at home, and don't treat symptoms at home for more than twenty-four hours unless you are following your veterinarian's specific directions:

Benadryl. This common medication can be a godsend if your cat is swelling from a bee sting or spider bite. Use a liquid pediatric formulation to ensure that you give an accurate dose. In humans, Benadryl sometimes causes drowsiness, but some cats may respond differently, becoming anxious and excitable after taking it. It's a good idea to give your cat a "test dose" to see how he reacts so you'll know what to expect in case he ever needs it therapeutically.

Dose: Once every six hours, give 25 milligrams for pets up to 30 pounds.

Pedialyte. If your cat is dehydrated from vomiting or diarrhea, you can help to replenish his fluids with the same stuff you'd give a baby with tummy problems. Pedialyte is designed to rehydrate and restore the balance of electrolytes in a child's system after a bout of vomiting or diarrhea. Anytime you need to get a cat to take in fluids, it's always best if you can get him to do it on his own rather than forcing liquid down his throat and running the risk of aspiration pneumonia. The easiest way to do that is to give him canned food, which contains as much as 70 to 90 percent water, or moisture. Adding Pedialyte to the canned food enhances the moisture content even more. If you need to help him eat it, mix the Pedialyte with canned food to make a paste and then gently put it into the front of the cat's mouth. Do this slowly so that nothing gets forced down the wrong pipe.

Dose: Give unflavored Pedialyte—a tablespoon or so—mixed with canned food.

Say No to Pepto

Be extra cautious about giving this bright pink liquid to a cat with an upset stomach. It's challenging enough to medicate cats because they metabolize substances so differently than humans or dogs, and use of Pepto-Bismol is especially tricky because it contains multiple drugs. One of those drugs is aspirin. By itself, aspirin can be used safely in cats in small doses under the direction of a veterinarian, but the effects are long-lasting. You can't give it more often than every three days. Because of that, you can't really give Pepto-Bismol to a cat frequently enough for it to have any real effect on a bilious belly. And bismuth, the other active ingredient in the pink stuff, has the potential to be toxic in cats if they get a little too much of it. Think twice and then put the bottle away before dosing your cat with this drug.

Hydrogen peroxide. The first use that comes to mind is cleaning wounds, but hydrogen peroxide can also be used to induce vomiting. Check with your veterinarian before doing this, because some substances cause more damage coming back up than they do going through the system. Then be sure you are using the household variety, a 3 percent solution, which you can purchase at the drugstore. Some homeopathic remedies contain a 20 percent solution, and that is high enough to perforate a cat's stomach. It's also important to use hydrogen peroxide that is fresh. If the bottle has been sitting around in your medicine cabinet for years, don't use it. Check the expiration date and make sure the bottle has not been open for more than one month.

Vomiting 101

Cats are what veterinarians call "easy vomiters"—except, of course, when you need them to. I'd like to throw up—um, out—some tips to help you get the job done if it's ever necessary. Again—I can't emphasize this enough—check with your veterinarian first to make sure inducing vomiting is the right thing to do for the situation.

Whenever you want an animal to vomit, you'll have an easier time of it if his stomach is full. Add the appropriate amount of hydrogen peroxide to some canned food. Choose something that your cat is likely to eat right away, like tuna or some stinky brand of cat food. It may seem a little counterintuitive, but when your cat eats, the food will expand the stomach and your cat will vomit more, emptying the stomach more effectively. Adding the hydrogen peroxide to food doesn't reduce its effectiveness, and it's a lot easier to get it down the hatch.

Dose: Use a medicine syringe to give your cat 3 ml of hydrogen peroxide per kilogram of body weight. For a ten-pound cat, about 3 teaspoons would be the appropriate dose to induce vomiting. Do not repeat unless directed by a veterinarian. If you're concerned enough about something your cat ate to induce vomiting, you should be talking to your veterinarian to be sure your pet doesn't need to come in.

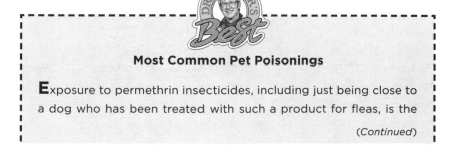

Most Common Pet Poisonings

Exposure to permethrin insecticides, including just being close to a dog who has been treated with such a product for fleas, is the

(Continued)

number one cause of accidental poisoning in cats. Ingesting medications meant for humans is another source of toxicity to cats. Cats are less likely than dogs to down an entire bottle of pills, but on the other hand it often takes less of a substance to poison them than it does dogs. And cats are attracted to the taste of some pills, including an antidepressant called Effexor.

Always store your own medications, including cough medicines and lozenges, out of sight and out of reach of your curious cat. Remind houseguests to do the same. It's typical for people who don't have pets to put medications on the nightstand, or in an easily accessible purse or piece of luggage. When you have visitors, explain the situation and ask them to put whatever they have behind secure cupboard doors.

WHEN A CRISIS HAPPENS

If you find yourself coping with a seriously sick or injured cat, you're going to have to dig deep and calm yourself before you can be much help. As first responders like to say, "Take your own pulse first."

That means take a deep breath, ask for help if you've got anyone nearby who can pitch in, and approach your cat's emergency step-by-step.

Later, when he's recovering nicely, you can allow yourself a little breakdown. You'll have earned it.

First Things First: Restraint

You love your cat. Your cat loves you. But in the event of an injury that requires any of the following procedures, *any cat*, even yours, may instinctively lash out and try to protect himself from further injury during first aid. The best way to protect both your cat and you is to restrain him. Wrap your cat up like a burrito in a blanket or towel with his head out so he can breathe, and enlist the help of an assistant if possible. A blanket will help you to immobilize your cat during treatment. It may also calm your cat so you can help him.

Bleeding

If your cat is bleeding heavily, your priority is to stop the flow. Use a clean cloth, towel, or gauze to push down on the wound. Once you start applying pressure, do not let up! Don't lift your bandage to look at the wound beneath or to replace it, as this can interfere with clotting and restart bleeding. Instead, if your bandage soaks through, put another one on top of it and keep applying pressure.

Open Wound

If your cat has an open wound but isn't heavily bleeding, rinse the wound with hydrogen peroxide, Betadine, or saline solution, and coat the area with K-Y jelly. This will help keep dirt and infection away from the wound until your cat's veterinarian can treat it properly. If you have to bandage a wound at home, cover it with sterile pads and then secure them by wrapping the area in an Ace bandage. Bandaging a cat can be a complicated business. Be creative—a clean ankle sock pulled up over a leg bandage may keep it in place. A long-sleeved T-shirt can be wrapped around your cat's torso and tied together at the arms to help keep a temporary bandage in place.

Bite or Puncture Wound

When cats get in fights, they often develop an abscess, a swollen, pus-filled area that is hard and hot to the touch, where they have been bitten or scratched. To treat the abscess until your veterinarian can drain it and prescribe antibiotics if needed, clip the fur around the area and clean the skin using a gauze pad moistened with water, wiping away from the wound. Then take a clean towel that has been soaked in a solution of hot water and two teaspoons of salt and apply it to the abscess. Hold it there for ten to fifteen minutes. (Yes, you'll likely need help.) Repeat every two hours or as often as possible.

Overheating

Overheating is one of the biggest hidden threats to cats and one of the most deadly. Your cat can overheat in the car, in the house, or in his own yard. It can happen if he is confined to an unshaded enclosure or left to sit in a carrier on a hot day. Cats overheat much more quickly than people because they can't sweat much to adjust their body temperature. Instead, a cat's temperature can quickly rise with the conditions. Flat-faced cats such as Persians are especially vulnerable, as are fat cats or cats with asthma. As a watchful pet owner, it's your job to avoid the obvious dangers—like the inside of a closed car, even on a seventy-five-degree day. But it also falls to you to watch for the signs of overheating when the conditions aren't so obvious. Always err on the side of keeping your cat cool and protected.

The most obvious signs of overheating are rapid breathing, panting, drooling, or vomiting. An overheated cat may also seem weak. If your cat is overheated, you are facing a true emergency. Start cooling him down with water immediately. Cool water on his belly will get his temperature heading in the right direction. You can also wrap him in cool, wet towels. **Do not use ice cold water or ice to cool an overheated cat!** It could send him into shock. Even if he seems to be improving under your care, get your cat to his veterinarian as soon as possible. He needs to be evaluated and treated by a pro. If needed, your veterinarian can administer oxygen to prevent brain damage and give fluids to reverse dehydration.

Broken Bones

If your cat falls off your balcony, gets hit by a bike or car, or otherwise breaks a bone, there's not a lot you can do at home to help him. Your job is to try to immobilize the broken bone and get him to a veterinarian as soon as possible. A quick way to splint a broken leg is with a rolled-up magazine or piece of poster paper. Wrap it around the wound and tape it. Transporting your cat may be easier for both of you if you carry him wrapped in a towel, blanket, or small rug. The less your cat moves between the moment of the break and the time his veterinarian sets it, the better.

Poisoning Risks for Your Cat

There are many items—both edible and not—in your cat's environment that can make him very sick or even kill him. Plant poisoning is more common than chemical poisoning for cats, but knowing the most common poisons will help you be more vigilant about your cat's exposure to them in and near your home:

❧ **Poisons.** Every year thousands of cats are sickened or killed by poisons intended for other animals. Two of the most common culprits are mouse/rat baits and insecticides. The easiest way to avoid this potential tragedy in your home is to not use poisons at all. If you do use them, put them in places your cat cannot possibly reach or, better yet, use secure bait stations that are inaccessible to pets.

   If you have any contractor who visits your home to chemically treat for insects or other pests, be sure that person understands you have cats and are concerned about their health.

❧ **Household chemicals.** This is a broad range of poisons, and many of them are ingested by cats accidentally rather than deliberately. For example, your cat may nibble grass that has just been treated with insecticide. Most cats have no interest in poking around your cleaning caddy looking for snacks (though, to be safe, the cleaning caddy should always be stored out of reach). When it comes to chemicals, you have to think one step further and consider your cat's access to their point of use. Until the product has dried, keep your cat away from lawns, floors, or other surfaces where chemicals have been used.

❧ **Plants.** Many household and landscape plants are poisonous for cats. If you have a cat who enjoys chewing grass or nibbling from your garden—and many of them do—take extra care to limit your cat's exposure to the following commonly seen poisonous plants: azalea, tulip bulbs, cyclamen, crocus, chrysanthemum, dieffenbachia, peace lily, philodendron, English ivy, yew, and Sago palm. And don't forget about jewelry made from natural but poisonous "beads" such as castor beans. A cat who chews on or eats them could be in serious trouble. If you'd like to look up any specific plant to see if it is dangerous for your cat, the ASPCA Animal Poison Control

Center (ASPCA.org/APCC) has an extensive searchable database online.

❧**Medications.** Yours, your children's, your dog's. It really doesn't matter much what the medicine is—if your cat helps himself, he's in danger from any pharmaceutical, even in small amounts. Always keep all meds in a place where your cat cannot see or reach them.

❧**Surprising things around the house.** Pet-proofing your home means looking at everything your cat can get to—and making sure it's out of the way. Candles, coins, mothballs, nutshells, potpourri—the list of things a cat (especially a kitten) can and will eat is astonishing.

Got Milk?

Some plant poisonings look scary, but they can easily be dealt with at home. Some common houseplants—pothos, dieffenbachia, philodendrons, and peace lilies (which are not true lilies)—contain tiny calcium oxalate crystals in their leaves. When cats chew on them, these plants eject little microcrystals into the gums and tongue. The immediate result is salivation, drooling, and sometimes vomiting. The cat may start tossing his head because he's in pain. You can quickly dissolve and neutralize the crystals by giving your cat a bowl of milk, some yogurt, or some other dairy product that's high in calcium, such as cottage cheese. That will soothe the cat almost immediately. Because he's in pain, you may have to coax him a bit to take the "remedy," but most cats like milk and other dairy products so they may be willing to drink up. And call your veterinarian.

The best way to pet-proof the poisons in your home is to treat them with the same kind of full effort you'd use if you were toddler-proofing instead. In other words, assume your cat not only may stumble upon these items, but may actually go looking for them. Store all potentially toxic products both *inside* a cabinet and *above* counter height.

Antifreeze has a sweet flavor that makes it enticing to pets, but even a tiny amount of the sweet-tasting stuff is potentially fatal to cats who lap it up. The ethylene glycol in antifreeze is not toxic on its own, but the metabolites that occur when the body breaks down the antifreeze are toxic to kidney cells. They form oxalate crystals that damage and block the kidney tubules. Once the damage is done, few cats recover from the experience.

If you see your cat lick at antifreeze, take him to the veterinarian immediately for treatment. Better yet, store it up high in a closed cabinet, wipe up spills right away, and choose a brand with bittering agents added to it. It's also toxic, but because it has an unpleasant taste, it's less likely to cause a problem.

The majority of cats never get medication as prescribed because their owners have difficulty getting the drugs inside the cat. If you're having problems giving medication to your cat, talk to your veterinarian about techniques and options.

Chapter 19

GETTING THE BEST MEDICAL CARE

Even the healthiest of cats with the very best of preventive veterinary care and nutrition will get sick on occasion. The bodies of our cats, like our own, are complicated machines—although I like to think of them as miracles—that are constantly fighting for survival. But it's not just bacteria and viruses that can cause health problems in our cats.

One of the most fascinating things we've learned about feline well-being is how stress and the environment can affect a cat's health. We used to suspect that was the case, but now science has proven it.

In a lengthy study, cats exposed to unusual external events—in other words, changes in their environment—were more likely to develop "sickness behaviors" that included vomiting, lack of appetite, and excessive grooming. Those behaviors occurred in healthy cats and cats with idiopathic (meaning the cause was unknown) cystitis. Sudden movements, loud noises, changes in feeding schedules, and the presence of strangers were among the stresses that caused cats to hack up hairballs, stop using the litter box, develop chin acne, and reduce their interactions with people.

Researchers learned a couple of important things. First, sickness behaviors could be turned on in cats by making changes cats didn't like or expect, and then turned off by changing things back the way they were. And second, making the cat's environment more interesting with toys, playtime, and other social interaction, and places to perch, climb, and scratch reduced sickness behaviors in the cats with cystitis. So if your cat is acting sick, he might have something physically wrong with him, he might be bored, or, well, he might just object to your mother-in-law's visit.

When Your Cat Isn't Acting Normal

The easiest way to know if your cat is sick or not feeling well is to know what's normal for him. If your cat's behavior is out of the ordinary, it may be his only way of telling you that something is wrong. If your cat doesn't usually hide under the bed or in the closet, if he loves to eat, but stops showing up at the food bowl at dinner o'clock sharp, if he usually likes to be petted and suddenly starts hissing when you reach for him, those are all clues that he's not feeling his best. When behavior changes, it changes for a reason, so don't ignore it.

No matter how good your veterinarian is, you are the reason your cat has a fighting chance at a healthy life. That's because not only are you the one who notices when he needs a veterinarian's help, but you're the one who'll be caring for him after that appointment.

It's a partnership with your veterinarian—and the hospital staff, plus any specialists brought in to help—and yourself, and the goal is your cat's recovery, or at least the management of a disease so your pet can live a normal life.

My favorite clients are the ones who want to know more, who challenge me, who ask questions, and who get the help they need to help their pets. I want to help you be one of those clients, for your pet's sake. So read on!

MAGIC WANTS, FAIRY DUST, AND
INFORMATION FROM THE INTERNET

Pet lovers were second only to sci-fi fans in embracing the possibilities of the Internet. I've read—and really, there's no way to substantiate this, so I just can't—that the Internet has more images and video of pets than of people. I don't find it that hard to believe, really, considering how many pictures of the Almost Heaven animal family you can find online.

The Internet is a great place to share the love of pets and connect with other pet lovers. And it's also a great place to look for information on pets and their care.

But as a veterinarian, I can tell you this: it's also one of the worst places to find information, not only because there's information that's wrong and can waste your time and your money, but also because there's information that's even worse—it's deadly. My pet care team of veterinarians, behaviorists, trainers, and other pet care experts has been working online for a very long time. We get asked questions so often that we have most of the answers saved for a little cut-and-paste action.

The number one thing we tell people? *Get off the 'Net and call your vet.*

That's not because I'm trying to drum up business for my fellow veterinarians. It's because there's no way to offer treatment options that work without knowing what's actually wrong with a pet. And very few pet owners are knowledgeable or skilled enough to present their pet's symptoms accurately. Not to mention, they don't have access to diagnostic testing we veterinarians often need to know what's really going on.

So let me stress this as strongly as I can: No Internet search and no book is a substitute for an in-person visit with your cat's veterinarian. And no magic home remedy you read about is going to help, either.

Now that I have that out of the way, let's give the amazing Internet some credit for what it can help you with, and that's improving the relationship you have with your veterinarian by giving you the information you need to be a better-educated advocate for your pet. With the Internet, you can read many of the same peer-reviewed journal articles your veterinarian is reading. You can research the best care options and cutting-edge solutions. You can even—although this point is controversial among veterinarians, many of whom feel unfairly treated—see what other pet owners thought about how their pets were treated by any particular veterinarian. It's all there for the finding, but you have to know how to understand the respective value of a source to get the benefit of the information. Here are some suggestions:

* **Check the sources.** Look for citations to veterinary literature and specific references to studies and clinical research. While citations older than ten years may still be perfectly valid, claims based entirely on older research require additional scrutiny. Testimonials are not evidence, proof, or documentation. They are advertising. Don't rely on testimonials in making health decisions.
* **Look at the wording.** The best sites have straightforward language, free of sensationalism. If a site is badly organized, full of misspelled words and grammatical errors, and hard to navigate, the information is less likely to be reliable. Look for a track record of providing good information in the past and on other subjects.
* **What are they selling?** Websites with financial or professional affiliations that might compromise their objectivity should sound alarms. In particular, be extremely skeptical of information being provided by someone trying to sell something. When information providers have strong ideological beliefs, such as passionate agendas about health and nutrition, that could taint their objectivity. Watch out for all-or-nothing statements praising or condemning a specific drug, procedure, therapy, or approach to health.

What you find on the Internet is best seen as a jumping-off spot for an open, thoughtful discussion with your veterinarian. And remember: when you show your veterinarian some Internet advice she hasn't seen before, it's not a sign that she hasn't kept up. In the first place, the information may be wrong, and in the second, there's nothing wrong with a medical professional saying, "I don't know"—as long as she's prepared to go find the answers.

WHAT YOU NEED TO KNOW ABOUT
MEDICATION AND SURGERY

It's hard to imagine a cat who will get through life without dealing with two everyday realities of modern health care: taking medication and having surgery. And yet, few things cause more concern and problems than these common issues. So I want to cover them so you can know the latest and do your part to help your pet.

Pet Pharmaceuticals: Pet Meds and "People" Meds

Drugs such as Valium, Xanax, and Elavil may be prescribed to help cats who are fearful, aggressive, or suffer from compulsive behaviors such as excessive grooming. Aside from flea- and tick-control products, almost all of the medications your pets receive are crossovers from human medicine.

Some 80 to 90 percent of the drugs used in veterinary medicine come from human medicine. When you get into more specialized treatments, such as those for cancer, that figure goes even higher. This so-called off-label use of human drugs allows veterinarians to treat medical conditions (and species) that might not be priorities for big drug companies when it comes to developing and selling medications.

Knowing how and why certain drugs are prescribed can help pet owners understand health-care options—including some that save money. A good veterinarian will discuss medications, tell you what side effects to look for, and encourage you to call with questions or concerns. Treatment can often be more complicated in animals than in humans.

Veterinarians need to know more about pharmacology than their physician counterparts. In human medicine, all drugs are FDA-approved, meaning that they have undergone significant scrutiny for safety and efficacy—but only in one species. Vets must often use fairly limited evidence to treat other species with differences in drug metabolism and action.

When a veterinarian believes that a particular human medication can help an animal, she'll prescribe it. This has been the case for decades, of course, but the practice has only really been legal since 1994, when Congress passed the Animal Medicinal Drug Use Clarification Act regulating the conditions under which such use is acceptable.

Even before the legislation was in place, however, there was a working system for prescribing human drugs to pets. Veterinarians relied on peer-reviewed studies, clinical trials, and published formularies that included suggestions for safe uses and dosages of human medications given to companion animals.

Today, with the legal issues cleared up, veterinarians and their patients have more options and better access to medications. Veterinarians have always been glad to provide in-house pharmaceutical services, and general pharmacists, too, have usually been willing to fill prescriptions written by vets. But recently, online retailers and specialty pharmacists have recognized that pets are an expansion market. These developments open the door to even more progress, including discussions on generic meds and price-shopping.

Chances are you won't be walking out with a prescription for Viagra or Valium the next time you go to the veterinarian's office, but you should still talk with the doctor about your pet's treatment options. More variety means better care for your favorite animal, and that's good news for everyone.

Good Stuff That's Not Really a "Drug"

The word *nutraceutical* is a combination of *nutrition* and *pharmaceutical*, and it refers to products, supplements, and dietary ingredients known or believed to have some kind of specific medical benefit. While not as well-tested or strictly regulated as drugs, nutraceuticals such as omega-3 fatty acids, glucosamine and chondroitin, antioxidants, and many other supplements and herbs have found their way into the world of veterinary medicine.

Conditions that can be helped by these kinds of supplements include age-related cognitive deficits, arthritis, side effects of prescribed medications, and many kinds of skin and digestive problems. The next time your pet's veterinarian diagnoses a health problem, ask if there are any nutraceuticals that could be a helpful part of his treatment plan.

"Natural" Therapies: Complementary Treatments That Can Help Your Cat

You are probably familiar with the use of acupuncture, herbal remedies, supplements, and other alternative, or complementary, treatments to help people with health problems, but did you know they can help your cat as well? Veterinarians in traditional practices are incorporating these as well as massage and low-level laser treatments to provide pain relief, organ support, and other positive effects.

For instance, acupuncture is a type of neurophysiologic stimulation with effects that have been studied in humans, cats, dogs, and other species. It can be used to relieve muscle spasms, increase blood circulation, and, in conjunction with pain-relief medications, improve a cat's comfort after surgery. The herb milk thistle is so valuable in the management of liver disease that it's not really considered alternative anymore. And cranberry keeps bacteria in the urine from being able to attach to the bladder wall.

Before going ahead with any therapy, be sure it has been safely used in cats—ask your veterinarian. Just because something has been used safely in humans or dogs doesn't always mean it will be safe to use in cats. And seek out a veterinarian who has training in the technique being used through a certification program or continuing education. Complementary and alternative techniques alone aren't a cure-all, and you should avoid any practitioner who says they are, but used in combination with traditional medicine they can be an important part of your cat's veterinary care.

Medications Don't Work If You Don't Give Them

One of the most maddening experiences you as a cat owner will ever have is attempting to get medicine into your pet. The reason is simple: it's hard to give medication to a pet who absolutely doesn't want it, especially when you're dealing with an animal as squirmy and stubborn as a cat.

However hard it is, your cat needs that medication in the dosage, for the length of time, and at the intervals his veterinarian has prescribed. Fortunately, help is available for most medications in the form of compounded drugs. Compounding pharmacies can make big pills tiny, bitter pills sweet, and turn your cat's worst nightmare into his favorite tasty treat. How? By mixing the medication into savory liquids or pastes that pets will lap up eagerly. We call it putting the TREAT into TREATment. There are other alternatives like pill pockets (stuff the pill into a yummy treat) and pill guns that pop the pill straight into your pet's throat. They can even put some medicines into what are called transdermals that can be wiped into the inside of the cat's ear.

If your pet's veterinarian prescribes medication and you find you can't follow his instructions, ask for help; there's plenty of it out there.

The Big Sleep: What You Need to Know About Anesthesia

If there's one part of veterinary medicine that seems to concern the average pet lover most, it's anesthesia. The simplest definition of anesthesia is putting an animal into an unconscious state so the pet will be immobile and pain free while a procedure is performed. But some pet lovers consider anesthesia so high-risk that they hesitate to okay or will even refuse procedures that have long-term benefits to an animal's health and comfort. Other pet lovers think anesthesia is too expensive, blaming changes in protocols for increased cost.

The good news about veterinary anesthesia is that although it can never be risk free, it's safer and more comfortable than ever. The bad news is that those things that improve safety for pets do indeed increase the cost.

One of the reasons anesthesia is safer now is because better monitoring of a cat's pulse, respiration, and even blood oxygen level is available. Monitors warn of problems early, and it's more likely these days for there to be someone whose sole job is to watch those machines and watch that patient—letting the veterinarian concentrate on performing surgery. Even without monitoring machines, it's important to have someone checking heart rate and breathing.

While many pet lovers probably think of veterinary anesthesia as a gas given through a mask over the animal's face, in fact the modern practice of preparing an animal for surgery is a combination of injectable medications (often blending anesthesia and pain-control agents), anesthesia-inducing gas, and pure oxygen, the latter two delivered through a breathing tube to maintain an animal's unconscious state.

In addition to constant anesthetic monitoring by machines and trained technicians, the use of intravenous fluids during anesthesia is another safety measure, meant to allow a veterinarian to react rapidly if something unexpected happens during surgery. If there's an emergency, you want instant access to a vein. Another important safety protocol is keeping pets warm during surgery and recovery. A cold animal doesn't recover as quickly, and shivering increases oxygen consumption.

Preanesthetic screening is also important when it comes to reducing risk. A good physical exam is the place to start. Your veterinarian needs to determine the underlying problems and recommend preanesthetic blood work based on what's found in the exam. In a young pet, that could be just checking for anemia. In an older pet, that means a complete blood count, determining kidney and liver function, making sure all organs are okay.

Even in older pets, health problems don't necessarily rule out the benefits of procedures that require a pet be put under. You have to balance risks with benefits, and discuss them with your veterinarian.

How much pain is the animal in? Has your pet stopped eating because of a rotting tooth? That needs to be addressed.

Veterinary anesthesiology specialists have modified anesthetic protocols and techniques so they can do a better job of helping cats. Examples include the careful use of NSAIDs (these must always be cleared or prescribed by your veterinarian), opiates, and narcotic drugs such as morphine and hydromorphone. It used to be thought that some of these drugs weren't suited for use with cats, but research has shown that they can be helpful under certain circumstances. Techniques such as epidurals, constant-rate infusion, and regional blocks are also being used to reduce pain in cats before and during surgery.

Most important are the advances in the way that general anesthesia is induced. The most up-to-date method is intravenous injection of induction drugs, a more controlled way of putting a cat under anesthesia than the use of a cat box or a mask procedure. Masking a cat asleep with gas or putting him in a box that has anesthetic gas delivered to it are not safe techniques because they aren't controlled ways of inducing anesthesia. Injectable anesthesia helps the cat go to sleep smoothly and wake up smoothly.

Have a frank discussion with your veterinarian before your cat has surgery, to understand how your pet will be treated and why—and what you need to do before surgery to help keep your animal safe, such as withholding food and water as recommended. You'll also need to know what to look for after your pet goes home so you can call and get help for your pet if anything abnormal pops up.

Urine Trouble

Some of the most frustrating conditions to treat in cats are urinary problems, ranging from urinary tract infections (also known as lower urinary tract disease) to urinary stones that form in the bladder, urinary tract, or ureter and cause dangerous blockages.

If you've ever suffered a bladder infection, you know that urgent feeling of needing to go *right now* and then dribbling out only a tiny bit of urine. You call your doctor, describe your symptoms, she prescribes antibiotics, and that's the end of it.

Cats are not so easy to treat. Depending on their age or gender, the problem could be any number of things. Cats younger than ten years get bladder stones, idiopathic cystitis, and, in males, urethral plugs. Bladder infections are rare in cats, and when they do occur it's usually in cats older than ten years. The one thing all these conditions have in common is that antibiotics are rarely the answer and can even make the problem worse if they're used when they aren't really called for.

Diagnosing bladder problems in cats is a challenge, and taking the time to do a complete workup that includes a urinalysis or even a urine culture is well worth the effort and cost. If stones are suspected, fancier diagnostic techniques may be necessary: blood work, X-rays with dye, ultrasound, or using an endoscope to look at the urethra and bladder.

Once the problem is identified, your veterinarian may suggest a special diet to dissolve stones; recommend switching from dry food to canned food to increase the amount of water your cat takes in; prescribe antibiotics to clear up an infection; or propose stress-relief techniques—keeping the litter box extra clean, switching to a larger or different type of box, or providing playtime for indoor cats. Those tips, known as enrichment, often help in cases where no cause is apparent.

Signs of Urinary Tract Problems

Your cat may not speak in words, but he'll let you know loud and clear if he has a urinary problem. Take him to your veterinarian straightaway if you notice any of the following signs: frequent urination; urinating in strange places, such as on a kitchen counter or in the bathtub; blood in the urine, identifiable by a pink tinge on light-colored carpets; dribbling urine; crying out while urinating; straining to urinate; and obsessively licking the genital area.

If a male cat is vomiting and stops eating, he may have a life-threatening urethral plug. That's an emergency, so don't wait to see if he gets better. Get him to a vet.

IS IT TIME TO CALL IN A SPECIALIST?

Although not as many specialists exist in veterinary medicine as in human medicine, the kinds and the number of certified veterinary experts grow every year. That's good news for our pets.

Companion-animal specialties include cardiology, dentistry, dermatology, nutrition, oncology, and radiology. Behavior specialists are becoming more common as well. These veterinarians help people and their pets work through such problems as house-soiling or separation anxiety with the aid of medication and behavior modification techniques. There are even veterinarians who specialize in feline medicine.

Many urban centers support independent specialists or specialty practices, but in less populated areas you're more likely to find a full complement of specialists at the closest university with a school or college of veterinary medicine. Only veterinarians who are board certified are allowed to call themselves specialists.

Specialists are usually called on a case-by-case basis to work on specific problems in which they have more experience than most veterinarians. While it used to be that primary care veterinarians were reluctant to refer, these days the advances in veterinary medicine and the growth of independent specialist groups have made getting the help of a specialist much more common—and your veterinarian may even recommend sending your cat to one.

If your veterinarian doesn't suggest a referral and you believe it could help your cat, open the discussion. The final decision on what treatment and who offers the care is yours. If you have a good relationship with your veterinarian, bringing in a specialist should never be a problem.

Many cats live comfortably into their teens if given good care and nutrition. How comfortable those years are depends on your ability to spot and get help for problems such as arthritis that prevent a cat's senior years from being as happy as they can be.

Chapter 20

SPECIAL CARE FOR AGING AND SPECIAL-NEEDS CATS

He has gone gray around the muzzle. She sleeps a little longer and doesn't seem to hear things that used to wake her up. He yawns when you bring out his favorite fishing-pole toy, instead of performing amazing flips the way he used to. When she looks up at you lovingly, her eyes are clouded.

Yes, there's no denying it: your cat is officially old.

No cat lover likes thinking about the fact that cats have much shorter life spans than we do. But I want to make you feel better by making sure you know a couple of things about the last few years of your cat's life.

First, the final third or so of your cat's life is often the best years you have together, the time when you understand each other well and work to make each other happy. You've reached the point where you're comfortable with each other, when your cat's behavior issues and training challenges are mostly behind him. You know where your cat likes to nap and which brand of catnip is his favorite. He is a comfort when you've had a hard day, and a daily play session does you both a world of good. There's an easy companionship with a cat you've loved for his whole lifetime.

The other thing you need to know: aging is inevitable, but suffering is not.

Since your cat may spend several years in this phase of life, try thinking of him not as a tired old guy, but as a pal just entering retirement.

There are a million ways people tackle their own retirement years, and the happiest of them stay busy and fit.

Your cat can do the same. She will regain a bit of her youth with interactive toys that challenge her, and she will love the times you and other family members spend talking to her or petting her. With your veterinarian's help in providing guidance for new strategies to slow, stop, and even reverse the aging process, the senior years of your cat's life really will be golden.

HOW OLD IS OLD? FORGET THAT "SEVEN YEAR" THING

Better care at home and at the veterinarian's, combined with changes in the way cats are protected from harm (many cats live indoor lives now, putting them at less risk of disease or death by car), has made the lives of many cats not only longer but also better. How well cats age also depends on factors such as weight, activity level, and sometimes the breed or breeds behind their genetic code. For instance, breeds such as Siamese and Abyssinians seem to have an edge when it comes to really stretching out that ninth life. But cats in general seem to live a long time. It's not unusual for them to reach fifteen or twenty years of age, or even older. I know of a feline-only practice in San Antonio, Texas, that routinely celebrates twenty-year-old cats' birthdays on their bulletin board!

One Year Equals...

There isn't an easy way to remember the formula for cats—and even that old "dog years" thing doesn't work as well as most people think it does.

Some people use a "one year equals four" formula, figuring that a twenty-year-old cat is about equivalent to an eighty-year-old person. Problem is, that formula doesn't work, since a one-year-old cat would be the equivalent in terms of mental and physical maturity to a human four-year-old, and that's clearly off.

A better equation is to count the first year of a cat's life as being comparable to the time a human reaches the early stages of adulthood—age fifteen or so. Like a human adolescent, a year-old cat looks fairly grown up and is physically capable of becoming a parent but is lacking in emotional maturity.

The second year of a cat's life picks up some of that maturity and takes a cat to the first stages of full adulthood in humans—a two-year-old cat is roughly equivalent to a person in his mid-twenties.

From there, the "four equals one" rule works pretty well. A cat of three is still young, comparable to a person of twenty-nine. A six-year-old cat, similar to a forty-one-year-old person, is in the throes of middle age; a twelve-year-old cat, similar to a sixty-five-year-old person, has earned the right to slow down a little.

It's all relative, though. Some cats live more risky lives than others. Feral cats—those poor, flea-bitten creatures wandering anywhere food can be scrounged, are lucky to live more than a year or two before being claimed by accident, predation, or disease. Pet cats who are allowed to roam are likewise more likely to meet with an early demise. With regular veterinary care and good nutrition, protected indoor cats can easily live into the late teens.

To help your cat achieve a comfortable old age, keep him active with play and toys. Even if he's not a top athlete anymore, batting at a feather toy or pawing at a ball inside a track helps to maintain muscle strength around arthritic joints and keeps cats more mobile. Feed your cat carefully so he doesn't get overweight. And take him to the veterinarian once or, better, twice a year. A strong preventive program ensures that problems are identified early so they can be corrected. That's way better than dealing with a crisis after damage has already been done.

Keep your cat indoors. As we mentioned, it's unquestionably true that cats allowed to go outdoors do not live as long as indoor cats. With plenty of interactive toys and play, as well as places to climb and lounge in the sun, your indoor cat can live a happy, interesting, and long life.

Bottom line: you know your cat best. You'll be able to see the signs of aging and start making adjustments for the best life possible when the prime of adulthood is past.

CHANGES IN VETERINARY CARE FOR SENIOR CATS

Every cat's senior years should be kicked off with an expanded veterinary exam. When your veterinarian recommends graduating your cat to senior status—around eight or so, usually—it's time for your cat to get the works—exam, blood screen, urinalysis, fecal exam, and possibly ultrasound, depending on what kinds of health problems your cat might be prone to. The purpose of all the testing is twofold. First, your cat will have up-to-date baseline values on all his lab tests. If and when health problems arise, these results will make it easier for your cat's veterinarian to spot the cause. Second, as time passes, cats are simply more likely to have ailments and for those problems to go undetected. For example, a cat can lose up to 75 percent of kidney function and still appear just fine during an exam. Lab tests are the key to discovering this kind of health problem early, so it can be treated or managed.

Consider your cat's senior exam a chance to ask the veterinarian what kinds of health concerns might be especially relevant as she ages. Do cats get arthritis? What are the signs of kidney problems or diabetes? Knowing what ailments are common will help you be vigilant in watching for early signs of trouble.

Take time at your cat's senior exam to talk with the veterinarian about diet and activity level. If your cat is just reaching old age and still feeling fine, you may not need to change a thing about his lifestyle. If he's got some weight creeping on, though, this is a good time to talk about changes to your cat's diet and routine. And don't forget to ask about medications and supplements that will make his life more comfortable.

Once your cat has had that super-senior physical, make his appointments at six-month intervals for routine checkups and stick with them.

BRAIN DRAIN?

As your cat gets older, you may notice that he prowls the house late at night, yowling despondently. He may wander into a room and then seem to wonder why he's there or how to get back out. Maybe he no longer gives that happy *mrrrp* when you come home from work or doesn't enjoy being petted as much. His hearing, vision, and sense of smell aren't as good as they used to be. Gradual slowing of the senses is a natural part of the aging process, but occasionally something more is going on.

Instead of writing off slowing senses or confusion as just the price of time, ask the veterinarian if your cat may be experiencing cognitive dysfunction syndrome (CDS). This condition, with signs similar to those of Alzheimer's disease in people, can start to affect cats who are well into their golden years.

The acronym DISH—Disorientation, Interactions, Sleep, House training—spells out the signs that generally accompany CDS. If your cat gets stuck in corners, changes his interactions with people, no longer sleeps through the night, or forgets where the litter box is, those are all good reasons to schedule a visit with your veterinarian for an evaluation. An overactive thyroid—hyperthyroidism—or high blood pressure can cause similar signs, and an underlying urinary tract infection can contribute to loss of house training. If a medical cause is ruled out, then CDS may be the reason for the changes.

Don't assume that nothing can be done to help your cat. Structure, limitations, and new routines can help him stay safe and secure. Consider limiting your cat's access to stairs or certain parts of the house such as basements or closets where he could get lost. Introducing a new routine that your cat will look forward to, such as giving a spoonful of a tasty canned food at a specific time, can help keep your cat's mind active. Adding high levels of omega-3 fatty acids or other supplements to your cat's diet may help to restore your cat's mental functioning. Melatonin sometimes reduces nighttime prowling and vocalizing, and a medication called selegiline (Anipryl) may benefit some cats with CDS.

A REVOLUTION IN THE TREATMENT OF PAIN

One of the most important considerations in improving the quality of life of an older cat is making sure he is as pain free as possible. And while pain medications have become the gold standard in every phase of veterinary medicine, their use is extremely important in dealing with the chronic pain that comes from aging.

Animals can feel all the same aches and pains that we can because they share the same physiologic structures. Treating pain doesn't just make the hurting stop; it also promotes healthy healing. Untreated pain slows healing time, interferes with sleep, and depresses the immune system. The treatment of pain improves respiration, shortens postsurgical hospitalization times, improves mobility, and can even decrease the spread of cancer after surgery.

Just as with human medicine, advancements in the way we think of and treat pain in animals is improving the quality of life for pets, with veterinarians now being able to choose from a wide array of products and strategies to ease the hurt. Most veterinarians prescribe pain medication when needed, but some older veterinarians were trained to believe—and still recommend—that pain will stop a pet from moving around and injuring himself during recovery from surgery or injury. This belief is no longer supported by studies. If an animal needs to be restrained, it's better to use a leash or a crate and have your pet's pain properly addressed.

Still, many owners don't give pets pain medications—even if they are prescribed—because of concerns about side effects. All drugs can cause unwanted effects, but those risks need to be balanced against the problems caused by untreated pain. Side effects can also be minimized by using drugs appropriately. If you have worries or concerns about the effects of pain medications—or any drug, in fact—call your veterinarian.

Complementary and alternative medicine also has much to offer cats suffering from chronic pain. Acupuncture, physical therapy, and supplements such as glucosamine and chondroitin can help relieve arthritis pain.

Pain control is never a "one size fits all" prescription. Drugs can be used alone and with other medications to relieve all but the most extreme pain in animals.

When a veterinarian isn't sure how to get to the bottom of a pet's pain, it's always worth asking for a consultation with a specialist to design a safe, individualized pain-management program. Veterinary specialists in oncology, surgery, and anesthesia are usually most familiar with the wide variety of drugs available today and their safe use.

Along with changes to diet, exercise, and environment, pain medications can make old cats feel young again. Don't ignore their important benefits.

MOVING MORE, AND MAKING MOVING EASIER

As your cat gets older, slower, and less active, the key thing to remember is that he still needs exercise. Regular, gentle play is truly one of the secrets to feline health and happiness. As your cat ages, continue to give him a minute or two of play here and there throughout the day. Batting at a big peacock feather or pouncing on a catnip mouse will help to keep his muscles, joints, and reflexes in good condition. And don't forget the benefits of "brain games" using food puzzles to keep his body moving and his mind active.

Above all, don't let him put on the pounds. Extra weight puts more pressure on your cat's joints and clogs up the efficient engine of his internal systems. If anything, keep your cat on the lean side of normal.

Don't forget environmental adjustments. Ask not what your old cat can do for you, but what you can do for your old cat. Keep in mind that for most cats, your presence and affection are the most pleasing thing of all. As they get older and when they're not feeling well, some cats become clingy. You can accommodate that need for closeness by giving your cat easy access to you. Steps can help him get onto the couch or bed, and comfy beds around the house will give him some soft spots to ease those old bones. (And don't forget heating pads in the cooler seasons, which can be added to your cat's favorite beds or sleeping spots.) More options to consider:

*   *   *

It's all about the bed. Choose beds that are well-padded and warm. If your cat has arthritis, consider adding egg-crate-type padding for extra cushioning. Offering a couple of different beds in separate rooms, ideally in sunny spots, will give your cat ways to both catch his naps and stay close to you. If you do have multiple beds, try mixing up the fabrics—you may find your cat's favorites change depending on the weather and his mood. And don't forget heating beds—many cats love them!

Flavorful food. If your cat seems to be losing his appetite, try a little extra flavoring for his food. I've used Stewart Pet Food Flavor Enhancer and Kitty Kaviar. A few little jars of strained-meat baby food (look for no- or low-salt varieties, and skip labels with onion and garlic on them as well) in the pantry will give you lots of healthy options to "kick it up" for your cat. A small spoonful of baby food will add new flavor and texture to your cat's food. To really amp it up, try putting the food in the microwave for a few seconds (no more than ten). Warming food releases its aromas and makes it more pungent. For a cat with sensory loss, the smell of his food warming in the microwave can be just the ticket to increase his appetite and his enjoyment of the meal.

Ramp it up or give him a lift. Many companies make stairs and ramps to help pets get to their usual favorite places. These are often lightweight, well designed, and collapsible, or attractive enough (in the case of stair-steps) to leave as a permanent part of the décor.

BE REALISTIC, FLEXIBLE, AND SOLUTION-ORIENTED

Your cat may breeze through years of senior citizenship without any significant health issues, but sooner or later, age catches up with even the most resilient of feline companions. You may one day discover your cat can't see or hear anymore, or that he's developed an irritable streak where he didn't have one before. In many cases, the first really distressing issue to come up is incontinence—an old cat may dribble urine in his bed or in the house—and suddenly you have a problem.

Anytime a new health issue develops, the best course of action is to have it checked out by your cat's veterinarian.

The good news: many problems are treatable at any age.

If it turns out your cat really is just running out of time, it's time to double down on the love and patience. As he begins to lose his health, he needs your care and assurance more than ever.

Some special situations you may deal with:

❧ **Vision loss.** Maintain your blind cat's environment with minimal change. Cats actually adapt amazingly well when they lose their eyesight—as long as you don't start rearranging the furniture. If your cat knows his way around your house and has a walking route that suits him, try to keep these things constant to prevent injuries and put him at ease.

❧ **Hearing loss.** For a cat who lives in a soundless world, sudden contact can be unnerving. Always be sure your cat sees you before you touch him, or step loudly as you approach him—your footfalls will cause a vibration that can be felt even if it's not heard. Teach any children in the home to approach him this way, too. Many cats are hearing impaired but not completely deaf, and for those a couple of simple hand claps are enough to get their attention.

❧ **Urine leakage.** If your cat has weakened urinary muscle tone from old age, he may dribble a bit on the way to the litter box or even be unable to make it all the way to the box before he has to go. Help him do the right thing by placing additional litter boxes throughout the house, especially if you live in a multistory home and he has achy joints that make it difficult for him to negotiate stairs. A simple, hard plastic dishpan is all you need to provide to make it easier for him to get to a box in time. The extra scooping is a small price to pay to ensure that your senior cat is comfortable.

Hearing and vision loss can cause cats to vocalize more loudly than they used to. Sometimes it's from distress because they can't see, but in the case of hearing loss your cat may simply not realize that he is "talking" more loudly than usual. Until a hearing aid for cats is developed, the best way to tone down your cat's vocalizations is to insert earplugs—into your own ears.

Will a Kitten Make an Older Cat Young Again?

A lot of cat lovers wonder about the right time to get another cat. Usually loyalty to a senior cat drives the debate—after all, the last thing anyone wants is to add stress or anxiety to the life of a beloved pet.

It's not the best idea to get a kitten or younger cat to rejuvenate a senior cat. Often, it leads to frustration or stress on both parts: the kitten wants to play and the senior cat wants to rest and not be bothered. Let your older cat be peaceful and comfortable.

If it's really important to you to have a younger cat, get a pair. Two siblings can play and wrestle and chase each other and leave your older cat alone.

Another option is to get your next cat while your first is still young and healthy enough to enjoy some companionship and be active. There are several reasons this is a good idea.

Pets who have a buddy are sick less often than those who live in single-pet households. When they do get sick, pets with partners recover more quickly. On average, pets from multipet households live longer than those alone. Your middle-aged cat may grouse a little bit if you bring home a kitten, but he'll likely come to enjoy the addition. Think of it as charging his batteries—in his new companion, he may rediscover some of the energy and enthusiasm he's lost over time.

GIVING YOUR CAT A COMFORTABLE END OF LIFE

At the end of your cat's life, you will have to make tough choices about what she can endure and what she should be spared. These are very personal decisions, and as you work with your cat's veterinarian to make them, know that there are no right or wrong choices—simply those that are best for your family and your cat.

Treatment, hospice care, and euthanasia are all options. When you choose treatment for your cat, consider what her quality of life is without it, what the treatment will involve, and what quality of life she can expect afterward. There are millions of pets whose lives are improved by veterinary care in their senior years, but there are also pets whose lives are prolonged by painful, costly procedures and treatments that do very little to improve their days. Consider the quality-of-life assessment guide in the previous section, and ask your veterinarian what the reasonable expectations are for your cat's condition after any intervention.

Hospice care, no matter who gives or receives it, is all about comfort and pain relief at the end of life. It starts at the point where a patient is no longer being given treatment with the goal of cure or recovery, but instead simply receiving whatever contributes to comfort and ease. Many families successfully give their cats excellent hospice care at home, buying weeks or months of high-quality time. Talk to your veterinarian about hospice options—you may be surprised at what can be done to care for a dying cat at home.

WHEN IS IT THE RIGHT TIME TO SAY GOOD-BYE?

A good death is the last, best, most loving thing you can do for your cat. It is also the most difficult decision you will ever make for your cat, even if he has reached an ancient age. No one can make this choice for you, and there is no wrong decision.

You know your cat best, so let him help you decide. Is his discomfort unmanageable, even with palliative care? Is food no longer of interest, even if made more palatable? Can he no longer do the things he used to enjoy? The end may come as a series of small and subtle changes, but it's usually clear when a cat is suffering and no longer enjoying life.

As hard as it is, talk to your veterinarian about euthanasia options. Decide whether you want to take your cat to the veterinary clinic for euthanasia or have the procedure done at your home. Veterinarians often make house calls these days, especially when euthanasia is necessary. If your cat is fearful of trips to the veterinarian and you want her to feel safe and comfortable, this may be something to consider.

Before the appointment, discuss what you want done with the remains (individual or group cremation, burial on your property if allowed by law, or simple disposal with no return). Your veterinarian and the entire staff are there to help you, to provide both you and your cat with what you need at this difficult time. They will help you through it, answering questions and scheduling your appointment so you won't have to wait.

If your cat's euthanasia is planned and not the result of an emergency situation, think about whether a particular time of day or of the week will be best for the procedure. For instance, a Friday afternoon would give you the weekend to be by yourself instead of having to go in to work the next day. Or late afternoon might be a better time for the entire family to gather to say their good-byes to Snowflake.

Whatever you do, don't wait too long. As I always say, "I'd rather be a week too early in euthanizing a pet than one minute too late."

Child-development experts say that children may be present, and saying good-bye to a beloved cat helps children learn to deal with the losses we all endure in our lives. You know your children—give them the opportunity to participate if they wish, and to find closure with memorials, such as drawings and storybooks, and even memorial ceremonies. (And do remember to tell your child's teacher, so she can be aware and help your child through the loss.) As hard as it may be to get through, seeing that your pet did not suffer and knowing that you were there at the end is usually quite comforting once the initial waves of grief have passed.

Pet Grief

Animals display a sense of loss when their companions die, and letting them sniff the body can help them know their feline friend won't be returning. Other pets may even show signs of grief when one of their fellows dies. These signs may include excessive grooming, loud or continuing vocalizations, a reduced appetite, and changes in sleeping habits. Give surviving pets extra attention (exercise, massage, and treats) to help them through the grief process.

The death of your cat is a tremendous loss. You'll find that some people completely understand how big a heartbreak this is, and others have no clue. The important thing is to know that it's okay to grieve. If you need someone to talk to, ask the veterinary office if there's a pet-loss support group in your area. Even if there's not a local group, there are pet-loss hotlines at many veterinary colleges and many online grief groups where pet owners can share their stories and struggles.

Doing something special in memory of your cat can help to ease the grief. Memorials can take the form of a simple candlelighting ceremony, placing an engraved slab in the garden, or even having a piece of jewelry made with a bit of fur or, astonishingly, DNA. Many people also like to do something for others in honor of their pet, such as making a donation to a feline health fund, veterinary school, or shelter.

In time, thinking of your cat will bring back happy memories along with your feelings of loss. Take comfort in everything you did to give your cat a good, healthy, happy life.

THE END, OR A NEW BEGINNING?

As a veteran veterinarian (over thirty years), a lifetime pet lover (well over fifty years), and a communicator in person and in all forms of media—traditional and new—I find themes or exercises that get repeated. After reading these pages you know how sacred I hold the human-animal bond, the appreciation I have for the healing power of pets, and how much I stress—to millions on TV in their living rooms or one-on-one in the exam room—the importance for pets of daily oral care, high levels of preventive care, good nutrition, and keeping pets and people fit.

For more than three decades I've enjoyed asking individuals ranging from clients and neighbors, celebrities and titans of industry, and groups ranging from ten to ten thousand the following question: who was the first pet you ever owned in your life? In the exercise I ask them to get specific: the species, breed, size, coloration, overriding memory of the pet, and, of course, my favorite...the genesis of the pet's name (my favorite cat's name is 11:30; it wasn't quite black enough to be called Midnight). In 99.99 percent of the cases, after asking the question I just sit back and watch the warm memories wash over the audience like a benediction. Most of these folks haven't thought about Puss Puss, Stinker (black with a white stripe), or Dirty Bung (the cat was chronically constipated, and as a young boy it was my job to check and, yes, help) (you may have guessed these were *my* childhood cats). As you think about your first pet, the vivid, warm memories come flooding back in an instant. They're warmed. Joyful. Thankful. First pets certainly rank ahead of first teacher, kiss, or car.

I trust in this book I've given you the tactics and tools to make the selection of the first pet for a child or your next pet as an adult.

I used to end a radio show by saying, "There's only one greatest pet in the world...and every family has that pet." Whether in the exam room at one of the veterinary hospitals I work at, in my church, on the street, or around the country (from people who recognize me from a book or the media), they get so exuberant when talking about their pet(s) and say in body language and words the same basic thing: "If you could just come over to where I live and be around for a few minutes, you'd see why I'm so crazy about her!"

By harnessing the hundreds of secrets, surprises, and solutions in this book you'll raise a happier, healthier cat. You'll have the greatest pet in the world seen by the greatest veterinarian in the world.

Next time you see me, tell me about it.

ACKNOWLEDGMENTS

No book is ever written alone, or even with the help of a coauthor, such as I have been fortunate enough to have found in Gina Spadafori, with whom I have now written more than a dozen books. We are also fortunate to have a team of experts working with us on every project, and on this one we thank Kim Campbell Thornton and Jana Murphy for their work on the writing and editing.

Gina and I are grateful as well for our editor, Karen Murgolo, and her most capable assistant, Philippa "Pippa" White. Members of "Team Becker" who also contributed a great deal to the book include top veterinarians Drs. Jacqui Neilson, Tony Buffington, Susan Little, Robin Downing, and Tony Johnson, as well as my daughter, Mikkel Becker, a trainer and behaviorist. I'm grateful, too, to Dr. Jane Brunt for contributing the foreword. Other colleagues I could not have done this book without include Drs. John Tegzes, Michael Dryden, Jane Brunt, Ilona Rodan Ganetzky, Alice Wolf, Kim Kendall, Andrew Luescher, Narda Robinson, Steve Garner, and Jan Bellows. Joan Miller of the Cat Fanciers' Association knows as much if not more about feline body language than anyone ever has.

Thanks, too, to the Team Becker folks who filled in on the writing and editing work we left to do this important project, or who contributed their considerable expertise, especially Christie Keith and David S. Greene. Thanks, too, to my agent, Bill Stankey, and to attorney Marc Chamlin.

Many, many other pet care experts have helped me a great deal over the years, and the list of folks would be longer than this book. To all of you, though, you know who you are and how much you mean to me. A special shout-out to fellow Washington State University College of Veterinary Medicine alum Dr. Bruce King, who let us use his stunning practice, Lakewood Animal Hospital in Coeur d'Alene, Idaho, for the pictures throughout and on the cover of this book, most of which were taken by Joel Riner and Dustin Weed of Quicksilver Commercial Photography, also in Coeur d'Alene. Thank you to all those who brought their cats in to be models for the book. Thank you, too, to Richard Schmidt, an award-winning photojournalist who allowed us to use some of his photos as well.

Thanks to Dr. King as well for letting me be his colleague at Lakewood, and to Drs. Dawn Mehra and Robert Pierce for letting me do the same at the North Idaho Animal Hospital in Sandpoint. Finding time to work as a hands-on veterinarian is difficult with my schedule, but I love it so much I can't do without. I also can't do without Angie Harmon and Madison Hill at Lakewood.

Thanks to my family, especially my incredible wife, Teresa. I just couldn't do what I do without her, and that's a fact. Thanks, too, to our son, Lex; our aforementioned daughter, Mikkel; granddaughter Reagan; and my mom, Virginia Becker. Love as well to the animal residents of our Almost Heaven Ranch in Bonners Ferry, Idaho.

Dr. Marty Becker
Almost Heaven Ranch
Idaho

RESOURCES

Cat Gear and Problem Solvers

Anti-Icky-Poo. Cat and dog urine odor eliminator; http://antiickypoo.com.

Arm & Hammer. Line of odor-cleaning products for pets; http://www.armandhammer.com.

Beastie Bands. Stretchable, lightweight collars that stay on most cats; http://www.beastiebands.com.

Bissell. Manufacturer of vacuums and hard floor cleaners; http://www.bissell.com.

Bitter Apple. Bitter-tasting liquid that discourages cats from biting themselves and creating hot spots; http://bitterapple.com.

Cat Dancer. Spring steel wire and rolled cardboard toy; http://www.catdancer.com.

Cat Fence-In. Containment system stops cats from climbing over fences and up trees; http://www.catfencein.com.

CatGenie. Litter-free, full-size litter box that uses permanent granules, connects to cold water line; http://www.catgenie.com.

Cats on Deck. Kits for solid, built-to-last cat enclosures; http://www.catsondeck.com.

Clipnosis Gentle Calming Clip. Causes a similar calming behavior to scruffing when clips are applied to cat's scruff; http://store.clipnosis.com.

Da Bird. Interactive toy that mimics the motions of a live bird in flight; http://go-cat.com.

Dirt Devil. Vacuums and floor cleaners; http://www.dirtdevil.com.

Dremel. Grinder for pet nails rather than cutting; http://www.dremel.com.

Drinkwell. Their pet fountains for cats and dogs filter and aerate continuously moving water so it's fresher than standing water; http://www.vetventures.com.

Dyson. Vacuum cleaners, including the Animal line; http://www.dyson.com.

Equalizer. Removes stains and eliminates odor, by Vétoquinol; http://vetprofenusa.com.

Feline Pine. Natural, 100 percent pure pine litter; http://www.felinepine.com.

Feliway. Synthetic copy of the feline facial pheromone, creates a state of familiarity and security; http://www.feliway.com.

Fresh Step. Scoopable and clay litters with odor-fighting carbon, some with crystals to absorb wetness; http://www.freshstep.com.

Freshpet Select. A line of freshly prepared cooked meals with all-natural ingredients; http://www.freshpetselect.com.

FroliCat. Interactive automatic laser toy; http://www.frolicat.com.

Funkitty Egg-Cersizer. Treat/feeding ball adjustable to your cat's level of play from the outside; http://www.premier.com.

FURminator. Deshedding tool for long and short coats; http://www.furminator.com.

Galkie Kitty Tease. Simple but effective string toy; http://www.kittytease.com.

Greenies. Dental treats; http://www.greenies.com.

Kitty Kaviar. Shaved bonito fish treat; http://www.kittykaviar.com.

LeBistro food dispensers. From Petmate, programmed automated portion control feeders; http://www.petmate.com.

Marmalade Pet Care Cheeky Chaise Cat Bed. A floor cradle for cats to sleep in; http://www.marmaladepets.com.

Nature's Miracle. Liquid stain and odor remover; http://www.naturemakesitwork.com.

OurPet's. Products for pets under a large umbrella of brands; http://ourpets.com.

Pat the Cat. Baby-preschool-level touch-and-feel book by Golden House; http://www.randomhouse.com.

PETCO. Nationwide pet supply store; http://www.petco.com.

Petfinder.com. Adoptable cats across the United States; available cats can be sorted by geographic area, breed, size, age, and sex; http://www.petfinder.com.

Petlinks System Dream Curl Curved Scratcher. A curved floor scratcher; http://petlinkssystem.com.

Petmate Deluxe Fresh Flow Fountain. Purifying pet fountain providing filtered water; http://www.petmate.com.

Pill Pockets. Treats in which you can hide a tablet or capsule to make medicating your cat easier; http://www.greenies.com.

Pledge Fabric Sweeper for Pet Hair. A tool that you slide picks up more fur from furniture and car interiors than sticky paper; http://www.pledge.com.

Purrfect Fence. Cat fence enclosure system, freestanding or added to fence or wall; http://purrfectfence.com.

Refined Feline. Stylish scratching posts and cat furniture; http://www .therefinedfeline.com.

Stewart Pet Food Flavor Enhancer. Dry food additive to enhance eating; http://www.miraclecorp.com/stewartpet/.

Sticky Paws. Adhesive strips apply directly to furniture to prevent scratching; http://www.stickypaws.com.

Swheat Scoop. Clumping litter that neutralizes odor even with multiple cats; http://www.swheatscoop.com.

Swiffer. Cleaning tools that pick up dirt and cat hair and help eliminate allergens from a cat; http://www.swiffer.com.

Tick Key. Tool to safely remove ticks, including the head; http://www .tickkey.com.

Ticked Off. Tool to safely remove ticks, including the head; http://www .tickedoff.com.

Whisker Studio. Modular cat trees that meet cat's behavioral needs; http:// whiskerstudio.com.

Whoa Buddy Blanket. Mylar-lined throw that mimics aluminum foil to keep your cats off the furniture; https://secure.whoabuddyblanket.com/tv .aspx.

Wobbler. Food-dispensing toy and feeder by Kong; http://www.kongcompany .com.

World's Best Cat Litter. All-natural clumping litter that is easy to scoop and fights odor; http://www.worldsbestcatlitter.com.

Yesterday's News. Litter made from recycled material is unscented and tough on odors, from Purina; http://www.yesterdaysnews.com.

ZoomGroom. Comfortable rubber brush that makes brushing easy; http:// www.kongcompany.com.

Health-Care Management Products

CareCredit. A patient financing program similar to a personal line of credit for health-care treatments and procedures; http://www.carecredit.com.

Oral Assessment, Treatment, and Prevention (ORAL ATP). Protocol helps prevent oral disease in cats; http://www.oralatp.com.

Organizations of Interest

Adiga Life Sciences. A company established at McMaster University to develop and commercialize Canadian research in medical science and technology; http://www.adiga.ca.

American Association of Feline Practitioners. Improves the health and welfare of cats by supporting high standards of practice, continuing education, and scientific investigation; http://www.catvets.com.

American Association of Feline Practitioners/American Animal Hospital Association. Feline Life Stages Guidelines, a convenient life stage classification; http://www.aahanet.org/PublicDocuments/FelineLifeStageGuidelines.pdf.

American Cat Fanciers Association. Promotes the welfare, education, knowledge, and interest in all domesticated, purebred, and nonpurebred cats; http://www.acfacat.com.

American College of Veterinary Behaviorists (ACVB). Professional organization of veterinarians who are board certified in animal behavior; http://www.dacvb.org.

American Veterinary Dental College (AVDC). Clinical specialist organization for veterinary dentists; http://www.avdc.org.

American Veterinary Medical Association (AVMA). Professional trade association for veterinarians, also offers information for pet lovers on the site; http://www.avma.org.

Animal Medicinal Drug Use Clarification Act. Allows veterinarians to prescribe extralabel uses of certain approved animal and human drugs under certain conditions; http://www.fda.gov/AnimalVeterinary/GuidanceCompliance Enforcement/ActsRulesRegulations/ucm085377.htm.

ASPCA Poison Control Hotline. Animal-specific poison control center providing information articles and case-specific help for a fee; http://www.napcc .aspca.org.

Association of American Feed Control Officials (AAFCO). Trade association for manufacturers of animal foods; http://www.aafco.org.

Cat Fanciers' Association. Registry of pedigreed breeds; http://www.cfa.org.

CATalyst Council. Organization reaching out to various communities to ensure cats receive the proper care and attention; http://www.catalystcouncil .org.

Certified Applied Animal Behaviorist Referrals. Provides list of certified applied animal behaviorists (CAAB), who have advanced degrees in animal behavior, some of whom are veterinarians; http://www.certifiedanimal behaviorist.com.

Fanciers Breeders Referral List. Pedigreed cat breeder referral service; http://www.breedlist.com.

Feline Advisory Bureau. Fabcats is a charity promoting the health and welfare of cats through improved knowledge; http://www.fabcats.org.

Healthy Cats For Life. A campaign to educate cat owners about how to watch for subtle signs of sickness; http://healthycatsforlife.com.

International Cat Association. International cat breed registry; http://www.tica.org.

US Food and Drug Administration. Sign up for pet health notices at http://fda.gov.

Veterinary Oral Health Council (VOHC). Association awards seal of approval to pet dental care products; http://www.vohc.org.

Vetstreet. Comprehensive pet health information as well as private secure web pages that allow twenty-four-hour web access to veterinarians, which can be used to request appointments, order pet products online, view pet's vaccine history, receive e-mail reminders, and research health information for pets; http://www.vetstreet.com.

Over-the-Counter Treatments

NOTE: Check with your veterinarian before giving your pet any medication, even over-the-counter.

Benadryl. Human allergy medication that can be used in cats with appropriate dosing instructions; http://www.benadryl.com.

Betadine. A povidone-iodine solution used as first aid to kill germs and help prevent infection in minor cuts; http://www.betadine.com.

C.E.T. Cat Toothbrush. Gentle, with a unique shape to reach the small areas of a cat's mouth; http://www.virbacpets.com.

C.E.T. Dental Chews. Chews that improve dental health; http://www.virbacpets.com.

Fleabusters. Flea powder kills fleas physically rather than chemically so they cannot build up an immunity; http://www.fleabuster.com.

Pedialyte. Children's over-the-counter liquid oral medication replaces lost fluids and electrolytes; http://pedialyte.com.

Pets in the Media: Broadcast, Print, and Web

The Dr. Oz Show. A syndicated television show about health, starring Dr. Mehmet Oz, MD. Dr. Becker is the regular veterinarian; http://www.doctoroz.com.

Good Morning America. Dr. Becker is the resident veterinarian on this ABC national morning news show; http://abcnews.go.com/GMA. You can find "The Pet Doctor" podcasts with Dr. Becker and Mikkel Becker on the site.

Home-Prepared Dog & Cat Diets: The Healthful Alternative. Written by veterinarian Donald Strombeck; easy-to-follow recipes that can easily be prepared at home, from publisher Wiley-Blackwell; http://www.wiley.com.

Prescription Foods, Medications, and Therapies

NOTE: These items should be given by prescription only, in consultation with your vet.

Advantage Multi. Topical liquid flea control that causes paralysis and subsequent death of fleas; http://www.petparents.com.

Anipryl. Improves cognitive dysfunction, by Pfizer Animal Health; https://animalhealth.pfizer.com.

Assurity. Cat-only flea control, can be used for kittens eight weeks of age and older; http://www.assurity4cats.com.

Clomicalm. For obsessive-compulsive disorders, from Novartis Animal Health; http://www.petwellness.com.

Frontline Plus for Cats. Topical monthly flea and tick killer; http://www.frontline.com.

Heartgard. Chewable tablets to prevent heartworm in cats; http://www.heartgard.com.

Hill's Pet. Food formulated to keep teeth clean and help control the oral bacteria found in plaque; http://www.hillspet.com/hillspet/utilities/selectLanguage.hjsp.

OraVet Barrier Sealant and Plaque Prevention Gel. Gel improves dental health; http://www.oravet.us.merial.com.

Prozac/Reconcile. Reconcile is a chewable, beef-flavored tablet of Prozac for separation anxiety; http://www.reconcile.com.

Revolution. Preventive for heartworms, fleas, and other parasites; https://animalhealth.pfizer.com.

Valium. Generically called diazepam, an appetite stimulant, muscle relaxer, and anticonvulsant medication by Roche; http://www.roche.com.

Xanax. Medication to treat panic disorder in people and cats; http://www.xanax.com.

INDEX

Abyssinians, 25–27, 171, 208, 241, 276
accidents, 216, 218, 245–46, 277
adult cats, 12, 93, 168, 231
    choosing cats and, 18, 22–24, 39–40,
      44, 46
affectionateness, 13
aging, 215, 221, 231
    senior cats and, 275–83
    urinary problems and, 270–71
aggressiveness, 41, 102, 157, 164, 191
    behavior correction and, 193, 198
air purifiers, 32
allergies, 55, 73, 113, 178, 237
    choosing cats and, 30–34
    emergencies and, 246, 250
    food and, 90, 94
American Wirehairs (breed), 30
anesthesia, 224, 242, 281
    in surgeries, 221, 240, 268–70
antifreeze, 78, 246, 259
antihistamines, 32, 250–51
appetite loss, 97–99, 115, 261, 282, 287
arthritis, 10–11, 51, 78, 80, 113, 177, 267
    litter box problems and, 182–83, 187
    senior cats and, 274, 278, 280, 282
asthma, 11, 78, 80, 101, 117, 125, 256
attention, 13

bathing, 31, 111, 119–20, 124
behavior, 6, 77, 101, 272, 275
    cat supplies and, 50, 53

compulsive, 193–94, 196, 199, 261, 287
correction of, 192–200
development of, 153–57
hardwired, 49, 103, 200
house rules and, 167, 173, 175, 177
of kittens, 20, 37, 41, 46, 71–72, 74,
    153–55, 196
litter boxes and, 184–88, 191, 193–94,
    197
medications and, 196, 198–200
sickness, 261–62
spraying and, 188–91
training and, 14, 71, 73–74, 159, 161,
    203–4
behaviorists, 13, 154, 189–91, 263
    cat supplies and, 52, 55
    correcting bad behaviors and, 194–99
    exercise and, 104, 108
    medications and, 196, 198–99
    questions asked by, 196–97
    spraying and, 189–90
    who they are and what they do,
      195–99
Benadryl, 251
birds, 60, 64, 126, 158, 161, 164, 210
biting, 162, 193
    communicating and, 156–57
    emergencies and, 246, 251, 255
    of fleas, 232, 236
    house rules and, 164, 169, 172–73
    preventable catastrophes and, 133–35

bleeding, 219, 223–24
  emergencies and, 246, 250, 255
body language, 78, 96, 102, 134, 155–59,
  172, 198, 288
body temperature, 112, 135, 235, 256
body types, 26–29
bones, 28–29, 97, 256
boredom, 3, 76–77, 101, 126, 262
bowls and dishes, 49, 55–56, 105, 146,
  166, 174, 176, 197, 262
breed types, 9, 159, 171, 208, 276
  body types and, 26–27
  choosing cats and, 19, 23–30, 34, 37,
    39, 41–44
brushing, 31, 66, 146
  home care and, 111, 118, 120, 124

calories, 94, 96, 99
cancer, 78, 80, 101, 113, 265, 280
CareCredit, 142
car engines, 71, 128
car rides, 10, 12, 49, 64, 71–72, 160–61,
  250, 256
carriers, 49, 117, 202
  exercise and, 103–4
  plastic, 64–65
  in vet visits, 12, 103–4, 160, 207–8,
    222
catastrophes, 127–36
  bites and, 133–35
  illnesses and, 128, 131–33, 135–36
  outdoor cats and, 127–29, 131–33, 136
  and potential dangers at home, 131–33
  scratches and, 134–35
cat fights, 134, 193, 197–98
  emergencies and, 245, 255
  after vet visits, 168–69
cat gear, 49–66, 291–93
catnip, 21, 24, 61–63, 76, 106, 133, 164,
  167, 246
  senior cats and, 275, 281
  training and, 159, 207–9
cats
  myths and misconceptions about, 9–16,
    24, 68, 71
  as predators, 10, 16, 50, 54, 56, 58–60,
    64, 78, 86, 103, 106, 123, 157,
    163–64
  as prey, 10, 50, 54, 157, 168
  sacrifices made by, 150–51
cat scratch disease, 135, 233

cat trees, 10, 24, 54–55, 74–75, 83, 103,
  105, 206
  house rules and, 166, 174, 176
ceramic dishes, 55
chewing, 176, 193
children, 1, 15, 73, 85, 93, 104, 136, 142,
  181, 187, 189, 206, 288
  choosing cats and, 19, 23, 37, 39–40
  house rules and, 163, 168, 170–72
  senior cats and, 283, 286
chocolate, 92
choosing cats, 6–7, 18–34, 37–46
  adult cats and, 18, 22–24, 39–40, 44,
    46
  breed types and, 19, 23–30, 34, 37, 39,
    41–44
  buying cats and, 37, 41–44
  cats choosing you and, 37, 44
  energy and, 21, 27–28, 37, 40
  healthy cats and, 6, 37–40, 43–44
  kittens and, 6, 18, 20–22, 24, 31,
    37–40, 43–46
  shelters and, 6, 37, 39–41
  two at once, 18, 24
claws. *See* nails
cleaning products, 49, 131, 147, 188, 191
cleanliness, 15, 134, 145–47
climbing, 58, 75, 123, 129, 132, 197
  choosing cats and, 20, 24, 27–28
  exercise and, 103, 105
  senior cats and, 277–78
  of trees, 17, 78
Clipnosis, 121
clothing for cats, 32
coats, 66, 94, 102, 134, 223
  choosing cats and, 6, 25, 29–34
  in healthy cats, 36, 38–40
  home care and, 113, 118, 120
  of kittens, 6, 21, 38
collars, 49, 63–64, 76, 129, 131
  emergencies and, 249–50
combing, 66, 146
  home care and, 118, 120, 124
"come" trick, 60, 73, 205–6, 209
communicating, 14, 184, 188
  with body language, 102, 134, 155–59,
    172
  house rules and, 165, 170–71
  training and, 161, 204
  See also vocalizations
complementary treatments, 267, 280

conditioner, 118
contact information, 249
Cornish Rex, 25, 27, 29–30, 171
crates, 103–4, 280
credit, 142
curtain cords, 70, 75

dairy products, 93, 258
death, 285–87
Devon Rex, 27, 30, 34
diabetes, 78, 94, 101, 113, 278
    litter box problems and, 182–83
dog food, 9–10, 93
dough, 92
drinking fountains, 57, 61, 87, 152
dryer danger, 132–33

ear mites, 113, 124–25, 236–37
ears, 59, 61, 72, 169–70, 219, 222
    communicating with, 102, 134,
        156–58, 172
    in healthy cats, 36, 38, 224
    home care and, 111, 113, 121
    in wellness exams, 223–24
electrical cords, 70, 75
electrostatic sheets, 146
emergencies, 73, 244–59, 269, 286
    in crises, 254–59
    expenses and, 140–41, 143, 246–47
    symptoms of, 245–46
    vets and, 91–92, 112, 132, 218–19, 225,
        245–47, 249–53, 255–56, 258–59,
        271
    and what to do before you can get help,
        248–53
enclosed spaces, 61–63, 78, 104, 200, 258
energy, 103, 171, 175, 284
    choosing cats and, 21, 27–28, 37, 40
entertainment, 58–60
euthanasia, 140–41, 285–86
exercise, 13, 223, 226, 281, 287
    behavior issues and, 194, 197, 200
    cat supplies and, 56, 58, 60
    choosing cats and, 20, 38
    food and, 60, 105–6, 108
    house rules and, 165–66, 177
    physical and mental, 60, 75, 77, 102–8,
        194, 197
    training and, 74, 103–4, 203, 206
expenses, 139–47, 240, 242, 285
    cutting of, 143–45

emergencies and, 140–41, 143, 246–47
food and, 88, 139, 143–45
keeping clean and, 145–47
medications and, 140, 144, 265, 269
planning and, 140–42
vets and, 139–45, 219, 227
eyes, 78, 94, 134, 219–20
    communicating and, 155, 157
    emergencies and, 246, 248
    in healthy cats, 36, 38
    home care and, 112–13
    of kittens, 21–22, 38, 58
    senior cats and, 275, 279, 282–83
    in wellness exams, 224–25

feline agility, 159
Feliway, 12, 160, 167, 172, 190, 207–8
    vet visits and, 221–22
feral cats, 45–46, 64, 234, 236, 277
first-aid kits, 250
fleas, 10, 38, 177, 232–38, 277
    control of, 124–25, 233–38, 248, 265
floors, 30, 61–62, 185, 234
    expenses and, 145–47
    house rules and, 165–66
food, 58, 82–99, 103, 135–36, 151,
        188–90, 223, 225, 234, 242, 248,
        261–62, 270–71, 296
    for adult cats, 23, 93
    behavior issues and, 153–55, 194,
        197–98
    brands of, 83, 87–88
    canned, 17, 73, 85, 87–90, 98–99,
        251–53, 271, 279
    for cats vs. dogs, 9–10, 93
    communicating and, 158–59
    cooking of, 15, 98
    dishes and bowls for, 49, 55–56, 105,
        146, 166, 174, 176, 197, 262
    dry, 56, 60, 77–78, 85–86, 89–90,
        98–99, 105–6, 108, 145, 271
    eating issues and, 97–98, 115
    exercise and, 60, 105–6, 108
    expenses and, 88, 139, 143–45
    favorite, 93, 98–99, 120
    feral cats and, 45–46
    forbidden, 91–93
    home care and, 115, 118
    homemade, 90–91
    house rules and, 164, 166, 170, 172,
        174–79

food (*cont.*)
    labels on, 87–88, 92, 145
    litter box problems and, 183, 188
    medications and, 98, 251–53
    nutritional needs and, 9–10, 86–87
    overeating and, 99, 226
    overfeeding and, 77–78, 94
    professional advice on, 85, 87–92,
        94–95, 97–99
    raw, 91, 136
    rejecting diet change and, 98–99
    schedules for, 88, 99, 183, 188, 190
    senior cats and, 274, 277–79, 281–82, 284
    training and, 73, 205–9
    varieties of, 85, 87–91, 99
    vets and, 83, 85, 87–91, 94–95, 97–99,
        219, 271
    See also treats
food puzzles, 56, 60, 78, 105, 198, 281
furniture, 10, 54–55, 61–62, 66, 71, 103,
        122, 145–46, 223, 234
    choosing cats and, 30, 32
    correcting bad behaviors and, 192–93
    house rules and, 163, 165, 167, 172, 176
    spraying and, 189, 191, 193
    training and, 159, 207

gaits, 123, 223
garlic, 92, 282
genetic diseases, 41, 43
gentling techniques, 72–73
"go to your place" trick, 206–7
GPS, 131
grass eating, 16
grief, 286–87
grooming, 10, 26, 72, 100, 144, 155–56,
        222
    choosing cats and, 24–25, 31
    compulsive, 193–94, 196, 199, 261, 287
    front-to-back guide for, 116–18
    home care and, 111, 115–24
    tools for, 49, 66, 118
gums, 38, 113, 115, 224
    preventive dental care and, 240–42

hairballs, 64, 66, 147, 156, 176
    home care and, 117–18
harnesses, 104, 208–9
health, 3, 48, 57–58, 78, 96, 102, 108,
        159, 221, 226, 229, 261–62, 284, 288
    behaviorists and, 195–96

choosing cats and, 6, 37–40, 43–44
    choosing vets and, 216–17, 219
    food and, 85–87, 89–92, 94–95, 172
    home care and, 111, 113–14, 116–17
    physical appearance of, 36–39
    senior cats and, 278, 282–83
health–care management products,
        293
hearing loss, 279, 282–83
heart, 97, 112, 115, 219, 223, 225, 269
heart disease, 43, 78, 94, 101, 117
heartworms, 80, 117, 125, 144, 234,
        237–39
HEPA filters, 31–32
hiding, 58, 60, 105
    preventable catastrophes and, 130–31
high-rise syndrome, 132
home, 153, 285
    emergencies and, 112, 248, 256–58
    expenses and, 139, 145–47
    kitten- and cat-proofing of, 69–71, 75,
        258
    parasites and, 124–25, 234–35
    potential dangers at, 131–33
    rules in, 163–79
home care, 111–25
    bathing and, 111, 119–20, 124
    body condition and, 114
    grooming and, 111, 115–24
    hairballs and, 117–18
    mouth and, 113, 115–16
    nail clipping in, 111, 121–22, 124
    physical appearance in, 112–13
    stress and, 112, 114–15, 119
    taking vital signs in, 112
household appliances, 71, 132–33
hydrogen peroxide, 250, 252–53, 255
hypoallergenic cats, 34

identification tags, 63, 76, 129
    emergencies and, 249–50
illnesses, 78, 108, 110–11, 127, 140–41,
        215, 244, 277, 284
    behavior issues and, 193, 196, 261–62
    choosing cats and, 19, 38, 41, 43
    food and, 92–95, 98
    home care and, 113–15, 125
    litter box problems and, 180–84, 187
    of overweight cats, 101, 110, 114, 126
    parasites and, 135–36, 232–33, 235,
        238

preventable catastrophes and, 128, 131–33, 135–36
prevention of. *See* preventive care
senior cats and, 276, 278–79
in wellness exams, 223–25
indoor cats, 13, 16, 101, 104, 126, 153, 163–64, 271
  life spans of, 3, 23, 79, 215, 277
  parasites and, 124, 136, 233–34, 238
  preventable catastrophes and, 127–29, 136
  senior cats and, 276–78
infections, 38, 159, 177, 237–38, 255
  home care and, 113, 115, 125
  litter box problems and, 182–84
  preventable catastrophes and, 128, 135–36
  urinary, 53, 77, 181, 270–71, 279
  in wellness exams, 223–25
injuries, 10, 17, 29, 78, 121, 140–41, 170, 173, 219, 280, 283
  emergencies and, 245–46, 254
  preventable catastrophes and, 128, 131–34
  in wellness exams, 224–25
Internet, 83, 91, 144, 232, 266
  emergencies and, 244–45, 258
  pros and cons of, 263–64
  selecting cats and, 34, 42, 44

jumping, 10, 60, 74–75, 223, 236
  choosing cats and, 26–27
  house rules and, 163, 172–74, 176
  training and, 161, 207

kidneys, 43, 95, 98, 115, 183, 269, 278
  emergencies and, 247, 259
kitten kindergartens, 20, 72, 166
kittens, 66, 229–31, 284
  behavior issues and, 20, 37, 41, 46, 71–72, 74, 153–55, 196
  choosing of, 6, 18, 20–22, 24, 31, 37–40, 43–46
  essentials for, 63–64
  eyes of, 21–22, 38, 58
  hazards in the home, 69–71, 75, 258
  healthy, 36–39
  house rules and, 164–65, 167–68, 175, 178
  important things to do with, 74–76
  parasite control and, 234, 236–37

play of, 20, 37, 58–60, 69, 75, 108, 162
preventive dental care and, 241–42
spaying/neutering of, 184, 189, 239
supplies for, 49, 52–53
training of, 71–74, 208
vaccinations for, 43, 230–31

laser pointers, 75, 108, 164
  play and, 58–59
leashes, 14, 250, 280
  walking on, 9, 26–27, 73, 104, 160, 171, 208–9
life spans, 46, 89, 240, 284
  of indoor cats, 3, 23, 79, 215, 277
  of outdoor cats, 3, 78–79, 128, 215, 277
  of overweight cats, 97, 110, 226
  senior cats and, 274–78
light sensitivity, 220
limit setting, 74–75
litter, 49–53, 77, 115, 139
  depth of, 53, 186, 197
  litter box problems and, 181, 185–87
  types of, 52–53, 185–86
litter boxes, 23, 49–53, 75, 83, 115, 135–36, 150, 153, 166, 170
  behavior issues and, 184–88, 191, 193–94, 197
  cleaning of, 15, 51–52, 77, 135–36, 181, 184–86, 197, 271
  locations of, 52, 186–88, 191, 197
  problems with, 180–88, 191, 261
  scooping and, 50–52, 77, 186–88, 197, 238, 283
  senior cats and, 182–83, 185, 187, 279, 283
  sizes of, 51, 184–85
  types of, 50–51, 187
litter liners, 53
liver, 97, 115, 219, 248, 267, 269
lost cats, 129–31, 250
lungs, 97, 219, 225, 238
lymph nodes, 135, 219, 225

Maine Coons (breed), 25, 28, 43, 51, 171
meats, 9–10, 15, 86, 88, 91, 136
medications, 61, 226, 265–72, 296
  administration of, 251–53, 260, 268
  for allergies, 32–33
  behavior issues and, 196, 198–200
  choosing cats and, 32–33, 38
  emergencies and, 246–47, 250–55, 258

medications (*cont.*)
  expenses and, 140, 144, 265, 269
  food and, 98, 251–53
  home care and, 121, 124–25
  pain and, 10, 79–80, 177, 183, 240–42, 251, 267–70, 280–81
  parasites and, 10, 233–39, 248, 265
  preventable catastrophes and, 131–32, 135–36
  senior cats and, 278–81
  shared between cats and people, 251–53, 265–66
  spraying and, 189–91
  toxicity of, 70, 79–80, 91–92, 131–32, 246–47, 251–52, 254, 258
  vets and, 218–19, 265–66, 268–70
  See also anesthesia
mental function, 279, 281
microchips, 63, 76, 129–31, 249
mouth, 113, 115–16, 223–24
  See also gums; teeth
mouth wash, 116

nails, 17, 59–61, 75, 85, 144, 150, 156–57, 160, 162
  clipping of, 61, 66, 72, 111, 121–22, 124, 144, 146, 160, 222
  declawing and, 39, 75–76, 146
  house rules and, 165–67
names, 288
neutering. *See* spaying/neutering
noses, 38, 173, 204–5, 219, 225

onions, 92, 282
organizations, 294–95
outdoor cats, 44, 63–64, 104, 181, 208–9, 231, 245
  behavior issues and, 153, 194
  dangers for, 13, 78, 127–28
  life spans of, 3, 78–79, 128, 215, 277
  parasites and, 128–29, 233, 238
  preventable catastrophes and, 127–29, 131–33, 136
overheating, 256
over-the-counter treatments, 295
overweight cats, 3, 94, 96–97, 101, 177, 185, 256, 277, 281
  illnesses of, 78, 101, 110, 114, 126, 144
  life spans of, 97, 110, 226

pain, 50, 78–80, 110, 115, 122, 129, 196, 212, 216, 218, 258
  cats' expression of, 10–11, 159
  litter box problems and, 182–84
  medications and, 10, 79–80, 177, 183, 240–42, 251, 267–70, 280–81
  preventive dental care and, 241–42
  senior cats and, 79, 177, 280–81, 285
  spay/neuter surgery and, 239–40
  wellness exams and, 221, 223
parasites, 10–11, 13, 66, 136, 177, 253–54, 277
  choosing cats and, 38–39
  control of, 10, 23, 94, 117, 124–25, 128–29, 135, 223, 229, 232–39, 248, 265
Pedialyte, 251–52
Persians, 171, 241, 256
  choosing of, 25, 28–29, 39, 43
pet health insurance, 76, 140–41
pets in the media, 295–96
petting, 12–13, 159, 262, 276, 279
  choosing cats and, 40–42, 45
  communicating and, 156–58
  house rules and, 170–71
  training and, 72–73
pheromones, 21, 50, 180
  house rules and, 167, 172, 178
  spraying and, 188–90
  vet visits and, 12, 160, 221–22
Ping-Pong balls, 59, 75, 106, 108, 175
plants, 16, 61, 214, 245
  toxicity of, 70, 79, 133, 247, 257–58
play, 9, 13, 56, 77, 159, 183, 197, 236, 262, 271
  choosing cats and, 20–21, 28, 37, 39
  exercise and, 102–3, 105–6, 108
  house rules and, 163–65, 168, 172, 175–76
  of kittens, 20, 37, 58–60, 69, 75, 108, 162
  rough, 162, 164–65
  senior cats and, 275, 277–78, 284
poisons, 92, 125
  emergencies and, 246–49, 253–54, 257–59
  preventable catastrophes and, 128, 131–33, 135
pregnancy, 15, 136, 238

preventive care, x, 11, 80, 138, 212–13, 215–16, 219, 229–42, 245, 261, 277
   dental, 240–42
   expenses and, 143, 242
   parasite control in, 229, 232–39
   spay/neuter surgery in, 229, 239–40
   See also vaccinations
problem solvers, 291–93
protein, 9–10, 34, 86, 88, 90, 95
punishment, 152, 154, 167, 173, 194
puzzle toys, 75, 108, 164, 178
   food and, 56, 60, 78, 105, 198, 281

rabies, 80, 136, 230–31
Ragdoll (breed), 24, 28, 43, 208
ramps, 282
rescue groups, 7, 37, 39, 236
resources, 291–96
restraint, 254
ringworm, 136
roundworms, 38, 124–25, 237

salmonella poisoning, 135
savings accounts, 141
scratching, 20, 46, 73, 150, 162, 207, 255
   crate training and, 103–4
   expenses and, 139, 145–47
   home care and, 121–22
   house rules and, 163–67, 169, 172–73, 177
   parasites and, 233, 236–37
   preventable catastrophes and, 134–35
   supplies for, 54, 61
scratching posts, 40, 54, 61, 74, 146–47, 163–67, 189, 204
senior cats, 51, 57, 194, 215, 274–86
   and end of life decisions, 284–85
   food and, 90, 95
   litter boxes and, 182–83, 185, 187, 279, 283
   mental function and, 279, 281
   pain and, 79, 177, 280–81, 285
   vets and, 276–78, 280–81, 283–86
shampoos, 10, 31, 118–20
shedding, 30–33, 117–18, 146, 223
shelters, 6, 37, 39–41, 63, 130–31, 181, 194, 236, 239
Siamese (breed), 171, 176, 193, 208, 241, 276
   choosing cats and, 25–27, 39
"sit" trick, 60, 73, 204–6

skin, 29, 38, 61, 66, 78, 101, 117, 120, 124, 136, 235–37, 255, 267
sleep, 10, 37, 101, 115, 135, 158, 287
   bedrooms and, 32, 178
   cat supplies and, 54, 59
   house rules and, 163, 170, 175–79
   senior cats and, 275, 279–82
smell, 14, 51, 72–73, 78, 168–69, 279
social discord, 191
socialization, 155–56, 210
   choosing cats and, 37, 41, 46
   of kittens, 20, 71–72, 74, 155
spaying/neutering, 18, 49, 75–76, 153, 221
   choosing cats and, 23–24, 34, 39
   in preventive care, 229, 239–40
   spraying and, 184, 188–89
specialists, 272, 281
Sphynx (breed), 19, 25, 27, 30
spraying, 184, 188–91, 193–95, 198
standoffishness, 12–13
sticky-tape rollers, 31
stress, 207, 223, 261, 271, 284
   behavior issues and, 188–89, 193–95, 198–99
   home care and, 112, 114–15, 119
   litter box problems and, 180, 183, 188
   vets and, 11–12, 216, 222
strollers, 104, 161, 171
supplements, 92, 177, 183, 266–67, 278, 280
surgery, 265, 280–81
   anesthesia in, 221, 240, 268–70
   See also spaying/neutering

tabbies, 6, 25, 39, 45, 96
tail chasing, 195–96
tapeworms, 38, 237–38
teeth, 38, 59, 66, 75, 89–90, 134, 144, 159, 222–24, 270
   dental problems and, 11, 80, 87, 113, 115, 241
   home care and, 111, 113, 115–16, 118
   preventive care and, 240–42
   See also bites, biting
therapies, 296
ticks, 10, 124–25, 234–35, 239, 248, 265
tinsel, 60, 107, 132
tolerance, 167–69
toxoplasmosis, 15, 135–36, 238

toys, 13, 40, 48–49, 54, 56, 70, 74, 77–78, 83, 189, 222, 242, 262
  behavior issues and, 72, 198
  exercise and, 75, 105–7
  expenses and, 139, 146
  fishing-pole, 28, 59, 107, 175–76, 209, 275
  house rules and, 164–66, 168–69, 175–76, 178
  senior cats and, 275–78
  training and, 159, 203–4, 207, 209
  See also puzzle toys
training, 20, 68, 159–61, 180, 227, 275
  behavior issues and, 14, 71, 73–74, 159, 161, 203–4
  clicker, 203–7, 210
  exercise and, 74, 103–4, 203, 206
  of kittens, 71–74, 208
  leash-walking and, 160, 208–9
  tricks and, 203–10
treats, 12, 14, 89, 95–96, 104, 158, 202, 216, 222, 242
  home care and, 116–17, 119–20
  house rules and, 167–69, 176
  training and, 73, 159, 161, 203–5, 207, 209–10
tricks, 60–61, 73, 203–10

urinary problems, 11, 53, 77, 181, 270–71, 279, 282–83

vaccinations, 33, 49, 129, 223, 228–32
  choosing cats and, 23, 39, 43–44
  frequency of, 80, 228–31
  preventable catastrophes and, 135–36
  what they are and how they work, 229–30
vacuuming, 31
veterinarians, ix–x, 10–12, 23, 39, 82–83, 138–45, 159, 177, 212–27, 261–72
  becoming a favorite of, 226–27
  behaviorists and, 52, 55, 195–97
  carriers in visits to, 12, 103–4, 160, 207–8, 222
  cat spats after visits to, 168–69

choosing of, 214, 216–20
  emergencies and, 91–92, 112, 132, 218–19, 225, 245–47, 249–53, 255–56, 258–59, 271
  euthanasia and, 140, 285–86
  expenses and, 139–45, 219, 227
  food and, 83, 85, 87–91, 94–95, 97–99, 219, 271
  home care and, 111–19, 121, 124–25
  litter box problems and, 181–83
  medications and, 218–19, 265–66, 268–70
  preventable catastrophes and, 129–30, 132–33, 136
  preventive care and, 138, 212–13, 215–16, 219, 229, 231–34, 237–42, 261
  and pros and cons of Internet, 263–64
  senior cats and, 276–78, 280–81, 283–86
  stress and, 11–12, 216, 222
  training and, 160–61, 207–8
  wellness exams and, 215, 220–27
vitamins, 10, 86, 92
vocalizations, 26, 156–59, 198, 287
  senior cats and, 279, 283
vomiting, induction of, 252–53

water, 78, 89–90, 152, 188, 256, 270–71
  cat supplies and, 49, 55–57
  correcting bad behaviors and, 197–98
  dishes and bowls for, 49, 55–56, 105, 146, 166, 174, 176, 197, 262
  in food, 86–87, 90
  process in drinking of, 57–58
  spraying and, 189–90
  squirting cats with, 173, 177, 198
weight loss, 78, 98, 102–3, 114
weights, ideal, 225–26
wellness exams, 142–43, 215, 220–27
whiskers, 29–30, 156–57
wounds, 135, 219, 246, 252, 255

xylitol, 92

ABOUT THE AUTHORS

Dr. Marty Becker

Dr. Marty Becker, "America's Veterinarian," is the popular veterinary contributor to ABC-TV's *Good Morning America*, the resident veterinarian on *The Dr. Oz Show*, and the pet expert for the American Association of Retired Persons (AARP). Along with his writing partner, Gina Spadafori, he has been a contributor to *Parade* magazine and other publications. Dr. Becker is the author of *Your Dog: The Owner's Manual*, and is the coauthor of *Chicken Soup for the Pet Lover's Soul*, *The Healing Power of Pets*, and, with Spadafori, *Why Do Cats Always Land on Their Feet?*, among many other books.

He is the veterinary spokesman and columnist for Vetstreet.com.

Dr. Becker is an adjunct professor at his alma mater, the Washington State University College of Veterinary Medicine, and also at the colleges of veterinary medicine at both Colorado State University and the University of Missouri. He has been named Companion Animal Veterinarian of the Year by the Delta Society and the American Veterinary Medical Association.

Dr. Becker lives with his wife, Teresa, in northern Idaho, a country drive away from his daughter, Mikkel; his son, Lex; and his granddaughter, Reagan Avelle.

Gina Spadafori

A longtime journalist and editor, Gina Spadafori has been writing primarily about pets and their care for almost thirty years as a syndicated columnist and book author. She has written more than a dozen books with Dr. Becker, including *Your Dog: The Owner's Manual*. Gina has also headed the Pet Care Forum, America Online's founding source of pet care information. She is a contributing editor to Vetstreet.com and does her recreational blogging at GoodFaithRanch.com.

Gina lives in northern California on a suburban micro farm with dogs, cats, chickens, and ducks. Her two horses are boarded nearby, and she is constantly looking for just the right property on which to keep all her animals together.